50% OFF Online PTCB Course!

Dear Customer,

We consider it an honor and a privilege that you chose our PTCB Study Guide. As a way of showing our appreciation and to help us better serve you, we have partnered with Mometrix Test Preparation to offer you **50% off their online PTCB Exam Course.** Many PTCB courses are needlessly expensive and don't deliver enough value. With their course, you get access to the best PTCB prep material, and **you only pay half price.**

They have structured their online course to perfectly complement your printed study guide. The PTCB Online Course contains **in-depth lessons** that cover all the most important topics, **30+ video reviews** that explain difficult concepts, over **500 practice questions** to ensure you feel prepared, and **300+ digital flashcards,** so you can study while you're on the go.

Online PTCB Prep Course

Topics Include:	Course Features:
• Medications	• PTCB Study Guide
○ Common and Life-Threatening Drug Interactions and Contraindications	○ Get content that complements our best-selling study guide.
○ Dosage Forms and Routes of Administration	• Full-Length Practice Tests
○ Drug Stability	○ With over 500 practice questions, you can test yourself again and again.
• Federal Requirements	
○ Handling and Disposal of Pharmaceutical Substances and Waste	• Mobile Friendly
○ Controlled Substances	○ If you need to study on the go, the course is easily accessible from your mobile device.
○ FDA Requirements	
• Patient Safety and Quality Assurance	
○ High-Alert/High-Risk and LASA Medications	• PTCB Flashcards
○ Error-Prevention Strategies	○ Their course includes a flashcards mode with over 300 content cards for you to study.
○ Event Reporting Procedures	
• Order Entry and Processing	
○ Procedures to Compound Nonsterile Products	
○ Formulas and Calculations	
○ And more	

To receive this discount, visit their website: mometrix.com/university/ptcb or simply scan this QR code with your smartphone. At the checkout page, enter the discount code: **TPBPTCB50**

If you have any questions or concerns, please contact Mometrix at support@mometrix.com.

Sincerely,

 in partnership with

FREE Test Taking Tips Video/DVD Offer

To better serve you, we created videos covering test taking tips that we want to give you for FREE. **These videos cover world-class tips that will help you succeed on your test.**

We just ask that you send us feedback about this product. Please let us know what you thought about it—whether good, bad, or indifferent.

To get your **FREE videos**, you can use the QR code below or email freevideos@studyguideteam.com with "Free Videos" in the subject line and the following information in the body of the email:

a. The title of your product

b. Your product rating on a scale of 1-5, with 5 being the highest

c. Your feedback about the product

If you have any questions or concerns, please don't hesitate to contact us at info@studyguideteam.com.

Thank you!

PTCB Study Guide 2024 and 2025
7 Practice Tests & PTCB Exam Prep Book
[8th Edition]

Lydia Morrison

Interested in buying more than 10 copies of our product? Contact us about bulk discounts:
bulkorders@studyguideteam.com

ISBN 13: 9781637751459

Table of Contents

Welcome

Dear Reader,

Welcome to your new Test Prep Books study guide! We are pleased that you chose us to help you prepare for your exam. There are many study options to choose from, and we appreciate you choosing us. Studying can be a daunting task, but we have designed a smart, effective study guide to help prepare you for what lies ahead.

Whether you're a parent helping your child learn and grow, a high school student working hard to get into your dream college, or a nursing student studying for a complex exam, we want to help give you the tools you need to succeed. We hope this study guide gives you the skills and the confidence to thrive, and we can't thank you enough for allowing us to be part of your journey.

In an effort to continue to improve our products, we welcome feedback from our customers. We look forward to hearing from you. Suggestions, success stories, and criticisms can all be communicated by emailing us at info@studyguideteam.com.

Sincerely,
Test Prep Books Team

FREE Videos/DVD OFFER

Doing well on your exam requires both knowing the test content and understanding how to use that knowledge to do well on the test. We offer completely FREE test taking tip videos. **These videos cover world-class tips that you can use to succeed on your test.**

To get your **FREE videos**, you can use the QR code below or email freevideos@studyguideteam.com with "Free Videos" in the subject line and the following information in the body of the email:

    a. The title of your product
    b. Your product rating on a scale of 1-5, with 5 being the highest
    c. Your feedback about the product

If you have any questions or concerns, please don't hesitate to contact us at info@studyguideteam.com.

1

Quick Overview

As you draw closer to taking your exam, effective preparation becomes more and more important. Thankfully, you have this study guide to help you get ready. Use this guide to help keep your studying on track and refer to it often.

This study guide contains several key sections that will help you be successful on your exam. The guide contains tips for what you should do the night before and the day of the test. Also included are test-taking tips. Knowing the right information is not always enough. Many well-prepared test takers struggle with exams. These tips will help equip you to accurately read, assess, and answer test questions.

A large part of the guide is devoted to showing you what content to expect on the exam and to helping you better understand that content. In this guide are practice test questions so that you can see how well you have grasped the content. Then, answer explanations are provided so that you can understand why you missed certain questions.

Don't try to cram the night before you take your exam. This is not a wise strategy for a few reasons. First, your retention of the information will be low. Your time would be better used by reviewing information you already know rather than trying to learn a lot of new information. Second, you will likely become stressed as you try to gain a large amount of knowledge in a short amount of time. Third, you will be depriving yourself of sleep. So be sure to go to bed at a reasonable time the night before. Being well-rested helps you focus and remain calm.

Be sure to eat a substantial breakfast the morning of the exam. If you are taking the exam in the afternoon, be sure to have a good lunch as well. Being hungry is distracting and can make it difficult to focus. You have hopefully spent lots of time preparing for the exam. Don't let an empty stomach get in the way of success!

When travelling to the testing center, leave earlier than needed. That way, you have a buffer in case you experience any delays. This will help you remain calm and will keep you from missing your appointment time at the testing center.

Be sure to pace yourself during the exam. Don't try to rush through the exam. There is no need to risk performing poorly on the exam just so you can leave the testing center early. Allow yourself to use all of the allotted time if needed.

Remain positive while taking the exam even if you feel like you are performing poorly. Thinking about the content you should have mastered will not help you perform better on the exam.

Once the exam is complete, take some time to relax. Even if you feel that you need to take the exam again, you will be well served by some down time before you begin studying again. It's often easier to convince yourself to study if you know that it will come with a reward!

2

Test-Taking Strategies

1. Predicting the Answer

When you feel confident in your preparation for a multiple-choice test, try predicting the answer before reading the answer choices. This is especially useful on questions that test objective factual knowledge. By predicting the answer before reading the available choices, you eliminate the possibility that you will be distracted or led astray by an incorrect answer choice. You will feel more confident in your selection if you read the question, predict the answer, and then find your prediction among the answer choices. After using this strategy, be sure to still read all of the answer choices carefully and completely. If you feel unprepared, you should not attempt to predict the answers. This would be a waste of time and an opportunity for your mind to wander in the wrong direction.

2. Reading the Whole Question

Too often, test takers scan a multiple-choice question, recognize a few familiar words, and immediately jump to the answer choices. Test authors are aware of this common impatience, and they will sometimes prey upon it. For instance, a test author might subtly turn the question into a negative, or he or she might redirect the focus of the question right at the end. The only way to avoid falling into these traps is to read the entirety of the question carefully before reading the answer choices.

3. Looking for Wrong Answers

Long and complicated multiple-choice questions can be intimidating. One way to simplify a difficult multiple-choice question is to eliminate all of the answer choices that are clearly wrong. In most sets of answers, there will be at least one selection that can be dismissed right away. If the test is administered on paper, the test taker could draw a line through it to indicate that it may be ignored; otherwise, the test taker will have to perform this operation mentally or on scratch paper. In either case, once the obviously incorrect answers have been eliminated, the remaining choices may be considered. Sometimes identifying the clearly wrong answers will give the test taker some information about the correct answer. For instance, if one of the remaining answer choices is a direct opposite of one of the eliminated answer choices, it may well be the correct answer. The opposite of obviously wrong is obviously right! Of course, this is not always the case. Some answers are obviously incorrect simply because they are irrelevant to the question being asked. Still, identifying and eliminating some incorrect answer choices is a good way to simplify a multiple-choice question.

4. Don't Overanalyze

Anxious test takers often overanalyze questions. When you are nervous, your brain will often run wild, causing you to make associations and discover clues that don't actually exist. If you feel that this may be a problem for you, do whatever you can to slow down during the test. Try taking a deep breath or counting to ten. As you read and consider the question, restrict yourself to the particular words used by the author. Avoid thought tangents about what the author *really* meant, or what he or she was *trying* to say. The only things that matter on a multiple-choice test are the words that are actually in the question. You must avoid reading too much into a multiple-choice question, or supposing that the writer meant

3

something other than what he or she wrote.

5. No Need for Panic

It is wise to learn as many strategies as possible before taking a multiple-choice test, but it is likely that you will come across a few questions for which you simply don't know the answer. In this situation, avoid panicking. Because most multiple-choice tests include dozens of questions, the relative value of a single wrong answer is small. As much as possible, you should compartmentalize each question on a multiple-choice test. In other words, you should not allow your feelings about one question to affect your success on the others. When you find a question that you either don't understand or don't know how to answer, just take a deep breath and do your best. Read the entire question slowly and carefully. Try rephrasing the question a couple of different ways. Then, read all of the answer choices carefully. After eliminating obviously wrong answers, make a selection and move on to the next question.

6. Confusing Answer Choices

When working on a difficult multiple-choice question, there may be a tendency to focus on the answer choices that are the easiest to understand. Many people, whether consciously or not, gravitate to the answer choices that require the least concentration, knowledge, and memory. This is a mistake. When you come across an answer choice that is confusing, you should give it extra attention. A question might be confusing because you do not know the subject matter to which it refers. If this is the case, don't  eliminate the answer before you have affirmatively settled on another. When you come across an answer choice of this type, set it aside as you look at the remaining choices. If you can confidently assert that one of the other choices is correct, you can leave the confusing answer aside. Otherwise, you will need to take a moment to try to better understand the confusing answer choice. Rephrasing is one way to tease out the sense of a confusing answer choice.

7. Your First Instinct

Many people struggle with multiple-choice tests because they overthink the questions. If you have studied sufficiently for the test, you should be prepared to trust your first instinct once you have carefully and completely read the question and all of the answer choices. There is a great deal of research suggesting that the mind can come to the correct conclusion very quickly once it has obtained all of the relevant information. At times, it may seem to you as if your intuition is working faster even than your reasoning mind. This may in fact be true. The knowledge you obtain while studying may be retrieved from your subconscious before you have a chance to work out the associations that support it. Verify your instinct by working out the reasons that it should be trusted.

8. Key Words

Many test takers struggle with multiple-choice questions because they have poor reading comprehension skills. Quickly reading and understanding a multiple-choice question requires a mixture of skill and experience. To help with this, try jotting down a few key words and phrases on a piece of

scrap paper. Doing this concentrates the process of reading and forces the mind to weigh the relative importance of the question's parts. In selecting words and phrases to write down, the test taker thinks about the question more deeply and carefully. This is especially true for multiple-choice questions that are preceded by a long prompt.

9. Subtle Negatives

One of the oldest tricks in the multiple-choice test writer's book is to subtly reverse the meaning of a question with a word like *not* or *except*. If you are not paying attention to each word in the question, you can easily be led astray by this trick. For instance, a common question format is, "Which of the following is...?" Obviously, if the question instead is, "Which of the following is not...?," then the answer will be quite different. Even worse, the test makers are aware of the potential for this mistake and will include one answer choice that would be correct if the question were not negated or reversed. A test taker who misses the reversal will find what he or she believes to be a correct answer and will be so confident that he or she will fail to reread the question and discover the original error. The only way to avoid this is to practice a wide variety of multiple-choice questions and to pay close attention to each and every word.

10. Reading Every Answer Choice

It may seem obvious, but you should always read every one of the answer choices! Too many test takers fall into the habit of scanning the question and assuming that they understand the question because they recognize a few key words. From there, they pick the first answer choice that answers the question they believe they have read. Test takers who read all of the answer choices might discover that one of the latter answer choices is actually *more* correct. Moreover, reading all of the answer choices can remind you of facts related to the question that can help you arrive at the correct answer. Sometimes, a misstatement or incorrect detail in one of the latter answer choices will trigger your memory of the subject and will enable you to find the right answer. Failing to read all of the answer choices is like not reading all of the items on a restaurant menu: you might miss out on the perfect choice.

11. Spot the Hedges

One of the keys to success on multiple-choice tests is paying close attention to every word. This is never truer than with words like *almost*, *most*, *some*, and *sometimes*. These words are called "hedges" because they indicate that a statement is not totally true or not true in every place and time. An absolute statement will contain no hedges, but in many subjects, the answers are not always straightforward or absolute. There are always exceptions to the rules in these subjects. For this reason,

you should favor those multiple-choice questions that contain hedging language. The presence of qualifying words indicates that the author is taking special care with his or her words, which is certainly important when composing the right answer. After all, there are many ways to be wrong, but there is only one way to be right! For this reason, it is wise to avoid answers that are absolute when taking a multiple-choice test. An absolute answer is one that says things are either all one way or all another. They often include words like *every*, *always*, *best*, and *never*. If you are taking a multiple-choice test in a subject that doesn't lend itself to absolute answers, be on your guard if you see any of these words.

5

12. Long Answers

In many subject areas, the answers are not simple. As already mentioned, the right answer often requires hedges. Another common feature of the answers to a complex or subjective question are qualifying clauses, which are groups of words that subtly modify the meaning of the sentence. If the question or answer choice describes a rule to which there are exceptions or the subject matter is complicated, ambiguous, or confusing, the correct answer will require many words in order to be expressed clearly and accurately. In essence, you should not be deterred by answer choices that seem excessively long. Oftentimes, the author of the text will not be able to write the correct answer without offering some qualifications and modifications. Your job is to read the answer choices thoroughly and completely and to select the one that most accurately and precisely answers the question.

13. Restating to Understand

Sometimes, a question on a multiple-choice test is difficult not because of what it asks but because of how it is written. If this is the case, restate the question or answer choice in different words. This process serves a couple of important purposes. First, it forces you to concentrate on the core of the question. In order to rephrase the question accurately, you have to understand it well. Rephrasing the question will concentrate your mind on the key words and ideas. Second, it will present the information to your mind in a fresh way. This process may trigger your memory and render some useful scrap of information picked up while studying.

14. True Statements

Sometimes an answer choice will be true in itself, but it does not answer the question. This is one of the main reasons why it is essential to read the question carefully and completely before proceeding to the answer choices. Too often, test takers skip ahead to the answer choices and look for true statements. Having found one of these, they are content to select it without reference to the question above. The savvy test taker will always read the entire question before turning to the answer choices. Then, having settled on a correct answer choice, he or she will refer to the original question and ensure that the selected answer is relevant. The mistake of choosing a correct-but-irrelevant answer choice is especially common on questions related to specific pieces of objective knowledge.

15. No Patterns

One of the more dangerous ideas that circulates about multiple-choice tests is that the correct answers tend to fall into patterns. These erroneous ideas range from a belief that B and C are the most common right answers, to the idea that an unprepared test-taker should answer "A-B-A-C-A-D-A-B-A." It cannot be emphasized enough that pattern-seeking of this type is exactly the WRONG way to approach a multiple-choice test. To begin with, it is highly unlikely that the test maker will plot the correct answers according to some predetermined pattern. The questions are scrambled and delivered in a random order. Furthermore, even if the test maker was following a pattern in the assignation of correct answers, there is no reason why the test taker would know which pattern he or she was using. Any attempt to discern a pattern in the answer choices is a waste of time and a distraction from the real work of taking the test. A test taker would be much better served by extra preparation before the test than by reliance on a pattern in the answers

6

Bonus Content & Audiobook

We host multiple bonus items online, including all 7 practice tests in digital format and our audiobook. Scan the QR code or go to this link to access this content:

testprepbooks.com/bonus/ptcb

The first time you access the tests, you will need to register as a "new user" and verify your email address.

If you have any issues, please email support@testprepbooks.com.

Introduction to the PTCB

Function of the Test

The Pharmacy Technician Certification Exam (PTCE) is administered by the Pharmacy Technician Certification Board (PTCB) and is used as part of the licensing process for pharmacy technicians. In many U.S. states, the PTCB reports that certified pharmacy technicians earn more money and have more access to promotions than those who are not certified. Test scores are typically used only in the certification process; employers do not typically request or consider the scores directly.

Most people taking the test are individuals looking to enhance their credentials to make progress in a career as a pharmacy technician. The test is administered nationwide, and states that use it are distributed around the country.

Test Administration

Test candidates must apply to take the PTCE and pay the test fee. Candidates whose applications are approved will receive an authorization at which time they will have ninety days to schedule their exam. The exam is given at any available time at Pearson VUE testing centers around the country.

Candidates are allowed up to four attempts to pass the PTCE. Candidates who do not pass must wait sixty days before a second or third attempt, and six months before a fourth attempt. After four attempts, interested individuals must submit a written request for additional attempts, which will be evaluated by the PTCB on a case-by-case basis. Such a request must spell out the specific steps that the candidate plans to take to obtain a successful result.

The PTCB will grant accommodations for students with disabilities, in cases where the requested accommodations are reasonable and consistent with the Americans with Disabilities Act (ADA).

Test Format

The PTCE consists of ninety questions, each with four multiple-choice answers. Ten of the ninety questions are unscored, although test takers do not know which ten. The test lasts 110 minutes, with another ten minutes set aside for a tutorial and post-exam survey. There are no breaks included in the testing time.

The test is administered on a computer. Test takers are not allowed to bring their own calculator, but they may request a calculator from the testing staff, and there is an on-screen calculator built into the testing program.

The content of the PTCE is divided between four domains, which are as follows:

Domain	Percentage of Test
Medications	40%
Federal Requirements	12.5%
Patient Safety and Quality Assurance	26.25%
Order Entry and Processing	21.25%

Scoring

Scores for the PTCE are based on the total number of correct answers given by the test taker. There is no penalty for incorrect answers or guesses and no benefit to leaving responses blank. The PTCB creates a reference score based off of an analysis of test items in which experts estimate the percentage of qualified pharmacy technicians that would be able to answer a given question. Those percentages are averaged together and scaled to a standard scale ranging from 1000 to 1600, with a passing score set at 1400. In 2015, 56,253 PTCEs were administered with 31,823 passing marks achieved, for an overall passing rate of 57 percent.

Recent/Future Developments

The PTCE is updated approximately every five years. The content outline was recently updated with an effective date of January 1, 2020. The domains were decreased from nine to four with only essential knowledge applicable to most practice settings being tested.

Study Prep Plan for the PTCB Exam

1 **Schedule -** Use one of our study schedules below or come up with one of your own.

2 **Relax -** Test anxiety can hurt even the best students. There are many ways to reduce stress. Find the one that works best for you.

3 **Execute -** Once you have a good plan in place, be sure to stick to it.

One Week Study Schedule		
Day 1	Medications
Day 2	Federal Requirements
Day 3	Order Entry and Processing
Day 4	Practice Test #1
Day 5	Practice Test #2
Day 6	Practice Test #3
Day 7	Take Your Exam!

Two Week Study Schedule			
Day 1	Medications	Day 8	Practice Test #1
Day 2	Drug Interactions and Contraindications	Day 9	Practice Test #2
Day 3	Drug Stability	Day 10	Practice Test #3
Day 4	Federal Requirements	Day 11	Practice Test #4
Day 5	Patient Safety and Quality Assurance	Day 12	Practice Test #5
Day 6	Order Entry and Processing	Day 13	Practice Test #6
Day 7	Equipment/Supplies for Drug Administration	Day 14	Take Your Exam!

One Month Study Schedule						
Day 1	Medications	Day 11	Issues that Require Pharmacist Intervention	Day 21	Practice Test #2
Day 2	Common Classes of Drugs for Different Diseases	Day 12	Types of Prescription Errors	Day 22	Answer Explanations #2
Day 3	Therapeutic Equivalence	Day 13	Order Entry and Processing	Day 23	Practice Test #3
Day 4	Drug Interactions and Contraindications	Day 14	Formulas/Calculations	Day 24	Answer Explanations #3
Day 5	Side Effects, Adverse Effects, and Allergies	Day 15	Calculating Doses Required	Day 25	Practice Test #4
Day 6	Drug Stability	Day 16	Medical Terminology and Abbreviations	Day 26	Answer Explanations #4
Day 7	Physical and Chemical Incompatibilities Related to Non-Sterile Compounding	Day 17	Equipment/Supplies for Drug Administration	Day 27	Practice Test #5
Day 8	Federal Requirements	Day 18	Identifying and Returning Medications and Supplies	Day 28	Practice Test #6
Day 9	Controlled Substances	Day 19	Practice Test #1	Day 29	Practice Test #7
Day 10	Patient Safety and Quality Assurance	Day 20	Answer Explanations #1	Day 30	Take Your Exam!

Build your own prep plan by visiting:
testprepbooks.com/prep

11

As you study for your test, we'd like to take the opportunity to remind you that you are capable of great things! With the right tools and dedication, you truly can do anything you set your mind to. The fact that you are holding this book right now shows how committed you are. In case no one has told you lately, you've got this! Our intention behind including this coloring page is to give you the chance to take some time to engage your creative side when you need a little brain-break from studying. As a company, we want to encourage people like you to achieve their dreams by providing good quality study materials for the tests and certifications that improve careers and change lives. As individuals, many of us have taken such tests in our careers, and we know how challenging this process can be. While we can't come alongside you and cheer you on personally, we can offer you the space to recall your purpose, reconnect with your passion, and refresh your brain through an artistic practice. We wish you every success, and happy studying!

Medications

Generic and Brand Names of Pharmaceuticals

Generic drugs are subjected to a similar review process as brand-name drugs to ensure safety, efficacy, and quality. Generally, **generic drugs** are copies of the brand-name drug and allow more affordable access to treatment and care. Pharmacy technicians should be familiar with the major therapeutic classifications of medications and should be able to match brand names of medications with the corresponding generic names.

Drug Abbreviations

There are common abbreviations that are used for certain medications. The table below provides the abbreviations and the drug names for some of these medications:

Common Abbreviation	Medication
APAP	Acetaminophen
ASA	Aspirin
EE	Ethinylestradiol
Fe	Iron
HCTZ	Hydrochlorothiazide
INH	Isoniazid
MgSO4	Magnesium sulfate
MOM	Milk of magnesia
MVI	Multivitamin
NS	Normal saline
NTG	Nitroglycerin
PCN	Penicillin
PNV	Prenatal vitamins
SMZ/TMP	Sulfamethoxazole/trimethoprim
TAC	Triamcinolone
TCN	Tetracycline

Brand vs. Generic Names

Brand Name	Generic Name	Class of Medication (Treatment of)
Medications Acting on the Nervous System		
Desyrel®	Trazodone	SARI (depression)
Celexa®	Citalopram	SSRI (anxiety and depression)
Lexapro®	Escitalopram	SSRI (anxiety and depression)
Prozac®	Fluoxetine	SSRI (anxiety and depression)
Paxil®	Paroxetine	SSRI (anxiety and depression)
Zoloft®	Sertraline	SSRI (anxiety and depression)
Effexor®	Venlafaxine	SNRI (anxiety and depression)
Cymbalta®	Duloxetine	SNRI (anxiety and depression)
Wellbutrin®	Bupropion	NDRI (anxiety and depression)
Elavil®	Amitriptyline	TCA (anxiety and depression)
Remeron	Mirtazapine	TeCA (anxiety and depression)
Buspar®	Buspirone	Anxiolytic (anxiety)
Atarax®	Hydroxyzine	Antihistamine (anxiety)
Seroquel®	Quetiapine	Anti-psychotic (schizophrenia, bipolar disorder)
Risperdal®	Risperidone	Anti-psychotic (schizophrenia, bipolar disorder)
Zyprexa®	Olanzapine	Anti-psychotic (schizophrenia, bipolar disorder)
Abilify®	Aripiprazole	Anti-psychotic (schizophrenia, bipolar disorder)
Geodon®	Ziprasidone	Anti-psychotic (schizophrenia, bipolar disorder)
Topamax®	Topiramate	Anticonvulsant (seizure, migraine)
Dilantin®	Phenytoin	Anticonvulsant (seizure)
Keppra®	Levetiracetam	Anticonvulsant (seizure)
Depakote®	Divalproex	Anticonvulsant (seizure)
Tegretol®	Carbamazepine	Anticonvulsant (seizure)
Trileptal®	Oxcarbazepine	Anticonvulsant (seizure)
Depakote®	Valproic acid	Anticonvulsant (seizure)
Lamictal®	Lamotrigine	Anticonvulsant (seizure)
Dilantin®	Phenytoin	Anticonvulsant (seizure)
Neurontin®	Gabapentin	Anticonvulsant (seizure, neuropathic pain)
Lyrica®	Pregabalin	Anticonvulsant (seizure, neuropathic pain)
Aricept®	Donepezil	Cognition enhancer (Alzheimer disease)
Namenda®	Memantine	Cognition enhancer (Alzheimer disease)
Requip®	Ropinirole	Dopamine agonist (Parkinson's disease)
Mirapex®	Pramipexole	Dopamine agonist (Parkinson's disease)
Sinemet®	Levodopa/carbidopa	Dopamine agonist (Parkinson's disease)
Ambien®	Zolpidem	Sedative (insomnia)
Lunesta®	Eszopiclone	Sedative (insomnia)
Restoril®	Temazepam	Sedative (insomnia)
Ativan®	Lorazepam	Sedative (anxiety, seizure)
Xanax®	Alprazolam	Sedative (anxiety)
Klonopin®	Clonazepam	Sedative (anxiety)
Valium®	Diazepam	Sedative (anxiety)
Catapres®	Clonidine	Sedative (hypertension)
Strattera®	Atomoxetine	SNRI (ADHD)
Ritalin®	Methylphenidate	Stimulant (ADHD)
Concerta®	Methylphenidate	Stimulant (ADHD)
Dexedrine®	Dextroamphetamine	Stimulant (ADHD)

Brand Name	Generic Name	Class of Medication (Treatment of)
Adderall®	Mixed salt of amphetamine	Stimulant (ADHD)
Vyvanse®	Lisdexamfetamine	Stimulant (ADHD)
Intuniv®	Guanfacine	Stimulant (ADHD)
Tenex®	Guanfacine	Stimulant (ADHD)
Provigil®	Modafinil	Stimulant (sleep disorder)
Maxalt®	Rizatriptan	Triptan (migraine)
Imitrex®	Sumatriptan	Triptan (migraine)
Medications Acting on the Cardiovascular System		
Zestril®	Lisinopril	ACE inhibitor (hypertension)
Zestoretic®	Lisinopril/HCTZ	ACE inhibitor & diuretic (hypertension)
Altace®	Ramipril	ACE inhibitor (hypertension)
Altace® HCT	Ramipril/HCTZ	ACE inhibitor & diuretic (hypertension)
Vasotec®	Elanapril	ACE inhibitor (hypertension)
Diovan®	Valsartan	ARB (hypertension)
Diovan® HCT	Valsartan/HCTZ	ARB & diuretic (hypertension)
Cozaar®	Losartan	ARB (hypertension)
Hyzaar®	Losartan/HCTZ	ARB & diuretic (hypertension)
Avapro®	Irbesartan	ARB (hypertension)
Avalide®	Irbesartan/HCTZ	ARB & diuretic (hypertension)
Atacand®	Candesartan	ARB (hypertension)
Atacand® Plus	Candesartan/HCTZ	ARB & diuretic (hypertension)
Micardis®	Telmisartan	ARB (hypertension)
Micardis® Plus	Telmisartan/HCTZ	ARB & diuretic (hypertension)
Benicar®	Olmesartan	ARB (hypertension)
Benicar® HCT	Olmesartan/HCTZ	ARB & diuretic (hypertension)
Tenormin®	Atenolol	Beta-blocker (hypertension)
Inderal®	Propranolol	Beta-blocker (hypertension)
Toprol®	Metoprolol	Beta-blocker (hypertension)
Coreg®	Carvedilol	Beta-blocker (hypertension)
Bystolic®	Nebivolol	Beta-blocker (hypertension)
Norvasc®	Amlodipine	CCB (hypertension)
Lotrel®	Amlodipine/benazepril	CCB & ACEI (hypertension)
Cardizen®	Diltiazem	CCB (hypertension)
Adalat®	Nifedipine	CCB (hypertension)
Verelan®	Verapamil	CCB (hypertension)
Lasix®	Furosemide	Diuretic (CHF)
Microzide®	HCTZ	Diuretic (hypertension, CHF)
Aldactone	Spironolactone	Diuretic (CHF)
Zocor®	Simvastatin	Statin (hyperlipidemia)
Lipitor®	Atorvastatin	Statin (hyperlipidemia)
Crestor®	Rosuvastatin	Statin (hyperlipidemia)
Pravachol®	Pravastatin	Statin (hyperlipidemia)
Altoprev®	Lovastatin	Statin (hyperlipidemia)
Zetia®	Ezetimibe	Absorption inhibitor (hyperlipidemia)
Vytorin®	Ezetimibe/simvastatin	Absorption inhibitor & statin (hyperlipidemia)
Tricor®	Fenofibrate	Fibrate (hyperlipidemia)

Brand Name	Generic Name	Class of Medication (Treatment of)
Lopid®	Gemfibrozil	Fibrate (hyperlipidemia)
Nitrostat	Nitroglycerin	Nitrate (coronary artery disease)
Plavix®	Clopidogrel	Blood thinner (blood clot)
Coumadin®	Warfarin	Blood thinner (blood clot)
Xarelto®	Rivaroxaban	Blood thinner (blood clot)
Eliquis®	Apixaban	Blood thinner (blood clot)
Lanoxin®	Digoxin	Glycoside (heart failure)
Digitek®	Digoxin	Glycoside (heart failure)
Klor-Con®	Potassium	Potassium supplement (hypokalemia)
Medications Acting on the Respiratory System		
Singulair®	Montelukast	Anti-inflammatory (asthma)
Nasonex®	Mometasone	Steroid (asthma, allergy)
Flovent®	Fluticasone	Steroid (asthma, COPD, allergy)
Qvar®	Beclometasone	Steroid (asthma)
Deltasone®	Prednisone	Steroid (asthma, autoimmune disorders)
Medrol®	Methylprednisolone	Steroid (asthma, allergy, inflammation)
Cortef®	Hydrocortisone	Steroid (asthma, COPD)
Ventolin®	Albuterol	Bronchodilator (asthma)
Combivent®	Albuterol/ipratropium	Bronchodilator (asthma, COPD)
Spiriva®	Tiotropium	Bronchodilator (COPD)
Rhinocort®	Budesonide	Steroid (nasal allergy)
Pulmicort®	Budesonide	Steroid (asthma, COPD)
Advair®	Fluticasone/salmeterol	Steroid & bronchodilator (asthma, COPD)
Symbicort®	Budesonide/formoterol	Steroid & bronchodilator (asthma, COPD)
Zonatuss®	Benzonatate	Local anesthetic (cough)
Medications Acting on the Digestive System		
Prilosec®	Omeprazole	PPI (GERD)
Nexium®	Esomeprazole	PPI (GERD)
Prevacid®	Lansoprazole	PPI (GERD)
Protonix®	Pantoprazole	PPI (GERD)
AcipHex®	Rabeprazole	PPI (GERD)
Pepcid®	Famotidine	PPI (GERD)
Zofran®	Ondansetron	Antiemetic (nausea and vomiting)
Anzemet®	Dolasetron	Antiemetic (nausea and vomiting)
Aloxi®	Palonosetron	Antiemetic (nausea and vomiting)
Motilium®	Domperidone	Antiemetic (nausea and vomiting)
Compro®	Prochlorperazine	Antiemetic (nausea and vomiting, migraine)
Bonine®	Meclizine	Antiemetic (nausea and vomiting, vertigo)
Colace®	Docusate	Stool softener (constipation)
Medications Acting on the Urinary System		
Flomax®	Tamsulosin	Urinary retainer (BPH)
Propecia®	Finasteride	Urinary retainer (BPH)
Cardura®	Doxazosin	Urinary retainer (BPH)
Detrol®	Tolterodine	Bladder relaxant (urinary incontinence)
Viagra®	Sildenafil	Vasodilator (erectile dysfunction)
Cialis®	Tadalafil	Vasodilator (erectile dysfunction)
Levitra®	Vardenafil	Vasodilator (erectile dysfunction)
Medications Acting on the Endocrine System		

Brand Name	Generic Name	Class of Medication (Treatment of)
Glucophage®	Metformin	Anti-diabetic (type 2 diabetes)
Glucotrol®	Glipizide	Anti-diabetic (type 2 diabetes)
Actos®	Pioglitazone	Anti-diabetic (type 2 diabetes)
Januvia®	Sitagliptin	Anti-diabetic (type 2 diabetes)
Janumet®	Sitagliptin/metformin	Anti-diabetic (type 2 diabetes)
Amaryl®	Glimepiride	Anti-diabetic (type 2 diabetes)
Lantus®	Insulin glargine	Anti-diabetic (type 1 and type 2 diabetes)
Humalog®	Insulin lispro	Anti-diabetic (type 1 and type 2 diabetes)
Byetta®	Exenatide	Anti-diabetic (type 2 diabetes)
Synthroid®	Levothyroxine	Hormone (hypothyroidism)
Levoxyl®	Levothyroxine	Hormone (hypothyroidism)
Premarin®	conjugated estrogens	Hormone (postmenopausal symptoms)
Yuvafem®	Estradiol	Hormone (postmenopausal symptoms)
Previfem®	Norgestimate/EE	Hormone (postmenopausal symptoms)
Yasmin®	Drospirenone/EE	Hormone (postmenopausal symptoms)
Plan B®	Levonorgestrel/EE	Hormone (postmenopausal symptoms)
Norlyda	Norethindrone	Hormone (menstrual disorders)
Medications Acting on the Immune System		
Amoxil®	Amoxicillin	Antibiotic (infections)
Zithromax®	Azithromycin	Antibiotic (infections)
Vibramycin®	Doxycycline	Antibiotic (infections)
Levaquin®	Levofloxacin	Antibiotic (infections)
Omnicef®	Cefdinir	Antibiotic (infections)
Avelox®	Moxifloxacin	Antibiotic (infections)
Biaxin®	Clarithromycin	Antibiotic (infections)
Flagyl®	Metronidazole	Antibiotic (infections)
Clindagel®	Clindamycin	Antibiotic (infections)
Bactrim®	SMZ/TMP	Antibiotic (infections)
Neosporin®	Neomycin/polymyxin B/ bacitracin	Antibiotic (skin infections)
Ciprodex®	Ciprofloxacin/dexamethasone	Antibiotic/steroid (ear infection)
TobraDex®	Tobramycin/dexamethasone	Antibiotic/steroid (eye infection)
Valtrex®	Valacyclovir	Anti-viral (herpes)
Viread®	Tenofovir	Anti-viral (hepatitis B, HIV)
Lamisil®	Terbinafine	Anti-fungal
Medications Acting on the Muscular and Skeletal System		
Fosamax®	Alendronate	Bone density modifier (osteoporosis)
Actonel®	Risedronate	Bone density modifier (osteoporosis)
Boniva®	Ibandronate	Bone density modifier (osteoporosis)
Evista®	Raloxifene	Estrogen modulator (osteoporosis)
Skelaxin®	Metaxalone	Muscle relaxant (musculoskeletal conditions)
Fexmid®	Cyclobenzaprine	Muscle relaxant (musculoskeletal conditions)
Zyloprim®	Allopurinol	Xanthine oxidase inhibitor (gout)
Uloric®	Febuxostat	Xanthine oxidase inhibitor (gout)
Lidoderm®	Lidocaine	Anesthetic (pain)
Vicodin®	Hydrocodone/acetaminophen	Opioid/NSAID (pain)
Oxycontin®	Oxycodone	Opioid (pain)
Percocet®	Oxycodone/acetaminophen	Opioid/NSAID (pain)

19

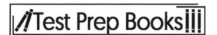

Brand Name	Generic Name	Class of Medication (Treatment of)
Ultram®	Tramadol	Opioid (pain)
Statex®	Morphine	Opioid (pain)
Advil®	Ibuprofen	NSAID (pain)
Bayer®	Aspirin	NSAID (pain)
Celebrex®	Celecoxib	NSAID (pain)
Mobic®	Meloxicam	NSAID (pain)
Aleve®	Naproxen	NSAID (pain)
Cambia®	Diclofenac	NSAID (pain)
Medications Acting on the Eyes		
Xalatan®	Latanoprost	Anti-glaucoma (increased intraocular pressure)
Lumigan®	Bimatoprost	Anti-glaucoma (increased intraocular pressure)
Travatan®	Travoprost	Anti-glaucoma (increased intraocular pressure)
Cosopt®	Dorzolamide/timolol	Anti-glaucoma (increased intraocular pressure)
Alphagan®	Brimonidine	Anti-glaucoma (increased intraocular pressure)
Claritin®	Loratadine	Antihistamine (allergy)
Zyrtec®	Cetirizine	Antihistamine (allergy)
Allegra®	Fexofenadine	Antihistamine (allergy)
Flonase®	Fluticasone	Antihistamine (allergy)
Astelin®	Azelastine	Antihistamine (allergy)
Patanol®	Olopatadine	Antihistamine (eye allergies)

Abbreviation key: **ADHD**: attention-deficit hyperactivity disorder, **ACEI**: angiotensin converting enzyme inhibitor, **ARB**: angiotensin receptor blocker, **CCB**: calcium channel blocker, **CHF**: congestive heart failure, **GERD**: gastroesophageal reflux disease, **NDRI**: norepinephrine dopamine reuptake inhibitor, **NSAID**: non-steroidal anti-inflammatory drug, **PPI**: proton pump inhibitor, **SARI**: serotonin agonist and reuptake inhibitor, **SNRI**: serotonin norepinephrine reuptake inhibitor, **SSRI**: selective serotonin reuptake inhibitor, **TCA**: tricyclic antidepressant, **TeCA**: tetracyclic antidepressant.

Common Classes of Drugs for Different Diseases

The following section will discuss different classes of medications referenced in the prior tables. It is important to recognize that drugs with a similar therapeutic effect might have different mechanisms/modes of action. For example, ACE inhibitors (e.g., ramipril), calcium channel blockers (e.g., amlodipine), and antihypertensive agents have similar therapeutic effects, but their mechanisms of action are different. When filling a prescription, it is important to understand how a drug works. Not only does knowledge about the pharmacology of a medicine help to identify possible drug interactions, but it also helps to facilitate patients' understanding of why medications are prescribed for them.

Medications Acting on the Nervous System
Antidepressants and Anxiolytics
Antidepressants are used to treat different mood disorders including depression, anxiety, phobias, and obsessive-compulsive disorder (OCD). Treatment for depression includes various medications, in addition to cognitive behavioral therapy (e.g., counseling).

The following are some of the symptoms frequently observed with depression:

- Difficulty concentrating

- Decreased interest or no interest in activities that used to be enjoyable
- Fatigue or lack of energy
- Sense of worthlessness or hopelessness
- Difficulty sleeping
- Changes in appetite
- Suicidal thoughts

Antidepressants exert their therapeutic effects by modulating the release or action of various neurotransmitters in the brain. **Neurotransmitters** are chemical messengers that transmit signals from one neuron to another. The common side effects of antidepressants are serotonin syndrome (headache, agitation, tremor, hallucination, tachycardia, hyperthermia, shivering and sweating), sexual dysfunction, weight changes, gastric acidity, diarrhea, sleep disturbances, and suicidal ideation.

Commonly prescribed antidepressant medications include:

- Sertraline
- Fluoxetine
- Paroxetine
- Citalopram
- Escitalopram
- Venlafaxine
- Desvenlafaxine
- Duloxetine
- Trazodone
- Bupropion
- Amitriptyline
- Nortriptyline

Benzodiazepines are a class of medications used for the short-term treatment of anxiety. They are often combined with antidepressants during initial treatment to increase treatment compliance. Benzodiazepines have the potential for significant physical dependence and withdrawal symptoms. These drugs can be used as sedatives and hypnotics and are also utilized as an add-on therapy with anti-convulsant medications. Benzodiazepines are often used to treat symptoms from alcohol withdrawal. The majority of benzodiazepines are labeled as Class IV controlled substances. The common side effects of these medications include physical dependence, sedation, drowsiness, dizziness, and lack of coordination.

The following are commonly prescribed benzodiazepines:

- Diazepam
- Lorazepam
- Clonazepam
- Alprazolam
- Midazolam
- Temazepam

Antipsychotics

Antipsychotics are used to treat psychosis, including schizophrenia and bipolar disorder. Psychosis is often characterized by a cluster of symptoms including delusions (false beliefs), paranoia (fear or anxiety), hallucinations, and disordered thoughts. The most common side effects of antipsychotics are dyskinesia (movement disorder), loss of libido or sex drive, gynecomastia (breast enlargement) in males, weight gain, heart diseases (QT prolongation), and metabolic disorders including type 2 diabetes.

The following are examples of commonly prescribed antipsychotics:

- Chlorpromazine
- Fluphenazine
- Haloperidol
- Aripiprazole
- Olanzapine
- Risperidone
- Ziprasidone
- Clozapine

Stimulant Medications

Stimulant medications are also called sympathomimetic agents, as they work by augmenting the sympathetic neurotransmitter activity (e.g., epinephrine and norepinephrine). These drugs are often used during emergencies to treat cardiac arrest and shock. Stimulant medications are also commonly used to treat attention-deficit hyperactivity disorder (ADHD). The common side effects of such medications include irritability, weight loss, insomnia, dizziness, agitation, headache, abdominal pain, tachycardia, growth retardation, hypertension, and cardiovascular disturbances, and death.

The following are examples of sympathomimetic drugs that are used in the treatment of ADHD:

- Methylphenidate
- Dextroamphetamine
- Lisdexamfetamine
- Mixed salts of amphetamine
- Atomoxetine

Anticonvulsant Medications

Anticonvulsants are also called antiepileptic or anti-seizure medications. They are used in the treatment of epileptic seizures. They suppress excessive firing of neurons and therefore prevent the initiation and spread of seizures. This class of medications is often used to stabilize mood in bipolar disorder or for the treatment of neuropathic pain. The common side effects are dizziness, sedation, weight gain, hepatotoxicity, hair loss, blood disorders, etc. Anticonvulsants are teratogenic and can cause significant harm to a fetus and result in birth defects. Therefore, female patients on anticonvulsant therapy should consult with their physicians before planning pregnancy.

The common medications in this class include the following:

- Carbamazepine
- Oxcarbazepine

- Phenytoin
- Valproic acid
- Divalproex
- Levetiracetam
- Lamotrigine
- Topiramate
- Clobazam

Medications Acting on the Cardiovascular System

Lipid-Lowering Medications

Lipid-lowering medications are used for the treatment of high blood lipids (**hyperlipidemia**), including high cholesterol (**hypercholesterolemia**) and high triglycerides (**hypertriglyceridemia**). Although a patient with hypercholesterolemia typically will not experience symptoms, the condition leads to the accumulation of fatty deposits in the blood vessels and liver, called atherosclerotic plaques. As time progresses, the deposits slow, impede, or block the flow of blood through the vessels. When blood flow is compromised to the heart muscle, ischemic heart disease can result. If the blood flow to the brain decreases, there is a possibility of ischemic stroke. Compromised blood supply in peripheral tissues and limbs can cause the development of peripheral vascular diseases (PVD). Lifestyle changes, such as a healthy diet and regular exercise, can significantly reduce the risk of hypercholesterolemia, even in the presence of predisposing genetic risk factors. Total cholesterol is determined from two components: **high-density lipoproteins (HDL) cholesterol**, considered the "good" cholesterol, and **low-density lipoproteins (LDL) cholesterol**, considered the "bad" cholesterol. Although it is helpful to keep a lower total cholesterol level for health and reduced disease risk, it is more critical to keep the ratio of HDL to LDL elevated.

Examples of lipid-lowering agents include:

- Statins: pravastatin, simvastatin, atorvastatin, rosuvastatin
- Cholesterol absorptions inhibitors: ezetimibe, cholestyramine, colestipol
- Fibrates: Gemfibrozil, fenofibrate

Antihypertensive Medications

Antihypertensive medications are used to treat high blood pressure. Although hypertensive individuals generally do not have symptoms, some people experience headaches, blurred vision, and dizziness. When high blood pressure is left untreated, it can lead to different clinical conditions including coronary artery disease, heart failure, kidney failure, or stroke. There are two values that comprise a blood pressure measure. The top number is the systolic pressure (the pressure on the arterial walls when the heart muscle contracts) and the bottom number is the diastolic pressure (the pressure on the arterial

23

walls when the heart muscle relaxes). Normal, healthy blood pressure in adults should be a systolic reading less than 120 mmHg and a diastolic pressure less than 80 mmHg.

There are three stages of high blood pressure, as outlined below:

- Prehypertension is characterized by systolic pressure between 120-139 mmHg and diastolic pressure between 80-89 mmHg

- Stage 1 hypertension is characterized by systolic pressure between 140-159 mmHg and diastolic pressure between 90-99 mmHg

- Stage 2 hypertension is characterized by systolic pressure of 160 mmHg and higher and diastolic pressure of 100 mmHg and higher

ACE Inhibitors (ACEIs): "ACE inhibitors," or angiotensin-converting enzyme inhibitors, are used to treat hypertension and cardiovascular diseases. The most common side effect of ACE inhibitors is a chronic dry cough, which, in many cases, is so annoying for a patient that it results in switching the medication to a different class. Other frequent side effects are low blood pressure (hypotension), dizziness, fatigue, headache, and hyperkalemia (increased blood potassium levels).

Examples of some ACE Inhibitors include:

- Ramipril
- Enalapril
- Lisinopril
- Captopril
- Quinapril
- Perindopril

Angiotensin Receptor Blockers (ARBs): ARBs have similar therapeutic effects as ACE Inhibitors; however, they tend to have better compliance, due to their lower incidence of persistent cough. They block the effect of angiotensin at the receptor site and are widely used for hypertension and cardiovascular disease. The common side effects are hypotension, fatigue, dizziness, headache, and hyperkalemia.

Examples of ARBs include:

- Losartan
- Irbesartan
- Valsartan
- Candesartan
- Telmisartan
- Olmesartan

Calcium Channel Blockers (CCBs): CCBs work by decreasing calcium entry through calcium channels. By regulating the movement of calcium, contraction of vascular smooth muscle is controlled, which causes blood vessels to dilate. This reduces blood pressure and workload on the heart, so this type of medication is used to treat hypertension and angina, and to control heart rate. Common side effects of CCBs include dizziness, flushing of the face, headache, edema (swelling), tachycardia (fast heart rate),

24

bradycardia (slow heart rate), and constipation. In combination with other medications that treat hypertension, calcium channel blocker toxicity is possible. Combinations, like verapamil with beta-blockers, can lead to severe bradycardia.

The following are examples of common calcium channel blockers:

- Amlodipine
- Nifedipine
- Felodipine
- Verapamil
- Diltiazem

Beta Blockers: Beta blockers are an important class of antihypertensive medications and are widely used to treat hypertension and cardiovascular disease. Some of them are also used to treat migraines, agitation, and anxiety. The side effects of beta blockers include hypotension, dizziness, bradycardia, headache, bronchoconstriction (trouble breathing), and fatigue.

Commonly prescribed beta blockers include:

- Atenolol
- Metoprolol
- Propranolol
- Sotalol
- Nadolol
- Carvedilol
- Labetalol

Vasodilators: Vasodilators cause blood vessels to dilate, lowering resistance to flow and reducing the workload on the heart. Vasodilators are used to treat hypertension, angina, and heart failure. The common side effects associated with their use include lightheadedness, dizziness, low blood pressure, flushing, reflex tachycardia, and headache. Vasodilators should not be combined with medications for erectile dysfunction, as this interaction can cause a fatal drop in blood pressure.

Examples of common vasodilators include:

- Nitroglycerin (available as sublingual tablets, sprays, patches, and extended release capsules)
- Isosorbide mononitrate
- Isosorbide dinitrate
- Hydralazine
- Minoxidil (limited use)

Alpha-1 Receptor Blockers: Alpha-blockers decrease the norepinephrine-induced vascular contraction, causing relaxation of blood vessels and a resultant reduction in blood pressure. This type of medication is used to treat high blood pressure and benign prostatic hyperplasia (BPH). The common side effects of this class of medications include hypotension, dizziness, headache, tachycardia, weakness, and nausea.

Examples of alpha blockers include:

- Prazosin
- Doxazosin
- Terazosin
- Tamsulosin (primarily used to treat BPH)
- Alfuzosin (primarily used to treat BPH)

Diuretics: Diuretics are used alone and in combination with other medications to treat hypertension. They are often used to eliminate excess body fluid to treat swelling/edema. Diuretics inhibit the absorption of sodium in renal tubules, resulting in increased elimination of salt and water. This action increases urine output, decreases blood volume, and lowers blood pressure. Side effects of diuretics include hypotension, dizziness, hypokalemia, dehydration, hyperglycemia, polyuria (frequent or excessive urination), fatigue, syncope (fainting), and tinnitus (ringing in ears).

Examples of commonly prescribed diuretics include:

- Furosemide
- Bumetanide
- Hydrochlorothiazide
- Spironolactone
- Amiloride
- Triamterene

Medications Acting on the Respiratory System
Antiasthmatics
Antiasthmatics are used to prevent and treat the acute symptoms of asthma, which is a disease characterized by wheezing, cough, chest tightness, and shortness of breath. Acute asthma can be life-threatening and needs to be treated promptly. **Asthma** is caused by inflammation and constriction of the airways, which results in difficulty breathing. Acute asthma may be exacerbated by certain triggering factors including environmental allergens, certain medications (e.g., aspirin), stress or exercise, smoke, and lung infections. It is important to avoid the triggering factors to prevent acute symptoms. The common side effects of antiasthmatics are cough, hoarseness, decreased bone mineral density, growth retardation in children, mouth thrush, agitation, tachycardia, and a transient increase in blood pressure.

There are two categories to asthma medications that can be used alone or in combination:

1. Bronchodilators (dilate the airway to ease breathing)

- Salbutamol
- Formoterol (generally used in combination with inhaled corticosteroids)
- Salmeterol (generally used in combination with inhaled corticosteroids)

2. Anti-inflammatory agents

- Fluticasone (inhaled corticosteroid)
- Budesonide (inhaled corticosteroid)
- Beclomethasone (inhaled corticosteroid)

26

- Montelukast
- Zafirlukast

Medication to Treat COPD (Chronic Obstructive Pulmonary Disease)

COPD is an obstructive airway disease that is characterized by coughing, wheezing, shortness of breath, and sputum production. COPD is a progressive disease that worsens over time. COPD is a combination of two common conditions: chronic bronchitis and emphysema. **Chronic bronchitis** is inflammation of the smooth lining of bronchial tubes. These tubes are responsible for carrying air to the alveoli, which are the air sacs in the lungs responsible for gaseous exchange between the lungs and blood. **Emphysema** results from alveolar damage, reducing the ability for healthy gas exchange. These two pathologies cause breathing difficulties in patients with COPD. The contributing factors for the development of COPD include smoking, environmental pollutions, and genetic risk factors. The side effects of COPD medications are similar to that of antiasthmatics.

The medications commonly used to treat COPD include the following:

1. Bronchodilators (dilate the airway to ease breathing)

- Salbutamol
- Formoterol (generally used in combination with inhaled corticosteroids)
- Salmeterol (generally used in combination with inhaled corticosteroids)

2. Anti-inflammatory agents

- Ipratropium (Atrovent)
- Tiotropium (Spiriva)
- Fluticasone
- Budesonide

Medications Acting on the Digestive System

Gastric acid Neutralizers/Suppressants

Gastric acid neutralizers/suppressants either neutralize stomach acid or decrease acid production, and therefore, provide relief of symptoms associated with hyperacidity. They are also used to treat gastroesophageal reflux disease, or GERD. In **GERD**, the lower esophageal sphincter does not close properly, which causes the contents of the stomach to back up into the esophagus. This leads to irritation, which is why the common symptoms of GERD include heartburn, coughing, nausea, difficulty swallowing, and a strained voice. There are many factors that can cause or exacerbate GERD including obesity, pregnancy, eating a large meal, acidic foods, a hiatal hernia, and smoking. Lifestyle modifications such as avoiding trigger foods, losing weight (if obesity is a component), decreasing meal size, and trying not to lie down immediately after eating, can reduce symptoms.

The medications used to treat hyperacidity in the stomach include the following:

- Antacids (e.g., calcium carbonate)
- Ranitidine
- Famotidine
- Omeprazole
- Esomeprazole

- Lansoprazole
- Rabeprazole
- Pantoprazole

Medications Acting on the Endocrine System

Anti-Diabetic Medications

Anti-diabetic medications are used to treat diabetes, which is a chronic metabolic disease in which the body cannot properly regulate blood sugar levels. This dysregulation is caused by either inadequate or absent insulin production from the pancreas (Type 1 diabetes) or inadequate action of insulin in peripheral tissues (i.e., insulin resistance in Type 2 diabetes). Type 1 diabetes usually occurs in early childhood and is typically treated with insulin injections or medications. Type 2 diabetes generally develops later in adolescence or adulthood, and is related to poor diet, lack of physical activity, and obesity. Diabetes often does not cause daily symptoms, but symptoms do arise when blood sugar is either too high (from inadequate control) or too low (from inappropriate dosing of hypoglycemic [antidiabetic] agents, including insulin). A few of the symptoms of diabetes include increased thirst and hunger, fatigue, blurred vision, a tingling sensation in the feet, and frequent urination.

Examples of some antidiabetic medications include:

- Insulin
- Metformin
- Acarbose
- Gliclazide, glyburide, glimepiride
- Rosiglitazone, pioglitazone
- Sitagliptin, saxagliptin

Drug and Non-Drug Therapy in Type 2 Diabetes: The most effective way of treating Type 2 diabetes is to combine both drug and non-drug therapies. As a part of the treatment, drug therapy can stimulate the pancreas to produce more insulin or help the body better use the insulin produced by the pancreas. As part of the non-drug therapy, counseling is necessary to help patients understand the important diet and lifestyle modifications. Patients with Type 2 diabetes should try to decrease their consumption of processed foods, simple carbohydrates and refined sugars, and overall caloric intake, while increasing physical activity. These interventions help to decrease the requirement of antidiabetic medications and prevent long-term diabetes-related complications.

Glucometer: Patients with diabetes should test their blood sugar regularly to ensure that it is well-controlled. **Glucometers** are used to measure blood sugar. Patients insert a testing strip into the glucometer, prick a finger with a lancet, and then apply a drop of blood to the test strip. Upon applying the blood, the meter gives a blood sugar reading. Most modern machines need a very small amount of blood to obtain an accurate reading and can generate the result in seconds. Some more advanced meters can store readings for a period of time, so patients can present it to their physicians for review.

Female Hormones

Hormonal medications are generally used as oral contraceptives to prevent pregnancy. Female hormonal medications are also used to treat premenstrual symptoms (PMS), post-menopausal symptoms, acne, and endometriosis. They are also used as emergency contraceptives to prevent unwanted and accidental pregnancy. **Oral contraceptives** can provide hormones (estrogen and/or

progestin), which suppress the egg maturation and ovulation process. Additionally, hormonal contraceptives prevent the endometrium from thickening in preparation to hold the fertilized egg. A mucus barrier is created by progestin, which stops the sperm from migrating to the fallopian tubes and fertilizing the egg. There are many side effects associated with oral contraceptives, including increasing the risk of fatal blood clots, especially in women older than 35 or in women who smoke. More common and less severe side effects include:

- Nausea and stomach upset
- Headache
- Weight gain
- Spotting between periods
- Mood changes
- Lighter periods
- Aching or swollen breasts

More serious side effects that need immediate emergency care include:

- Chest pain
- Blurred vision
- Stomach pain
- Severe headaches

Examples of some commercially available brands of contraceptive include:

- Yasmin
- Ortho Tri-Cyclen
- TriNessa
- Sprintec
- Ovcon
- Plan B (emergency contraceptive)

Medications Acting on the Immune System

Antivirals

Antivirals are used to fight viruses in the body, by either stopping replication or blocking the function of a viral protein. They are used to treat HIV, herpes, hepatitis B and C, and influenza, among other viruses. Vaccines are also available to prevent some viral infections. Side effects of antivirals include headache, nausea, blood abnormalities including anemia and neutropenia (low neutrophil count), dizziness, cough, runny or stuff nose, etc.

Some examples of disease-specific antivirals include:

- Acyclovir, valaciclovir (Valtrex): Herpes simplex, herpes zoster, and herpes B
- Ritonavir, indinavir, darunavir: Protease inhibitor for HIV
- Tenofovir (Viread): Hepatitis B and HIV infection
- Interferon: Hepatitis C
- Oseltamivir (Tamiflu): Influenza

Antibiotics

Antibiotics are antimicrobial agents that are used for treatment and prevention of bacterial infections. The mechanism of action of an antibiotic involves either killing bacteria or inhibiting their growth. Antibiotics are not effective against viruses, and therefore, they should not be used to treat viral infections. Antibiotics are often prescribed based on the result of a bacterial culture to ascertain which class of antibiotic(s) the respective strain will respond to. The common side effects of antibiotics include allergies, hypersensitivity reactions or anaphylaxis, stomach upset, diarrhea, candida (fungal) infections, and bacterial resistance (superinfection, in which a strain of bacteria develops resistance to broad classes of antibiotics).

Commonly prescribed antibiotics include:

- Penicillin V
- Amoxicillin (with or without clavulanic acid)
- Ampicillin
- Cloxacillin
- Cephalexin
- Cefuroxime
- Cefixime
- Tetracycline
- Doxycycline
- Minocycline
- Gentamicin
- Tobramycin
- Ciprofloxacin
- Levofloxacin
- Erythromycin
- Azithromycin
- Clarithromycin
- Clindamycin

Antimetabolites

Antimetabolites are used to treat diseases including severe psoriasis, rheumatoid arthritis, and several types of cancer (breast, lung, lymphoma, and leukemia). The most commonly used medication of this class is methotrexate, which suppresses the growth of abnormal cells and the action of the immune system. Methotrexate is widely used to treat rheumatoid arthritis. This medication is typically prescribed as a once per week dose, and it should not be prescribed for daily dosing because overdosing can be lethal. Pharmacists should be alerted to any prescriptions for daily methotrexate, as the doctor must be contacted to confirm and correct the dosing.

The following are the potential side effects of methotrexate:

- Dizziness
- Drowsiness
- Headache
- Swollen gums
- Increased susceptibility to infections

30

- Hair loss
- Confusion
- Weakness

Steroids

Steroids are used to treat allergies, asthma, rashes, swelling, and inflammation. These medications are available in different forms, such as oral tablets, nasal sprays, eye drops, topical creams and ointments, inhalants, and injections. The common side effects of steroids include insulin resistance and diabetes, osteoporosis, depression, hypertension, edema, glaucoma, etc.

The following are examples of commonly prescribed corticosteroids:

- Prednisone
- Hydrocortisone
- Fluticasone
- Triamcinolone
- Mometasone
- Budesonide
- Fluocinolone
- Betamethasone
- Dexamethasone

Total Parenteral Nutrition: Total parenteral nutrition is used in situations where a patient cannot orally ingest food or digest food through the stomach and intestines. In such cases, total parental nutrition is essential to maintain patient nourishment and to prevent wasting or malnutrition.

The clinical conditions requiring total parenteral nutrition include the following:

- Any cause of malnourishment
- Failure of liver or kidneys
- Short bowel syndrome
- Severe burns
- Enterocutaneous fistulas
- Sepsis
- Chemotherapy and radiation
- Neonates
- Conditions requiring full bowel rest, such as pancreatitis, ulcerative colitis, or Crohn's disease

Therapeutic Equivalence

There are certain parameters (bioavailability, dosage form, active ingredients, safety profile, and clinical efficacy) that need to be identical or nearly identical to ensure that a specific medication and the reference medication are equivalent. The extent that one medication can be substituted for another depends on which type of equivalence (bio, pharmaceutical, and therapeutic) has been established. Therefore, pharmacy technicians must understand the different types of equivalence.

Pharmaceutical Equivalents

Pharmaceutical equivalents refer to two or more medications that have equal quantities/strength of the identical active ingredients in the same dosage form, and with the same route of administration. The active ingredients in pharmaceutical equivalent formulations should meet the official compendia (e.g., USP and NF) standard on identity, purity, strength, and quality. Pharmaceutical equivalent formulations, however, may vary in shape, scoring configuration, packaging, excipients (preservatives, colors, and flavors), labeling, and date of expiration.

Pharmaceutical Alternatives

Pharmaceutical alternatives refer to medications that have the same therapeutic moiety (structure), but are formulated as different salts, esters, or complexes. They might have different strengths and dosage forms. For example, tetracycline 250 mg formulated as hydrochloride and phosphate salts are pharmaceutical alternatives. Generally, different dosage forms and strengths of a single medication by a single manufacturer are pharmaceutical alternatives. The extended release formulations and the standard/immediate release formulations are, therefore, pharmaceutical alternatives, as they carry the same active ingredient.

Bioequivalents

Bioequivalents refer to two or more pharmaceutically-comparable products that demonstrate equivalent bioavailability when tested under similar experimental conditions. The rate and extent of absorption of bioequivalent products should be identical. Bioequivalence of two or more formulations is determined by comparing the rate and extent of absorption of those formulations with that of the reference standard formulation.

Therapeutic Equivalents

Therapeutic equivalents refer to two or more pharmaceutical products that provide identical clinical effect, safety, and efficacy. Therapeutic equivalents should meet the following criteria:

1. They should have identical safety and efficacy

2. They should be pharmaceutically-equivalent

3. They should be bioequivalent

4. They should be adequately labeled

5. They should be manufactured in accordance with the standards of Current Good Manufacturing Practice (cGMP)

Bioavailability

Bioavailability is a function of the rate and extent of absorption of a drug from a formulation. It is the fraction of a drug that reaches the blood circulation after administration. The bioavailability following an intravenous administration is 100%, since the medication is completely available in circulation.

The following are parameters which measure bioavailability on a concentration-time curve:

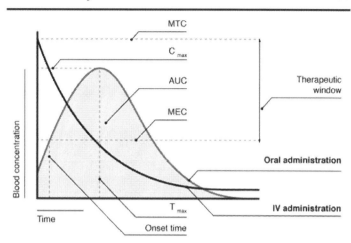

- **C$_{max}$**: The peak blood concentration of the medication.

- **T$_{max}$**: The time to reach the peak blood concentration of the medication; indicative of the rate of absorption of a drug from a formulation

- **MEC**: The minimum effective concentration (i.e., the minimum drug concentration required to exhibit the therapeutic effect)

- **MTC**: The maximum therapeutic concentration at which the greatest therapeutic effect of a drug is achieved

- **Therapeutic window**: The range of drug concentrations between which the desired therapeutic effect is obtained without any significant toxicity

- **AUC**: The area under the concentration-time curve; refers to the amount of the drug absorbed in the system following administration. It is the principal index of the bioavailability of a drug from a dosage form.

Below are explanations of two types of bioavailability:

- **Absolute bioavailability**: This refers to the comparison between the bioavailability of a drug following a non-intravenous route (e.g., oral, rectal, sublingual, subcutaneous, transdermal, etc.) of administration and the bioavailability of the same drug following intravenous administration. It is measured by the ratio of AUC from the non-IV route to that of the IV route.

- So, % absolute bioavailability is:

$$F_{abs} = \frac{AUC_{PO}}{D_{PO}} \times \frac{D_{IV}}{AUC_{IV}} \times 100$$

Where, AUC$_{po}$ = AUC from oral administration

AUC$_{iv}$ = AUC from intravenous administration

33

D_{po} = dose of oral formulation

D_{iv} = dose of intravenous formulation

- **Relative bioavailability**: This refers to the comparison of the bioavailability of a drug from one dosage form (e.g., tablet or capsule) to the bioavailability of the same drug from a reference dosage form (e.g., syrup or suspension). When the reference formulation is an IV dosage form, it also indicates absolute bioavailability.

- So, % relative bioavailability is:

$$F_{rel} = \frac{AUC_A}{D_A} \times \frac{D_B}{AUC_B} \times 100$$

Where, AUC_A = AUC from formulation A (test formulation)

AUC_B = AUC from formulation B (reference standard)

D_A = dose of formulation A (test formulation)

D_B = dose of formulation B (reference standard)

Generic Substitution

Generic substitution refers to filling a prescription with a generic, therapeutically-equivalent formulation instead of an original brand name formulation. For example, the generic form of Lipitor® is Atorvastatin; both have the same clinical efficacy and safety for treating high cholesterol. Dispensing generic Atorvastatin for a prescription written for Lipitor® is an example of generic substitution. There are different laws in each state for filling prescriptions with generic substitutions, and therefore, it is important to know and abide by the laws in the state of employment.

Generally, generic medications are less expensive for patients. Prescribers may deem the brand name medically necessary and order "dispense as written" or "no substitution" to prevent generic substitutions. It is also important to check the therapeutic index of a drug before substituting with a generic medication. Drugs with a narrow therapeutic index should be cautiously dispensed as generics, as minute changes in bioavailability can impose significant toxicity. Examples of such drugs include levothyroxine, lithium, warfarin, phenytoin, and digoxin.

Therapeutic Substitutions

Therapeutic substitution can be done in two different forms: substitution of an equally potent drug from within the same class or substitution of a drug from a different class of drugs, but with the same pharmacologic effect and similar potency yet a different mechanism of action. An example of the first type of substitution is dispensing enalapril for lisinopril, which is substitution of an ACE inhibitor with another ACE inhibitor. An example of the second type of substitution is giving enalapril in place of amlodipine, which is substituting a calcium channel blocker with an ACE inhibitor, where both drugs have similar antihypertensive effect but different modes of action. The frequency of therapeutic substitutions is low in community pharmacies and is more likely to happen in hospitals or federal facilities. It is imperative to make sure that these types of substitutions are discussed with the prescriber before making the substitution.

34

There are several consequences of therapeutic substitutions:

- Either over- or under-treating the patient
- The unfavorable effects either get better or worse
- There could be different adverse effects
- The cost of the prescription could be higher or lower for the patient

Orange Book

Orange Book is a reference to find drugs that have been approved and evaluated for therapeutic equivalence. The official name of the book is **Approved Drug Products with Therapeutic Equivalence Evaluations**, and it is now available online at the FDA's website.

Drug Interactions and Contraindications

Drug interaction refers to the alteration in pharmacology (absorption, distribution, metabolism, elimination, efficacy, side effects, etc.) of a medication by various factors including disease conditions, prescription and OTC medications, and foods or nutritional supplements. These interactions may result in either an augmentation or decrease in the efficacy and/or toxicity of the respective medication. Drug interaction should be carefully reviewed in order to avoid serious life-threatening conditions.

Examples of different types of drug interactions and examples within each type are described below.

Drug-Disease Interactions
NSAIDS and Peptic Ulcers
NSAIDs including aspirin, ibuprofen, naproxen, and indomethacin can cause stomach irritation and can aggravate peptic ulcer symptoms. Therefore, NSAIDs should not be used by patients with peptic ulcers or GERD. If NSAIDs are used by patients with hyperacidity, gastro-protective agents, such as proton pumps inhibitors (e.g., omeprazole, pantoprazole, lansoprazole, etc.), should also be used.

Diuretics and Diabetes
Diuretics are used to treat hypertension and edema. Hydrochlorothiazide is a commonly prescribed diuretic that can cause glucose intolerance and hyperglycemia. Therefore, if a patient with type 2 diabetes is prescribed a diuretic, blood sugar control becomes difficult, so routine monitoring of blood sugar is required. If blood sugar is not properly controlled, dose adjustments of the anti-diabetic medication or alternative diuretics should be considered.

Drug-Drug Interactions
Warfarin and NSAIDs
Warfarin is a commonly prescribed blood thinner, indicated to prevent blood clots in various cardiovascular diseases. Patients on warfarin should not take other prescription/OTC/herbal medications without consulting with their prescriber and pharmacist. For example, commonly available OTC NSAIDs can cause an increase in the blood-thinning effect of warfarin and result in internal hemorrhage.

The following medications can interact with warfarin:

- Aspirin
- Acetaminophen (at high doses)

- Ibuprofen
- Naproxen
- Celecoxib
- Diclofenac
- Indomethacin
- Piroxicam

Oral Contraceptives and Antibiotics

Antibiotics can decrease the effect of hormonal oral contraceptives, thus increasing the possibility of pregnancy even while taking the contraceptive. Non-hormonal back-up methods, such as condoms, should be used while a woman taking an oral contraceptive is prescribed an antibiotic. Other medications that can affect the efficacy of oral contraceptives include anti-fungals, a few anti-seizure medications, certain HIV medications, and a few herbal preparations, like St. John's Wort.

Nitroglycerin and Erectile Dysfunction Medications

Nitroglycerin is a vasodilator that is often used to treat episodes of angina. To prevent recurring angina, the extended release capsules of nitroglycerin are taken daily, whereas in cases of non-frequent occurrence, sublingual tablets or sprays can be used. Medications to treat erectile dysfunctions, such as sildenafil, tadalafil, and vardenafil, should not be taken with nitroglycerin. These medications augment the vasodilatory effect of nitroglycerin and can lead to irreversible hypotension and fatality. Emergency care should be sought immediately if this combination accidentally happens. The symptoms of hypotension include dizziness, fainting, and cold, clammy skin.

Drug-Food and Drug-Nutrient Interactions

Statins and Grapefruit Juice

Statins (e.g., pravastatin, simvastatin, atorvastatin, and rosuvastatin) are used to treat hypocholesteremia. Patients taking this medication should avoid drinking grapefruit juice or consuming large amounts of grapefruit because this juice decreases the metabolism of statins, resulting in a buildup of statins in the body. The risk of serious side effects is increased when statin buildup occurs, with possible resultant muscle or liver damage. Pharmacists should counsel patients about avoiding grapefruit juice while on statins. Although increasing statin dosage may seem to benefit the patient, the liver can only process so much. Accumulation of a statin in the body can cause muscle damage, pain, and rhabdomyolysis—a serious and potentially lethal side effect. In rhabdomyolysis, the skeletal muscle is rapidly catabolized. Patients taking statins should undergo routine blood tests and notify their doctors immediately about symptoms of muscle pain or fatigue. Undetected and unmanaged rhabdomyolysis can result in death.

MAOIs and Tyramine

Monoamine oxidase inhibitors (MAOIs) are used to treat chronic depression that does not respond to other medications or treatments. Due to side effects and drug interactions, MAOIs are not commonly prescribed. Examples of MAOIs are phenelzine (Nardil®), selegiline (Emsam®), and tranylcypromine (Parnate®). MAOIs can cause serotonin syndrome. There are many medications and foods that can lead to severe side effects when combined with MAOIs. Foods like wine, cheese, certain meats, and pickled foods carry tyramine, which leads to spikes in blood pressure, if co-administered with MAOIs.

Drug-OTC Interactions
Antihypertensives and Decongestants
Pseudoephedrine and **phenylephrine** are used as decongestants in different OTC cough and cold medications. These medications have sympathomimetic effects and can cause elevated blood pressure. Therefore, if a decongestant medication is taken by patients on antihypertensive medication, it reduces the blood pressure control of the antihypertensive agent. Hypertensive patients should avoid taking OTC medications containing sympathomimetic agents.

Antihistamines and Sedatives
OTC **antihistamines**, such as diphenhydramine and chlorpheniramine, are used to treat various allergic conditions. Antihistamines can cause sedation and drowsiness, which can potentiate the side effects of sedatives and hypnotics. Patients taking sedatives—such as diazepam, lorazepam, alprazolam, and midazolam—should be cautious when taking an OTC antihistamine.

Drug-Laboratory Interactions
Antibiotics and Bacterial Cultures
Treatment with certain medications can affect laboratory results. For example, the blood or urine sample collected from a patient taking an antibiotic for one infection might yield a false antibiotic sensitivity or culture report for a second infection. The lab work should, therefore, be scheduled after the wash-out period of the first antibiotic.

Polypharmacy
Polypharmacy occurs when a patient takes multiple medications to treat different medical conditions. This happens mostly in elderly patients who are being treated for several medical conditions. Polypharmacy can cause serious drug interactions. Polypharmacy also tends to happen when a patient sees multiple doctors to treat separate conditions. Pharmacy technicians can help to prevent adverse consequences of polypharmacy by alerting pharmacists to drug interactions.

Therapeutic Contraindications Associated with Medications
Alcohol
Alcohol should be avoided while patients are on prescription medications. Consumption of alcohol with medications can cause nausea, vomiting, fainting, loss of coordination, or extreme drowsiness. More severe reactions can lead to heart problems, internal bleeding, and difficulty breathing. Certain medications, when combined with alcohol, can cause toxicity. As alcohol is a strong CNS depressant, combining it with other depressants, like benzodiazepines or sleeping medications, can be dangerous and can cause respiratory failure. If alcohol is combined with a high dose of acetaminophen, there is potential for serious liver damage. Additionally, if alcohol is consumed while taking metronidazole, the patient can experience significant side effects including nausea, vomiting, abdominal pain, cramps, facial redness, headache, tachycardia, and liver damage.

Age
Age has a significant effect on the pharmacology of medications. Maturation during childhood causes various changes in body composition, accompanying growth and development. Therefore, newborns, infants, children, and adolescents often do not receive full adult dosages. As mentioned, medication doses should be appropriately calculated based on the age and weight of the child. There are many medications that are not approved by the FDA for children and yet are used "off label." Unexpected

reactions can happen when medications are not studied in pediatric populations. For example, tetracycline is contraindicated in children because it can bind with the calcium in bones, modify bone cartilage, and cause growth retardation. Generally, if a physician prescribes a medication that is not approved for use in children, pharmacy technicians should consult with the pharmacist, who will rely on their professional judgment about how to proceed (i.e., dispense the medication or talk with the physician).

In elderly adults, there can also be significant changes in pharmacokinetics and pharmacodynamics of a medication. Geriatric populations often have comorbid conditions, including cardiovascular disease, diabetes, and renal insufficiencies. Aging can decrease the body's clearance of a medication, resulting in buildup and manifesting in unwanted effects. Routine blood work and dose adjustments may be necessary in the geriatric population.

OTC Medications

Some OTC medications impose significant risks with certain disease conditions. A few OTC medications can lead to an increase in blood pressure, so these may be contraindicated in patients with hypertension. The following medications are known to cause problems for patients with hypertension:

- NSAIDS (ibuprofen and naproxen)
- Decongestants like pseudoephedrine
- Migraine formulations with caffeine

Patients with high blood pressure should talk to a pharmacist or a physician before taking OTC medications or herbal supplements.

Pregnancy

During pregnancy, medications should be prescribed carefully, to prevent harm to the developing fetus. For some medications, there might not be enough data available regarding safety during pregnancy, and therefore, they must be used cautiously after weighing the benefits versus the risks. Many medications are contraindicated during pregnancy, as they have teratogenic effects and can cause birth defects. If a patient is on a teratogenic medication prior to pregnancy, the medication should be stopped upon conception. A few examples of medications that are contraindicated in pregnancy include ACE inhibitors (e.g., ramipril, enalapril, lisinopril, etc.), ARBs (e.g., losartan, candesartan, irbesartan, etc.), isotretinoin, tetracycline antibiotics, hormonal therapies, and immunosuppressants (e.g., methotrexate).

Strength/Dose, Dosage Forms, Routes of Administration, and Duration of Drug Therapy

Dose and Dosage Forms
The list below shows the different dosage abbreviations and their meanings:

- **cap** = capsule
- **tab** = tablet
- **gtt** = drop
- **i, ii, iii, iv = 1, 2, 3, 4** (quantities are often identified with roman numerals on prescriptions)
- **mg** = milligrams
- **mL** = milliliter

- **tbsp**. = tablespoon (15 mL)
- **tsp**. = teaspoon (5 mL)
- **ss** = one-half
- **mcg/ ug** = microgram

Note that *ug* is not being used as much anymore, as it is confused with *mg*. If unsure, pharmacy technicians should check with the prescriber.

A **pharmaceutical dosage form** is a formulation type in which the active ingredient(s) (with excipients) is manufactured to be administered to patients. There are different types of pharmaceuticals dosage forms, some of which include the following:

1. **Tablets** are the most common oral dosage form. Tablets can be made from firmly condensed powder into the desired shape. Tablets are often coated to mask a bad taste/smell of a medication. There are also more complex types of tablets that are designed by using special polymers, which release the medication from the tablet core in a controlled pattern, often in slow-release formulations.

2. **Capsules** can use a hard or soft shell, which contains powder or liquid ingredients inside. Most capsules are made from gelatin, a collagen by-product of an animal protein. Other capsule shells contain plant-based polysaccharides such as carrageenan, modified starch, and cellulose.

3. **Liquid formulations** are primarily of two categories: elixirs and suspensions. An **elixir** is a clear liquid solution in which active ingredients are mixed in a liquid carrier (or formulation vehicle); shaking is *not* required to mix the ingredients. In **suspensions**, medication is suspended in a liquid carrier. It is essential to shake suspensions before administration, as some ingredients often collect at the bottom as sediment. Sometimes a suspension is supplied as a dry powder, which needs to be mixed with the appropriate volume of distilled water, before dispensing it to the patient.

4. **Suppositories** are solid dosage forms that are inserted into body cavities, including the rectum, vagina, and urethra, where they melt and provide local or systemic effects. Due to local administration, suppositories show fewer side effects compared to orally-administered medications. Suppositories also provide greater absorption of the medication, as they bypass the first pass metabolism in the liver.

5. An **injectable** is a pharmaceutical dosage form that follows the parenteral route to administer a medication locally or systemically. An injectable is manufactured in an aseptic environment and must be sterile in nature. Examples of some types of injectable routes are intravenous, intradermal, subcutaneous, intramuscular, intraperitoneal, intrathecal, intracardiac, epidural, etc.

Pharmacokinetics

Pharmacokinetics is the study of the fate of a medication in the body. The knowledge of a medication's pharmacokinetics helps to determine dosing. Pharmacokinetics of a medication includes four parameters: absorption, distribution, metabolism, and elimination. **Absorption** refers to the process of the medication entering blood circulation. **Distribution** is the process of dispersion of the medication throughout the body, including the site of action. **Metabolism** is the process of degradation of the parent molecule into different metabolites. **Elimination** refers to the process of removal of the parent molecule and the metabolites from the body.

39

The pharmacokinetic of a medication can be affected by various factors including:

- Age
- Race
- Gender
- Genetic factors
- Dosage form
- Disease conditions
- Foods
- Concurrent administration of other conditions

Pharmacodynamics

Pharmacodynamics refers to the study of the effects of a medication at the site of action. This helps to ascertain the mechanism of action of a medication and to determine the dose-response relationship by analyzing the interaction of a drug with its receptors at the target organ or site.

Half-Life

Half-life is a pharmacokinetic parameter that represents the unit of time over which the concentration of a medication in circulation drops to half of its initial concentration. For example, if a medication has a half-life of 15 hours, blood concentration of the drug decreases 50% every 15 hours. The longer a medication's half-life, the longer the effects persist; therefore, lower therapeutic doses or longer dosing intervals should be used. Medications in the same therapeutic class might have different half-lives, resulting in varying durations of action. Knowledge of a medication's half-life helps to determine the necessary dosage and the frequency of administration.

A medication's half-life depends on the elimination rate kinetics of the respective medication. There are two common types of elimination rate kinetics that are studied in pharmacology: first order kinetics and zero order kinetics.

First Order Kinetics

When a medication follows **first order elimination kinetics**, the medication undergoes a linear rate of elimination in proportion to its concentration. However, the elimination half-life remains constant independent of the initial concentration of the reactant. The metabolism and elimination of most of the drugs follow first order kinetics. Below is an example in which an IV administration of a medication follows first order kinetics with a constant half-life (i.e., $t_1 = t_2 = t_3$).

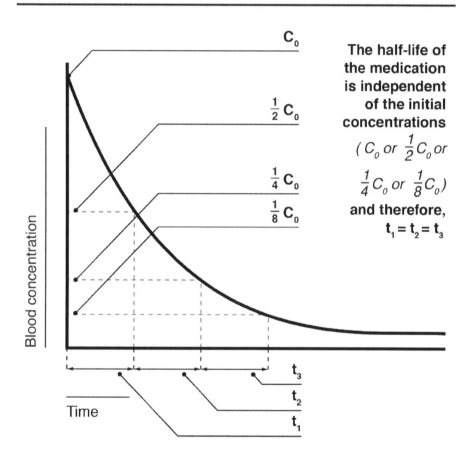

Concentration-time curve (IV)

1st order of elimination kinetics

The half-life of the medication is independent of the initial concentrations

$(C_0$ or $\frac{1}{2}C_0$ or $\frac{1}{4}C_0$ or $\frac{1}{8}C_0)$

and therefore,

$t_1 = t_2 = t_3$

Zero Order Kinetics

Zero order kinetics refers to a reaction that proceeds at a rate independent of the concentrations of the reactants. For example, alcohol metabolism in the liver follows zero order kinetics.

Routes of Administration and Duration of Therapy

There are different routes of administration for medications including the following:

- **Orally** or **by mouth**: oral tablets, capsules, liquid preparations (elixirs and suspensions)
- **Nasally**: sprays or drips
- **Intravenously (IV)**: goes through the veins and must be liquid
- **Intramuscularly (IM)**: goes into the muscle and must be liquid
- **Subcutaneously**: usually an injection under the skin
- **Epidurally**: may be infused into epidural space in the spinal cord
- **Transdermal route**: medication is absorbed through the skin via patches and creams
- **Rectally**: these usually are suppositories and some cream medications
- **Sublingually**: under the tongue
- **Inhalation route**: many sprays and nebulizer solutions are inhaled into the lungs
- **Ocular route**: into the eye, usually in the form of solutions and suspensions
- **Aurally**: into the ear, usually in the form of solutions and suspensions

Common abbreviations for administration of medications include:

- **au** = both ears
- **as** = left ear
- **ad** = right ear
- **ou** = both eyes
- **od** = right eye
- **os** = left eye
- **po** = by mouth
- **c** = with
- **sl** = sublingual (under tongue)
- **top** = topically (apply to skin)

The following are common abbreviations found in medication directions:

- **od** = once a day
- **bid** = twice a day
- **tid** = three times a day
- **prn** = as needed
- **qd** = everyday/ daily
- **q4h/q4°** = every 4 hours
- **qid** = four times a day
- **qod** = every other day
- **ac** = before eating (meals)
- **hs** = at bedtime
- **pc** = after eating (meals)

42

Side Effects, Adverse Effects, and Allergies

Patient's Medical History

To prevent possible adverse effects with medications, the following information should be included in a patient's medical history:

- All prescription medications, OTC drugs, and dietary supplements taken by the patient
- Chronic and acute medical conditions
- Patterns of prescription compliance
- Allergies to substances, medications, and foods
- Possible interactions that have previously occurred (drug-drug, drug-food, drug-disease etc.)

With access to a patient's medical history, the pharmacist can determine if there are any risks to the patient. Certain medications may be contraindicated with particular medical conditions or health concerns. Allergies or prior adverse reactions to one medication may also impose an allergy risk to other medications in the same class. A complete medical history helps the pharmacist prevent drug interactions and serious clinical consequences.

Common and Severe Side (or Adverse) Effects

An adverse drug reaction is a reaction that is undesirable, yet happens even when a medication is taken according to its standard dosing. Adverse drug reactions can manifest with the first dosing of the medication or can develop over time. They can happen in a limited area of the body (locally) or can affect the whole body (systemic). An intervention is needed in cases of serious adverse drug reactions that can cause injury and fatality.

The different types of adverse reactions to medications are as follows:

- Compounded pharmacologic effects that include tolerance and side effects
- Peculiar and unpredictable effects (idiosyncratic drug reaction, which could be life-threatening)
- Chronic effects
- Delayed effects
- Effects at the end of treatment
- Treatment failure
- Genetic reactions

Allergies

The following are symptoms that indicate an allergy to a medication:

- Hives
- Skin redness and rashes or other types of reactions
- Swelling in the face, throat, tongue or other area of the body
- Difficulty breathing, wheezing, or chest tightness
- Irregular or rapid heartbeat

Severe form of these reactions can indicate an **anaphylactic reaction**, which is life threatening and requires immediate emergency treatment. **Emergency Medical Services (9-11)** should be contacted right away in cases of suspected anaphylactic reactions to any substance. It is common for patients to

confuse allergic reactions and adverse effects. Therefore, it is important for the pharmacy staff to ask about the symptoms a patient experiences so the reaction can be categorized correctly.

Allergy with Foods and Excipients

There are some medications and supplements that contain food-based ingredients, and therefore, precautions need to be taken when prescribing such substances to a patient with food allergies. The coatings of medications, for example, can have excipients such as lactose, maltodextrin, and other starches that can cause allergic reactions in patients who are susceptible to those ingredients. Other medications, including Prometrium (a hormone medication), contain peanut oil so patients with peanut allergies should avoid such formulations. Some calcium products and omega-3 supplements are derived from shellfish; hence, a person with a seafood allergy may need to avoid these supplements. Patients with dietary restrictions, such as celiac disease or gluten intolerance, should avoid capsules made with gluten fillers or gelatin. If there are any questions about the ingredients, it is best to contact the manufacturer.

Indications of Medications and Dietary Supplements

Dosage and Indication of Legends

Legend drugs are those that require a prescription. The following information is required to be on prescription labels as mandated by the Food, Drug, and Cosmetic Act:

- The name and address of the pharmacy dispensing the medication
- The prescription number
- The date the prescription was filled
- The last date for refills
- The name of the prescriber
- The patient's name
- The instructions for use
- Any precautions or things to not take while on the medication

A prescription should include the following information:

- **Date written**: Prescriptions for non-controlled substances may be honored for up to one year after they are written.

- **Prescriber information**: Includes full name and title, office address, office telephone and fax number, and, if applicable, National Provider Identifier (NPI) number and medical registration/license number.

- **Patient information**: Includes full name and home address and, if applicable, weight, height, and allergies.

- **Inscription**: Includes name of medication, strength of medication, dosage form, and quantity to dispense.

- **Subscription**: Instructions to pharmacist.

- Number of refills

- Drug Enforcement Administration (DEA) number: Only required for prescriptions for controlled substances.

- Signature of prescriber

Patient Package Insert and Medication Guide Requirements

Written patient information refers to any written information about a prescription medication that is provided to the patient.

There are three categories of written information:

- Patient Package Insert (PPI)
- Medication Guide (MG)
- Instructions for Use (IFU)

The written patient information addresses various issues that are specific to the medication regarding its safe and effective use. It also discusses special directions and precautions to avoid medication-induced adverse events. Not all medications have written patient information. Patients can ask their healthcare provider or pharmacist for details about their prescriptions.

Patient Package Insert (PPI)

PPIs are developed and submitted voluntarily to the FDA by the manufacturer. PPIs are approved by the FDA.

For certain classes of medications, it is mandatory that PPIs be provided to patients—these include oral contraceptives and estrogen-containing products. The FDA warrants the safe and effective use of these products by requiring that patients be fully informed about the benefits and risks associated with the uses of these medications.

Manufacturers also voluntarily submit PPIs for other medications to the FDA for approval; however, distribution of these PPIs to patients is not mandatory.

Medication Guide (MG)

MGs are paper handouts that contain FDA-approved information about specific drugs and drug classes. They are provided in order to help patients avoid adverse events. The manufacturer of the medication develops the MG, and the FDA approves it. The FDA requires that MGs be supplied to patients receiving certain prescribed drugs and biological products. MGs help patients prevent serious adverse effects and make informed decisions (by providing information about serious side effects of a product). They also help patients adhere to the product's directions associated with product's effectiveness.

Instructions for Use (IFU)

IFUs refer to written patient information that is produced by the manufacturer and approved by the FDA. They are provided to ensure proper use of certain medications with complicated dosing instructions.

OTC Medications and Dietary Supplements

Some medications are available "**over the counter**," or **OTC**, without a prescription. OTC medications are still regulated by the FDA, as the manufacturing and sales of these medications are regulated under the

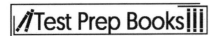

Federal Food, Drug, and Cosmetic Act. There are some medications that are classified as OTC, yet, due to federal or local laws, require pharmacy staff to intervene with patients buying the medication. The patient needs to sign a ledger before the sale can be completed. Examples include medications with pseudoephedrine or emergency contraceptives.

Dietary supplements, unlike OTC medications, are not regulated by the FDA. The Dietary Health and Supplement Act of 1994 defines the guidelines that dietary supplements must meet, including those that:

- Contain a vitamin, mineral, herb, botanical, and/or amino acid
- Are sold as a capsule, tablet, powder or liquid
- Are not purposefully marked to be the sole source of nutrition
- Has the labeling "dietary supplement"

OTC Medications Ingredients

OTC medications often contain various ingredients, especially those intended to treat coughs, colds, and flu. It is important to cross-check the ingredients to prevent duplication of treatment. Two medications that pose a risk for overdose are acetaminophen and dextromethorphan, which are commonly used in cough and cold preparations such as Theraflu and Nyquil. Moreover, OTC sleep aids often have identical ingredients found in antihistamines. It is, therefore, important to check the ingredients in OTC medications to prevent duplicate therapies. The pharmacist should help the patient to pick appropriate OTC medications and counsel them accordingly.

Dosage of Acetaminophen

The maximum daily dose of acetaminophen is 4,000 mg for people with a healthy liver. For those with compromised liver function, the maximum dose is only 2,000 mg per day. In some cases, people with liver disease cannot take acetaminophen at all. As acetaminophen is metabolized primarily in the liver, it is important to follow the dosing instructions to prevent liver damage. Consumption of excessive acetaminophen causes saturation of liver enzymes and buildup of acetaminophen. The metabolic by-products of acetaminophen damage liver cells (hepatocytes).

Dosage of Controlled Substances

The following are the usual range of dosages, available forms, and routes of administration for controlled substances:

- **Hydrocodone/acetaminophen**: There are two dosage components: the hydrocodone can range in strength from 2.5 mg to 10 mg, and the acetaminophen can range from 325 mg to 650 mg. Depending on the severity of pain, doses are either one or two tablets, as needed for pain. It is important not to exceed 4000 mg of acetaminophen each day with the dosing. The medicine is available in oral tablets of different strengths and as an oral solution.

- **Lorazepam**: This drug is usually taken PRN or as needed, with up to a total of 6 mg each day in divided doses. This medication is available in two forms: oral tablet and injectable solution.

- **Methylphenidate**: This drug can be dosed up to 72 mg each day. Immediate release tablets can be taken once or twice a day, while extended-release formulations are only taken once a day. This medication is available in two forms: oral tablets and oral extended-release tablets.

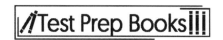

Dosages for Antibiotics

The following are the usual ranges for dosing and available forms for antibiotics:

- **Amoxicillin**: Usually dosed at 250 mg to 500 mg every 8 hours, or at a higher dose (500 to 875 mg) every 12 hours. This drug is available in a chewable tablet, a capsule, and a powder to make suspensions.

- **Penicillin VK**: This drug is usually dosed at 125 mg to 500 mg every 6-8 hours. It is available in either oral tablets or a powder to make suspensions.

- **Cephalexin**: The dose of this drug is 250 mg to 500 mg every 6 to 8 hours. It is available as oral capsules and powder for oral suspensions.

- **Cefuroxime**: The dose of this drug is usually 250 mg to 500 mg every 12 hours. The forms available are tablets and a powder for oral suspensions.

- **Azithromycin**: This drug can be taken in multiple combinations; the possibilities are as follows: a single dose of 1000 mg, 500 mg for three days, or one dose of 500 mg followed by four days of 250 mg. This drug is available either in oral tablets or a powder for oral suspensions.

Dosages for Antidepressants

The following are the typical dosages, form, and routes of administration for antidepressants:

- **Amitriptyline**: This medication can be started at a dose of 10 mg and can be increased to up to 300 mg per day. The dose can be taken at one time or divided over 2-3 occurrences. This drug comes in oral tablets and intramuscular injections.

- **Bupropion**: The usual daily adult dose for this drug is 150 mg to 300 mg, either in divided doses or in a single extended-release tablet. The maximum daily dose is 450 mg. This drug is available in standard or extended-release tablets.

- **Citalopram**: This drug is dosed at 20 mg to 40 mg daily; it is recommended not to exceed 40 mg per day. Citalopram can be taken in oral tablets or as an oral solution.

- **Mirtazapine**: This drug is usually dosed between 15 mg to 45 mg each day. It is available either in regular oral tablets or disintegrating oral tablets.

Dosage of Antihypertensive Medications

The usual dosage range, forms, and routes of administration of common antihypertensive medications are outlined below:

- **Hydrochlorothiazide (HCTZ)**: The dosage for HCTZ can range from 25 mg to 100 mg per day, which can be taken once or in divided doses throughout the day. This medication is available as tablets, capsules, and as a solution.

- **Atenolol**: Based on the medical conditions, the usual dose of atenolol is 25 mg to 100 mg daily, with a maximum daily dose of 200 mg. This medication is available in oral tablets and as IV injections.

- **Amlodipine**: This drug can be prescribed from 2.5 mg to a maximum of 10 mg each day and is available as an oral tablet.

- **Losartan**: This medication is usually prescribed at 25 mg to 100 mg each day and can be taken all at once or divided into two doses. This drug is available as an oral tablet.

Drug Stability

Prior to dispensing any formulation to a patient, it is important to ensure the accuracy and completeness of the formulation by reviewing each step of the compounding.

In the preparatory steps, the following criteria should be met:

- The ingredients, excipients, and equipment are appropriately selected for the formulation.
- The calculation of each of the ingredients and excipients is correct.
- The formulation ingredients are accurately measured.
- The formulation meets the requirements of intended use and ensures stability.

In the final formulation, the following criteria need to be met to ensure accuracy and stability:

- The actual yield is consistent with the calculated yield.

- The physical properties (e.g., color, odor, consistency, clarity) of the final formulation are consistent with what was predicted. Alteration in physical properties is an indicator of incompatibility.

- The formulation should be suitably labeled. The label should meet all legal requirements and must include the discard after date or beyond-use date.

It is recommended that samples of the formulations are sent to an analytical testing laboratory (or this can be done within the pharmacy) to assess the stability of the formulation over the storage period.

Analytical testing aims to assess the following:

- Physical characteristics (color, odor, consistency, taste, etc.)
- Homogeneity
- Concentration
- pH
- Sterility
- Nonpyrogenicity
- Expiration date and beyond-use date

During compounding, personnel should avoid ingredients and conditions that could result in a sub-potent formulation. Adequate knowledge about chemical reactions helps in ascertaining product stability and degradation over the period of compounding, dispensing, and storage.

Commercially-available pharmaceuticals carry an expiration date based on the stability data. The expiration date refers to the calculated timeframe within which a product retains its physical and chemical stability and therapeutic efficacy, based on a published monograph.

The **beyond-use date** refers to the date after which a compounded preparation should not be used and should be discarded. A beyond-use date should be assigned conservatively, utilizing professional judgement, and applying knowledge from pharmaceutical science and compounding experience. The beyond-use date should never be later than the expiration date of any of the ingredients.

These factors must be considered when specifying a beyond-use date:

- The chemical nature of the drug and its degradation kinetics
- The formulation dosage form and the ingredients
- Any possible microbial growth
- The packaging container
- The storage conditions
- The intended length of therapy
- Any information obtained from suppliers and published literature

In absence of stability information, the beyond-use date could be specified as illustrated in the following table:

Beyond-use Date by the Type of Formulation	
Non-aqueous formulations	Not later than the time remaining until the earliest expiration date of any of the ingredients or 6 months
Aqueous oral formulations	Not later than 14 days since compounded and when stored at controlled cold temperatures
Aqueous topical/dermal and mucosal liquid and semisolid formulations	Not later than 30 days

Environmental factors such as temperature, moisture, light, pH, and even the container in which a medication is packaged can affect the ability of a medication to retain its safety and efficacy. Improper storage of a drug can cause it to degrade, which may result in the loss of therapeutic capability and possible adverse effects to the patient. It is the responsibility of the pharmaceutical manufacturer to establish testing protocols, conduct stability testing, and ensure medications can maintain stability throughout the life and usage of the drug. Stability testing simulates these stresses using both long-term and accelerated protocols. The results from these stability studies are used to determine the temperature the medication should be stored at, the product expiration date, whether it is light sensitive, etc.

An **oral suspension** is composed of an insoluble active ingredient, the internal phase, suspended in an aqueous medium, and the external phase. Characteristics of a stable suspension include small particle size, minimal sedimentation, sedimentation that is easily redistributed with moderate shaking. Another type of oral suspension is one that requires reconstitution with water, such as amoxicillin or clarithromycin. These reconstituted antibiotic suspensions are packaged as dry powders, which are then reconstituted with water at time of use. These types of powders can have a shelf life of two to three years, but their stability decreases significantly with the addition of water. Amoxicillin and clarithromycin oral suspension are both stable for only fourteen days once reconstituted with water; however, while amoxicillin requires refrigeration once mixed, clarithromycin should not be refrigerated.

Insulins are sterile solutions composed of proteins that must be stored under refrigerated conditions until use. If left unrefrigerated the proteins can break down, which fosters bacterial growth within the vial. This instability can lead to an ineffective product and possibly serious complications for a diabetes patient. After opening, most insulin vials—for example Lantus and Humalog—can be left at room temperature and will remain stable for up to twenty-eight days. The stability of insulin pens, however, can vary once opened. For instance, Humulin 70/30 pens are a type of premixed insulin that is stable for only up to ten days at room temperature; the Tresiba FlexTouch pen is stable at room temperature for up to fifty-six days. It is therefore important for insulin dependent patients to understand the proper storage requirement of their insulin by reading the package insert or consulting with the pharmacist when uncertain.

For **vaccines** to retain stability, it is important to adhere to a cold chain protocol starting with the manufacturing process all the way through to vaccine administration. Temperature regulation is vital when it comes to ensuring a vaccine remains potent. For example, the influenza vaccine requires refrigeration, typically between 2°C and 8°C. However, the zoster vaccine for shingles and Varicella, or chickenpox vaccine, must remain frozen in order to maintain stability; this usually requires a special freezer. If a frozen vaccine thaws, the vaccine may begin to degrade.

Injectable antibiotics that require reconstitution are mixed with a diluent before being administered to the patient. The type of diluent used for reconstitution can vary due to incompatibility or stability concerns once reconstituted. Diluents might include sterile water, bacteriostatic water, lidocaine, and sodium chloride, to name a few. Rocephin, for example, is an antibiotic that is typically reconstituted with sterile water prior to administration, whereas Invanz is often reconstituted with lidocaine. After reconstitution, the stability decreases significantly, depending on how the reconstituted medication is stored.

Narrow Therapeutic Index (NTI) Medications

The efficacy and safety of a drug are determined quantitatively by comparing the amount of the drug needed to achieve a specific therapeutic goal and the amount at which toxicity occurs. The therapeutic index, or TI, compares the concentration of a drug in the blood at levels considered to be effective and at levels that are toxic. The therapeutic index is equal to the ratio of the toxic dose, or TD, for fifty percent of subjects and the effective dose, or ED, for fifty percent of subjects.

$$TI = \frac{Toxic\ dose}{Effective\ dose} = \frac{TD_{50}}{ED_{50}}$$

Generally, a medication with a high therapeutic index has a broader margin of safety and does not require close monitoring by a physician. For example, simvastatin, a statin medication, is used to reduce cholesterol and is available in strengths ranging from 5mg to 80mg. Statins require minimal monitoring, such as annual bloodwork for cholesterol screening. Like many medications, Simvastatin can have adverse effects, but overall, it is considered safe because of its broad therapeutic range.

Medications with a low therapeutic index are referred to as narrow therapeutic index drugs. Narrow therapeutic index, or NTI, medications have a small window between being effective and lethal. Some NTIs can have significant drug and dietary interactions which can complicate dosing. Examples of narrow therapeutic index medications include the anticoagulant warfarin, thyroid medications such as levothyroxine, transplant rejection medications like cyclosporine, and the anticonvulsant phenytoin, to

name a few. Narrow therapeutic medications require close monitoring of a patient by the physician to ensure its use does not result in therapeutic failure, serious injury, or death. **Vancomycin** is a narrow therapeutic antibiotic medication that is used to treat serious bacterial infections like Methicillin-resistant Staphylococcus aureus (MRSA).

The antibiotic vancomycin is typically delivered via intravenous infusions when treating these types of bacterial infections and requires extensive monitoring to ensure efficacy. To effectively inhibit bacterial growth, vancomycin must hit a peak blood concentration followed by a low concentration called a trough. Dosing is repeated until a steady state, or the balance between infusion and elimination of the medication in the body, is achieved. A trough level is usually drawn before the fourth dose in the course is administered, as this is when the drug is at its lowest concentration in the bloodstream. Vancomycin is cleared from the body by the kidneys; therefore, kidney function must also be monitored to ensure adequate elimination from the body. Renal impairment may allow for the buildup of the medication in the body, possibly leading to irreversible nephrotoxicity. Vancomycin is most effective at a specific and steady concentration in the bloodstream; it is vital to monitor the patient's level to determine adjustments in dosing.

The blood thinner warfarin is another example of a narrow therapeutic index medication. **Warfarin** is an anticoagulant used to prevent the formation of blood clots in the body. Achieving the correct dose can be challenging in warfarin patients because of its narrow therapeutic range. Warfarin dosing is further complicated by the fact that it interacts with other medications, dietary supplements, and some foods. A patient taking a blood thinner should avoid taking nonsteroidal anti-inflammatory drugs (NSAIDS) like aspirin or ibuprofen, or dietary supplements such as garlic, as these can increase bleeding. In some foods like leafy greens, which are rich in Vitamin K, warfarin acts to slow down the process of clotting factor production by blocking Vitamin K.

Vitamin K is a fat-soluble vitamin which is necessary to produce clotting factors like the protein prothrombin. A dose too low can allow for clot formation and potentially result in stroke, embolism, or heart attack. A dose too high can cause uncontrolled bleeding in the body. Warfarin patients require close monitoring by performing a PT/INR test to determine how quickly the blood is clotting. **Development of the International Normalized Ratio (INR)** helped to standardize these test results and account for any laboratory variations that may affect test results. The INR values range from zero to five with the standard therapeutic target INR for a patient taking warfarin being between two and three. A low INR value can put the patient at risk of clot formation, whereas a higher INR value can put the patient at risk for excessive bleeding.

Anticonvulsants are considered narrow therapeutic index medications and are used to minimize seizure activity in patients with seizure disorders such as epilepsy. Determining the correct therapeutic dose requires the patient to self-monitor any medication side effects they experience in addition to monitoring seizure activity, such as how frequently seizures occur or the duration of the seizure. In addition, bloodwork must be monitored to ensure organ function is within range and blood concentration of medication is at a steady state.

Physical and Chemical Incompatibilities Related to Non-Sterile Compounding

The preparation of nonsterile compounds requires the consideration of potential incompatibilities that can affect the stability, effectiveness, and overall safety of the product. The two types of incompatibility that must be addressed when compounding nonsterile preparations or reconstitutable medications are

physical incompatibilities and chemical incompatibilities. **Physical incompatibilities** seen in nonsterile compounds might result in the loss of product uniformity, change in odor, altered palatability, or an overall undesirable preparation. A **chemical incompatibility** is one in which the components in the compounded preparation undergo a chemical reaction resulting in the loss of potency and integrity of the active pharmaceutical ingredient.

A physical incompatibility often seen in topical emulsion preparations such as creams or lotions is immiscibility. **Immiscible liquids** do not mix easily with one another and tend to separate due to the differing polarity properties of the liquids. For example, oil-based liquids are hydrophobic, or nonpolar, whereas water-based liquids are hydrophilic, or polar. An **emulsifier**, or **surfactant**, is an agent used to stabilize immiscible preparations by forming a barrier and decreasing interfacial tension between the two liquids being mixed. Emulsifiers and surfactants are **amphiphilic**, meaning they have polar and nonpolar ends that act to create a barrier between the internal or dispersed phase and the external continuous phase.

Using the incorrect type of emulsifying agent or the incorrect quantity of an emulsifier are two factors that can cause the phase separation of an emulsion. A disruption of interfacial tension breaks down the barriers between the internal and external phases of an emulsion, which can result in coalescence between the two phases. Coalescence can lead to the formation of larger droplet sizes and unequal distribution of the dispersed phase within the continuous phase. A cracked emulsion appears as a clear separation of the oil and water layers in a compounded medication. Coalescence is an irreversible process that can ultimately affect the therapeutic effectiveness of the compounded preparation rendering the compounded preparation unusable.

Insolubility is a physical incompatibility in compounded medications that can be overcome with the addition of a wetting agent and by decreasing the particle size of the active ingredient. Wetting agents are a type of surfactant that can increase solubility of an active ingredient within a suspension by decreasing the surface tension. Reducing particle size increases the surface area of the solids, which allows the wetting agent to penetrate the molecules more easily. The wetting agent also lowers the surface tension of the liquid, allowing it to spread between the solid particles, increasing overall solubility. Two methods typically used to reduce particle size are trituration, a dry method, and levigation, a wet method. **Trituration** is the grinding of a solid ingredient, whether tablets or powders, into smaller particles using a mortar and pestle. **Levigation** is like trituration in that it involves the grinding of solids, but it is done in the presence of a wetting agent.

Liquification is an example of a physical incompatibility that can occur when certain solid ingredients with low melting points are combined, otherwise known as a eutectic mixture. While this may be useful in some preparations like fixed oil suspensions, it can be detrimental if a liquid preparation is not the desired dosage form.

Chemical incompatibility is a significant area of concern for intravenous and injectable medications that require reconstitution prior to administration. Using the incorrect diluent to reconstitute a medication can result in a chemical reaction between the active pharmaceutical ingredient and the diluent.

Precipitates and crystallization are examples of chemical incompatibilities that can occur in reconstituted intravenous medications when mixed incorrectly. Reconstituting with the incorrect diluent or at the incorrect concentration can cause the active ingredient to precipitate out of the solution causing the formation of solids or crystals within the solution. **Precipitates** and **crystal formation** are the

result of a chemical reaction that changes the chemical properties of the active drug. The formation of a precipitate or crystals within the IV lines can have a range of consequences for the patient. The chemical reaction can result in the patient receiving a toxic medication, embolism due to crystallized particulates entering the body, irritated tissues at the IV site, and therapeutic failure.

It is not always evident whether a compounded preparation has lost stability due to chemical incompatibility issues. While color changes, precipitation formation, and changes in odor can be observed, chemical incompatibilities such as pH changes or product degradation are not necessarily detectable by visual inspection.

Proper Storage of Medications

Drug manufacturers determine specific storage conditions for the medications they produce. In addition, the drug manufacturer determines the type of container and temperature for storage of the medication.

Outside factors such as light, whether natural or artificial, can influence molecular changes in the active pharmaceutical ingredient (API) of a drug. Such changes can cause impurities in the drug that may not only harm the patient but can also lead to therapeutic failure. It is therefore imperative for pharmaceutical manufacturers to develop measures that can protect light sensitive drugs during all aspects of development and distribution of their products. Efforts to protect medications might include coating tablets in a light-resistant film that can block natural and artificial light exposure. Extended release Verapamil tablets, for example, is a medication that is used for hypertension and is sensitive to both light and moisture. Applying a film coating to the tablet during the manufacturing process creates a seal around the tablet, preventing the degradation of the active ingredient by blocking light and moisture. Often these medications are packaged, stored, and dispensed in dark-colored amber bottles or vials in order to protect them from harmful light.

Prescription medications, as well as federally restricted over the counter (OTC) products, should be secured in the pharmacy, stored behind the counter, or locked in a cabinet that is accessible to pharmacy personnel only. Pseudoephedrine is the active ingredient in many OTC cold products, as well as the drug precursor for the illegal production of methamphetamine, a highly addictive stimulant. Federal law, mandated by the Combat Methamphetamine Epidemic Act, or CMEA, limits the sale of products containing ephedrine, pseudoephedrine, and phenylpropanolamine to 3.6 grams per day due to their abuse potential. Storage and access restrictions must be implemented by pharmacy staff to deter theft or the diversion of controlled drugs.

The Drug Enforcement Agency (DEA) has issued minimum guideline requirements for the proper storage and access of controlled substances. Controlled substances must be stored in a cabinet or safe that can be securely locked per DEA regulations. It is also permitted to disperse controlled drugs amongst noncontrol medications within the pharmacy. A safe or locked cabinet is typically reserved for storing schedule II medications rather than schedule III through V controlled drugs. The security of controlled drugs requires the thorough consideration of various factors including theft or diversion history, the physical location of the pharmacy, type of security system in place, the quantities of controlled drugs needing to be stored at a given time, and lastly, how many individuals have access to the drugs.

Storage Temperatures

Most medications may be stored safely at controlled room temperature. The United States Pharmacopeia has published the following standard parameters for medication storage:

- Freezer: Temperature maintained thermostatically between -13° and -14° Fahrenheit (-25° and -10° Celsius)

- Cold: Temperature not exceeding 46 °F (8 °C)

- Cool: Temperature between 46° and 59 °F (8° and 15 °C)

- Room temperature: Temperature prevailing in a working environment

- Controlled room temperature: Temperature maintained thermostatically between 68° and 77 °F (20° and 25 °C)

- Warm: Temperature between 86° and 104 °F (30° and 40 °C)

- Excessive heat: Temperature above 104 °F (40 °C)

- Protect from freezing: Freezing may lead to loss of potency or strength in a medication

- Dry place: Environment doesn't exceed 40% relative humidity

If the patient is to pick up medication from a community pharmacy, pharmacy staff should notify the patient of any special storage requirements. If the medication is being delivered by a pharmacy delivery service or mail-order pharmacy, special steps must be taken to ensure the medication is stored at appropriate temperatures (e.g., ice packs and coolers).

Glossary

Absolute Bioavailability	This refers to the comparison between the bioavailability of a drug following a non-intravenous route of administration and the bioavailability of the same drug following intravenous administration.
Absorption	This refers to the process of the medication entering blood circulation.
ACE Inhibitors (ACEIs)	Angiotensin-Converting Enzyme Inhibitors; these are used to treat hypertension and cardiovascular diseases.
ADHD	Attention-Deficit Hyperactivity Disorder
Alpha-1 Receptor Blockers	These decrease the norepinephrine-induced vascular contraction, causing relaxation of blood vessels and a resultant reduction in blood pressure.
Amphiphilic	This means they have polar and nonpolar ends that act to create a barrier between the internal or dispersed phase and the external continuous phase.
Anaphylactic Reaction	This is a life-threatening reaction and requires immediate emergency treatment.
Angiotensin Receptor Blockers (ARBs)	These have similar therapeutic effects as ACE Inhibitors; however, they tend to have better compliance, due to their lower incidence of persistent cough.
Antiasthmatics	These are used to prevent and treat the acute symptoms of asthma.
Antibiotics	These are antimicrobial agents that are used for treatment and prevention of bacterial infections.
Anticonvulsants	These are considered narrow therapeutic index medications and are used to minimize seizure activity in patients with seizure disorders such as epilepsy.
Antidepressants	These are used to treat different mood disorders including depression, anxiety, phobias, and obsessive-compulsive disorder (OCD).
Anti-Diabetic Medications	These are used to treat diabetes, which is a chronic metabolic disease in which the body cannot properly regulate blood sugar levels.
Antihistamines	These are used to treat various allergic conditions.
Antihypertensive Medications	These are used to treat high blood pressure.
Antimetabolites	These are used to treat diseases including severe psoriasis, rheumatoid arthritis, and several types of cancer.
Antipsychotics	These are used to treat psychosis, including schizophrenia and bipolar disorder.
Antivirals	These are used to fight viruses in the body, by either stopping replication or blocking the function of a viral protein.
ARB	Angiotensin Receptor Blocker
Asthma	This is caused by inflammation and constriction of the airways, which results in difficulty breathing.
AUC	This refers to the area under the concentration-time curve; refers to the amount of the drug absorbed in the system following administration.
Aurally	This refers to the ear, usually in the form of solutions and suspensions.
Benzodiazepines	These are a class of medications used for the short-term treatment of anxiety.
Beta Blockers	These are an important class of antihypertensive medications and are widely used to treat hypertension and cardiovascular disease.
Beyond-Use Date	This refers to the date after which a compounded preparation should not be used and should be discarded.
Bioavailability	This is a function of the rate and extent of absorption of a drug from a formulation.

Bioequivalents	These refer to two or more pharmaceutically-comparable products that demonstrate equivalent bioavailability when tested under similar experimental conditions.
Calcium Channel Blockers (CCBs)	These work by decreasing calcium entry through calcium channels. By regulating the movement of calcium, contraction of vascular smooth muscle is controlled.
Chemical Incompatibility	This is which the components in the compounded preparation undergo a chemical reaction resulting in the loss of potency and integrity of the active pharmaceutical ingredient.
CHF	Congestive Heart Failure
Chronic Bronchitis	This is inflammation of the smooth lining of bronchial tubes.
C_{max}	This is the peak blood concentration of the medication.
COPD	This is an obstructive airway disease that is characterized by coughing, wheezing, shortness of breath, and sputum production.
Development of the International Normalized Ratio (INR)	This is used to help to standardize these test results and account for any laboratory variations that may affect test results.
Distribution	This is the process of dispersion of the medication throughout the body, including the site of action.
Diuretics	These are used alone and in combination with other medications to treat hypertension.
Drug Interaction	This refers to the alteration in pharmacology of a medication by various factors including disease conditions, prescription and OTC medications, and foods or nutritional supplements.
Elimination	This refers to the process of removal of the parent molecule and the metabolites from the body.
Elixir	This is a clear liquid solution in which active ingredients are mixed in a liquid carrier (or formulation vehicle); shaking is not required to mix the ingredients.
Emphysema	This results from alveolar damage, reducing the ability for healthy gas exchange.
Emulsifier or Surfactant	This is an agent used to stabilize immiscible preparations by forming a barrier and decreasing interfacial tension between the two liquids being mixed.
Environmental factors	These include things such as temperature, moisture, light, pH, and even the container in which a medication is packaged can affect the ability of a medication to retain its safety and efficacy.
Epidurally	This means that something may be infused into epidural space in the spinal cord.
First Order Elimination Kinetics	The medication undergoes a linear rate of elimination in proportion to its concentration.
Gastric Acid Neutralizers/Suppressants	These either neutralize stomach acid or decrease acid production, and therefore, provide relief of symptoms associated with hyperacidity.
Generic Drugs	These are copies of the brand-name drug and allow more affordable access to treatment and care.
Generic Substitution	This refers to filling a prescription with a generic, therapeutically-equivalent formulation instead of an original brand name formulation.
GERD	This is the lower esophageal sphincter does not close properly, which causes the contents of the stomach to back up into the esophagus.
Glucometers	These are used to measure blood sugar.
Half-Life	This is a pharmacokinetic parameter that represents the unit of time over which the concentration of a medication in circulation drops to half of its initial concentration.
High-Density Lipoproteins (HDL) Cholesterol	This is considered the "good" cholesterol.
Hormonal Medications	These are generally used as oral contraceptives to prevent pregnancy.

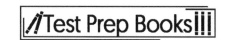

Hypercholesterolemia	High cholesterol
Hyperlipidemia	High blood lipids
Hypertriglyceridemia	High triglycerides
Immiscible Liquids	These do not mix easily with one another and tend to separate due to the differing polarity properties of the liquids.
Inhalation Route	This means that substance is inhaled into the lungs.
Injectable	This is a pharmaceutical dosage form that follows the parenteral route to administer a medication locally or systemically.
Insolubility	This is a physical incompatibility in compounded medications that can be overcome with the addition of a wetting agent and by decreasing the particle size of the active ingredient.
Instructions for Use (IFU)	This refers to written patient information that is produced by the manufacturer and approved by the FDA.
Insulins	These are sterile solutions composed of proteins that must be stored under refrigerated conditions until use, or the proteins can break down, which fosters bacterial growth within the vial.
Intramuscularly	This refers to something that goes into the muscle and must be liquid.
Intravenously	This revers to something that goes through the veins and must be liquid.
Legend Drugs	These are medications that require a prescription.
Levigation	This is like trituration in that it involves the grinding of solids, but it is done in the presence of a wetting agent.
Lipid-Lowering Medications	These are used for the treatment of high blood lipids.
Liquification	This is an example of a physical incompatibility that can occur when certain solid ingredients with low melting points are combined, otherwise known as a eutectic mixture.
Low-Density Lipoproteins (LDL) Cholesterol	This is considered the "bad" cholesterol.
MEC	This is the minimum effective concentration, i.e., the minimum drug concentration required to exhibit the therapeutic effect.
Medication Guides (MGs)	These are paper handouts that contain FDA-approved information about specific drugs and drug classes.
Metabolism	This is the process of degradation of the parent molecule into different metabolites.
Monoamine Oxidase Inhibitors (MAOIs)	These are used to treat chronic depression that does not respond to other medications or treatments.
MTC	This is the maximum therapeutic concentration at which the greatest therapeutic effect of a drug is achieved.
NDRI	Norepinephrine Dopamine Reuptake Inhibitor
Neurotransmitters	These are chemical messengers that transmit signals from one neuron to another.
Nitroglycerin	This is a vasodilator that is often used to treat episodes of angina.
NSAID	This refers to a non-steroidal anti-inflammatory drug that can cause stomach irritation and can aggravate peptic ulcer symptoms.
Ocular Route	This refers to something that has gotten into the eye, usually in the form of solutions and suspensions.

Oral Contraceptives	These can provide hormones (estrogen and/or progestin), which suppress the egg maturation and ovulation process.
Oral Suspension	This is composed of an insoluble active ingredient, the internal phase, suspended in an aqueous medium, and the external phase.
Orange Book	This is a reference to find drugs that have been approved and evaluated for therapeutic equivalence. (Approved Drug Products with Therapeutic Equivalence Evaluations)
Over The Counter (OTC)	These medications are available without a prescription.
Patient Package Inserts (PPIs)	These are developed and submitted voluntarily to the FDA by the manufacturer.
Pharmaceutical Alternatives	These refer to medications that have the same therapeutic moiety (structure), but are formulated as different salts, esters, or complexes.
Pharmaceutical Dosage Form	This is a formulation type in which the active ingredient(s) (with excipients) is manufactured to be administered to patients.
Pharmaceutical Equivalents	These refer to two or more medications that have equal quantities/strength of the identical active ingredients in the same dosage form, and with the same route of administration.
Pharmacodynamics	These refer to the study of the effects of a medication at the site of action.
Pharmacokinetics	This is the study of the fate of a medication in the body.
Physical Incompatibilities	If these are seen in nonsterile compounds, they might result in the loss of product uniformity, change in odor, altered palatability, or an overall undesirable preparation.
Polypharmacy	This occurs when a patient takes multiple medications to treat different medical conditions.
PPI	Proton Pump Inhibitor
Precipitates (Crystal Formation)	These are the result of a chemical reaction that changes the chemical properties of the active drug.
Pseudoephedrine and Phenylephrine	These are used as decongestants in different OTC cough and cold medications.
Rectally	These are usually suppositories and some cream medications.
Relative Bioavailability	This refers to the comparison of the bioavailability of a drug from one dosage form.
SARI	Serotonin Agonist and Reuptake Inhibitor
SNRI	Serotonin Norepinephrine Reuptake Inhibitor
SSRI	Selective Serotonin Reuptake Inhibitor
Statins	These are used to treat hypocholesteremia.
Steroids	These are used to treat allergies, asthma, rashes, swelling, and inflammation.
Stimulant Medications	These are also called sympathomimetic agents, as they work by augmenting the sympathetic neurotransmitter activity.
Subcutaneously	This is usually an injection under the skin.
Sublingually	This refers to something under the tongue.
Suppositories	These are solid dosage forms that are inserted into body cavities, including the rectum, vagina, and urethra, where they melt and provide local or systemic effects.

Suspensions	This is medication that is suspended in a liquid carrier. It is essential to shake suspensions before administration, as some ingredients often collect at the bottom as sediment.
TCA	Tricyclic Antidepressant
TeCA	Tetracyclic Antidepressant
Therapeutic Equivalents	These refer to two or more pharmaceutical products that provide identical clinical effect, safety, and efficacy.
Therapeutic Substitution	This can be done in two different forms: substitution of an equally potent drug from within the same class or substitution of a drug from a different class of drugs, but with the same pharmacologic effect and similar potency yet a different mechanism of action.
Therapeutic Window	This is the range of drug concentrations between which the desired therapeutic effect is obtained without any significant toxicity
T$_{max}$	This is the time to reach the peak blood concentration of the medication; indicative of the rate of absorption of a drug from a formulation.
Total Parenteral Nutrition	This is used in situations where a patient cannot orally ingest food or digest food through the stomach and intestines.
Transdermal Route	This is when medication is absorbed through the skin via patches and creams.
Trituration	This is the grinding of a solid ingredient, whether tablets or powders, into smaller particles using a mortar and pestle.
Vancomycin	This is a narrow therapeutic antibiotic medication that is used to treat serious bacterial infections like Methicillin-resistant Staphylococcus aureus (MRSA).
Vasodilators	These cause blood vessels to dilate, lowering resistance to flow and reducing the workload on the heart.
Vitamin K	This is a fat-soluble vitamin which is necessary to produce clotting factors like the protein Prothrombin.
Warfarin	This is a commonly prescribed blood thinner, indicated to prevent blood clots in various cardiovascular diseases.
Written Patient Information	This refers to any written information about a prescription medication that is provided to the patient.
Zero Order Kinetics	This refers to a reaction that proceeds at a rate independent of the concentrations of the reactants.

Practice Quiz

1. Which of the following carries information about the pharmacology of a medication?
   I. Prescription label
   II. PPI
   III. Product monograph
   a. I only
   b. II only
   c. II and III
   d. I, II, and III

2. Which of the following medications should not be taken in combination with nitroglycerin and what would be the result if they were taken together?
   a. Warfarin, excessive blood thinning
   b. Sildenafil, irreversible hypotension
   c. Allegra®, increased heart rate
   d. Sertraline, increased depression

3. If a patient is receiving chemotherapy, which of the following is likely to be prescribed to help with side effects?
   a. Anti-histamines
   b. Propranolol
   c. Ondansetron
   d. Nitroglycerin

4. What type of dosage form is dissolved under the tongue?
   a. Buccal
   b. Inhalation
   c. Subcutaneous
   d. Sublingual

5. Why is it important to collect the patient's medical history before filling a prescription?
   a. It is not usually important, unless the patient is elderly.
   b. It can provide an allergy history and prevent dangerous drug reactions.
   c. It can help the pharmacist predict the next medical condition.
   d. It can make it easier to provide refills.

See answers on the next page.

Answer Explanations

1. C: The PPI (patient package insert) carries detailed information about the medication including the pharmacology. The product monograph or product insert (PI) or prescribing information (PI) carries various details of the medication including pharmacology, toxicology, and clinical studies.

2. B: Sildenafil and nitroglycerin should not be taken together, as both cause blood vessel dilatation, leading to the potential of irreversible hypotension. The other listed combinations do not have documented direct effects when taken in combination with nitroglycerin.

3. C: Ondansetron is an anti-emetic, which can help the patient deal with nausea from the chemotherapy. The other drugs would not help with hair loss, nausea, memory problems, weakness, or other side effects associated with chemotherapy.

4. D: Sublingual means under the tongue. Inhalation is through the nose or the mouth. Subcutaneous is an injection that goes under the skin. Buccal refers to the cheek inside the mouth, but not under the tongue.

5. B: Collecting the patient's history can help identify allergic reactions or drug-drug interactions. Although in some cases having the patient's history can help track which medications may need to be refilled, it's not the primary intent.

Federal Requirements

Handling and Disposal Requirements

Safety Data Sheets (SDS)

Safety Data Sheets (SDS), formerly known as Material Safety Data Sheets (MSDS), are forms that contain information about hazardous materials and chemical compounds, including identifying the chemical and what should be done in the case of a spill (i.e., precautions and procedures). SDS forms are available as physical forms or on computers. Each pharmacy is required by the Occupational Safety and Health Administration (OSHA) to make sure that the SDS forms can be readily accessed by all employees who work with hazardous chemicals and must be immediately accessible at all times, even in the case of an emergency such as a power outage.

There are sixteen sections to the SDS. Note that, while Sections 12-15 are labelled non-mandatory and are not enforced by OSHA, they must be included to be compliant with the UN Globally Harmonized System of Classification and Labelling of Chemicals (GHS):

- Section 1: Identification
- Section 2: Hazard(s) Identification
- Section 3: Composition/Information on Ingredients
- Section 4: First-Aid Measures
- Section 5: Fire-Fighting Measures
- Section 6: Accidental Release Measures
- Section 7: Handling and Storage
- Section 8: Exposure Controls/Personal Protection
- Section 9: Physical and Chemical Properties
- Section 10: Stability and Reactivity
- Section 11: Toxicological Information
- Section 12: Ecological Information (non-mandatory)
- Section 13: Disposal Considerations (non-mandatory)
- Section 14: Transport Information (non-mandatory)
- Section 15: Regulatory Information (non-mandatory)
- Section 16: Other Information

The ingredients used in formulations should be handled cautiously in order to prevent contamination and degradation. Materials from the same container can be reused until they reach the expiration date labeled on the container. Staff should make sure to decrease exposure to the remaining content each time any material is withdrawn from the container.

The withdrawal of ingredients from the container should be performed by a trained individual who has expertise in handling the materials. If an ingredient is transferred from the original container to a different container, the new container should be labeled with the necessary information including name, supplier, lot number, and expiration date.

The pharmaceutical waste generated during compounding should be appropriately handled and disposed. In the past, pharmacies used to destroy waste materials by incinerating them, washing them

down a sink or toilet, or returning them to the sales representative/manufacturer. However, incineration pollutes the air, and dumping medications down a sink or toilet causes environmental pollution. Many medications are hydrophilic, biologically-active, and resistant to wastewater treatment. Therefore, disposal of pharmaceutical waste must comply with the corresponding state and federal regulations, as well as those regulations specified by the U.S. Environmental Protection Agency (EPA). A compounding pharmacy may contact a third party that has expertise in pharmaceutical waste collection, handling, and disposal.

There are three types of waste produced in a pharmacy:

- **Solid waste**: all solid, liquid, and gaseous waste

- **Hazardous waste**: any substance or combination of substances that could produce harmful effects on the health and safety of a person

- **Infectious waste**: blood, bodily fluids, blood products, sharps that are infectious, and waste from the laboratory

Waste receptacles are waste-specific. There is usually a specified container for biohazards and sharps (including infectious sharps); it is typically a red/dark orange receptacle that is labeled "bio-hazard."

For pharmaceuticals (expired or unused non-hazardous drugs), there are separate disposal containers (typically dark blue); these containers are appropriate for disposal of items such as antibiotics, IVs, and ibuprofen. For hazardous drugs, there are typically waste bags with the label "**Hazardous Drug Waste**"; these are leak-proof and come in a variety of colors, with the exception of white.

Hazardous Waste in Pharmacies

Pharmacies produce a variety of hazardous waste products, which necessitate proper disposal. Some of these items include the following:

- Expired medications

- Incorrectly compounded medications

- Items that have been contaminated with bodily fluids

- Equipment (not machine, but attachable items) that can be disposed of that was used to dispense or make hazardous materials

- Chemotherapy drugs

There should be a designated bin for hazardous waste, specifically designed for such collection. The waste should be stored in the hazardous waste bin until it is picked up by an outside company for disposal.

Hazardous items should be handled with care and placed in bags that are marked with symbols identifying them as hazardous or biohazards.

There are outside companies that will come to the pharmacy to pick up hazardous waste that is generated.

Reconciliation Between State and Federal Laws and Regulations

- State laws and rules can be different depending on which state the pharmacy is in
- Pharmacy law follows the strictest requirements if state and federal law differ

Controlled Substance Prescriptions

Drug Enforcement Administration (DEA)

The **DEA** is a governmental agency set up in 1973 to implement laws around drug use and to fight drug trafficking. The Controlled Substances Act serves as the guiding document. This agency shares jurisdiction with the Federal Bureau of Investigation and with Immigrations and Customs Enforcement.

The DEA focuses on the following objectives:

- Instructing the public, especially through programs in the community targeted at youth, to lower the use of illegal and diverted drugs

- Supporting local and state law enforcement to assist in lowering drug-related crime and fighting/violence

- Disrupting origins and providers of illegal and diverted drugs on a local, national, and international level

Controlled Substances Act (CSA)

The **CSA** was enacted in 1970 by the U.S. Congress as Title II of the Comprehensive Drug Abuse Prevention and Control Act. Through the CSA, every Federal law relating to the manufacture, regulation, and sale of certain controlled substances (narcotics as well) were made. Also, the CSA allowed for the creation of five controlled drug classes (Schedules I-V) and outlined the criteria for the medications in each class. Updates are made to the Act and the drug schedules to reflect up-to-date information and research.

Explanation of Schedules I-V Controlled Drug Classes

Classification is based on currently accepted medical use for treatment and the likelihood of abuse or dependence on the drug.

- **Schedule I**: Have a high potential for abuse and no accepted medical value. Examples include marijuana, heroin, lysergic acid diethylamide (LSD), and mescaline (peyote).

- **Schedule II/IIN**: Have a high potential for abuse but have an accepted medical use. Abuse of these drugs could lead to severe psychological or physical dependence. Examples include oxycodone, cocaine, and morphine. Examples of Schedule IIN controlled substances include amphetamine (Adderall®, Dexedrine®) and methylphenidate (Ritalin®).

- **Schedule III/IIIN**: Have a low to moderate potential for abuse (less than Schedule II, but more than Schedule IV). Abuse may lead to low or moderate physical dependence or high psychological dependence. Examples include combination medication products containing less than 15 mg of hydrocodone per dose, products containing no more than 90 mg of codeine per dose (e.g., Tylenol® with Codeine [Tylenol® #3]), and buprenorphine. Examples of Schedule IIIN controlled substances include ketamine and anabolic steroids, such as testosterone.

- **Schedule IV**: Have a low potential for abuse (less than Schedule III and more than Schedule V) and a low risk of dependence. Examples include clonazepam (Klonopin®), diazepam (Valium®), triazolam (Halcion®), and alprazolam (Xanax®).

- **Schedule V**: Have the lowest potential for abuse among the controlled substances. These consist mostly of preparations containing limited quantities of certain narcotics. Examples include cough preparations containing not more than 200 mg of codeine per 100 mL or per 100 g (e.g., Robitussin® AC), pregabalin (Lyrica®), and diphenoxylate/atropine.

Transfer of Controlled Substances

Pharmacies are responsible for the physical transfer of controlled substances and for the precision of the inventory and records. For two years after the transfer, the pharmacy must keep the records immediately available for inspection by the DEA.

An outside firm may be hired by the pharmacy to take stock, pack, and coordinate the transfer of its controlled substances to another location (pharmacy, original supplier, or original manufacturer).

Depending on the schedule category of the substance, DEA Form 222 (Schedule II) or other written documentation (Schedule III or IV) containing the drug name, dosage form, strength, quantity, and the date of transfer is filled out.

Record Keeping

The pharmacy is required to maintain a log or file of dispensed prescriptions. Each prescription needs to be kept for a minimum of two years. The authorities or Board of Pharmacy need to be able to review and inspect the log or file of records at any time.

The log or records of dispensed medications should contain the following information:

- Date the medication was dispensed
- Details of the prescription: drug name, strength, and dosage form
- The patient's name
- The quantity of medication dispensed
- The patient's address

It is important to note that Schedule II medication prescriptions need to have their own file, and Schedule III-V prescriptions need to have their own separate file as well. Additional prescription medications that are not controlled substances may also have their own file. If Schedule III-V prescriptions are filed together with noncontrolled substances, then they should be stamped with a red C no less than an inch high.

Disposal of Nonhazardous Waste

The proper disposal of pharmaceutical waste, including prescription medications, is regulated by the **Environmental Protection Agency (EPA)** under the guidelines set forth by the **Resource Conservation and Recovery Act, or RCRA**. The RCRA was enacted to prevent the improper disposal of unused hazardous medications. A medication that is not defined as hazardous under the RCRA is therefore categorized as nonhazardous. **Nonhazardous pharmaceutical waste** may include antibiotics, hormone medications, and OTC products. Despite being called nonhazardous pharmaceutical waste and not being

classified as hazardous under the RCRA criteria, it does not mean it is not still harmful to the environment.

Nonhazardous pharmaceutical waste should be processed by a DEA registered reverse distributor as such distributors are regulated and can ensure proper disposal methods are used. Reverse distributors are employed to retrieve unused and expired medications from the pharmacy to obtain manufacturer credit. Pharmaceutical medications that have expired or are considered unsaleable are called pharmaceutical waste. Once determined to be waste, the reverse distributor will process the waste according to regulations set by local environmental agencies as well as EPA guidelines. The EPA opposes the disposal of nonhazardous pharmaceutical waste in the sewer system. Preferred methods of disposal of nonhazardous pharmaceutical waste are incineration or a solid waste landfill. For patients who want to dispose of unwanted, unused, or expired medications at home, it is recommended to put the loose medications in an undesirable substance such as coffee grounds or cat litter and place them in the trash.

Controlled Substances

In 1970, the U.S. Food and Drug Administration (FDA) released drug classifications, or drug schedules, under the Controlled Substance Act (CSA). As mentioned, the **drug schedules** arrange drugs into groups based on risk of abuse or harm. Under the CSA, drugs and other substances considered controlled substances are divided into five categories, schedule I to schedule V.

Documentation Requirements for Receiving, Ordering, and Returning Controlled Substances

DEA Form 222 must be filled out, either electronically or on paper, by the pharmacy in order to transfer, order, or return Schedule II medications. Once filled out, the DEA Form 222 needs to be stored so that it can easily be accessed during an inspection if requested (this applies to both electronic and paper records). On the DEA Form 222, the date, the name of the medication ordered, and the amount are required.

There are several rules that need to be followed when filling out and filing the DEA Form 222:

- Do not make alterations to the form. If a mistake is made while filling out the form, a new form should be used.

- For triplicate paper versions (prior to October 30, 2021):

    - The blue copy of the form is kept by the recipient (the purchaser).

    - The green copy of the form is mailed to the local DEA office.

    - The brown copy of the form needs to be kept and filed at the supplying pharmacy for at least two years.

- For single-sheet forms (after October 30, 2021):

    - The recipient (the purchaser) must keep a paper or electronic copy for two years.

    - The supplier must keep the original form on record for two years.

> o The supplier can either report through the Automation of Reports and Consolidated Orders System (ARCOS) OR they can send a paper or electronic copy of the original form to the DEA office.

Older copies of DEA Form 222 (in triplicate on carbon paper) will no longer be acceptable past October 30, 2021, and the single-sheet form will become the standard. The filling procedure with the single-sheet forms is similar to the triplicate forms: the purchaser must keep a paper or electronic copy of the original for two years. The supplier must keep the original on record for two years. Suppliers who do not report through the **Automation of Reports and Consolidated Orders System (ARCOS)** must send a paper or electronic copy of the original to the DEA office.

Documentation Requirements for Loss/Theft of Controlled Substances

In the event of a loss or theft of any controlled substance at a pharmacy, the procedures outlined below must be carried out within one business day of discovering that theft or loss has occurred.

- Notify the local DEA Diversion Field Office in writing, as the theft of controlled substances is considered a criminal act and a source of deviation, which requires that the DEA be notified.

- It is not clearly required by federal law or policies, but it is important to also inform local law enforcement and state regulatory agencies.

- The DEA needs to be informed of the loss/theft precisely, without any intermediaries (i.e., other parts of the corporation) and the notice needs to be signed by an authorized individual of the registrant.

- DEA Form 106 (Report of Theft or Loss of Controlled Substances) must be filled out by the pharmacy. This form will document what happened to lead to this situation and the amount of controlled substances involved. The following information should be included on the form:

  - Pharmacy name and address

  - DEA registration number

  - Local Police Department name and phone number (if the pharmacy has contacted)

  - Kind of theft (for example: armed robbery, break-in, etc.)

  - Any identifying label features used on the containers (marks, symbols, or price codes)

  - Record of which controlled substances are missing, including the strength, dosage form, and size of container or National Drug code numbers

If the reported lost/stolen material is found after filing and notifying local authorities and the DEA, a written notification must be given to clear up why no Form 106 was filed after the initial notification.

Formula to Verify the Validity of a Prescriber's DEA Number

The formula is very specific for DEA numbers. In order to test the legitimacy of a DEA number, the following requirements must be met:

- DEA numbers have two letters accompanied by six numbers and a "check" number.

- The type of registrant is identified by the first letter in the DEA number. This could be **M** for a mid-level practitioner or **P/R** for manufacturer/researcher.

- The second letter in the DEA number represents the first letter of the registrant's last name.

- The sum of the first, third, and fifth numbers is SUM1.

- The sum of the second, fourth, and sixth numbers is SUM2.

- SUM2 multiplied by two is PROD2.

- The last digit in the result of adding SUM1 and PROD2 should be the same as the check number.

Disposing of Medications

Medications need to be properly disposed; the FDA recommends the following to adhere to safe procedures:

- Medications should not be flushed down the toilet unless the package explicitly says to do so.
- Community take-back programs should be used if they are offered in the area.
- The label should be destroyed or made illegible before the medication is thrown away.
- If medications are thrown in the garbage, the following should be done before doing so:

    o Medications should be removed from the original containers and mixed with a substance (coffee grounds or cat litter) and

    o Medications should be placed in a sealed bag or another empty container to avoid leakage.

DEA Take-Back Program

This program is a national event where pharmacies, community partners, and law enforcement agencies support collection sites where community members can return expired or unnecessary medications for proper disposal. After collection, the medications requiring disposal are retrieved by a local DEA representative. The main purpose of this program is to reduce the number of drugs that could possibly be used by unintended persons and to reduce risks to consumer safety by stopping the consumption of expired medication. Also, these events deter improper medication disposal and reduce possible environmental contamination.

Reverse Distribution

Pharmacies can dispose of unused or expired controlled substances by using a reverse distributor registered with the DEA. The controlled substances are transferred from the pharmacy to the reverse distributor where the drugs are evaluated to determine if credit can be given. The reverse distributor can also facilitate the return of controlled substances to a manufacturer for a credit. Upon transfer, a DEA Form 222 must be issued from the reverse distributor to the pharmacy when a schedule II controlled substance is accepted. When schedule III to V controlled substances are transferred, the pharmacy is responsible for recording the date of the transfer, the name of the medication, the dosage form, dosage, and quantity. If manufacturer credit cannot be given, the reverse distributor will dispose of the controlled substances according to DEA regulations. The reverse distributor must submit a DEA Form 41 to the DEA after the controlled substances have been destroyed.

68

Restricted Drug Programs and Related Medication Processing

Pharmacy personnel are responsible for providing dependable, safe, and effective care, which includes implementing strategies focused on the reduction of medication errors. **Risk management** refers to systems that identify, assess, and implement procedures aimed at reducing medication errors. Risk management has three components—quality control (QC), quality assurance (QA), and quality improvement. Pharmacies should include risk management guidelines and regulations in their SOPs. Risk management is an ongoing process and may require periodic adjustments.

Accuracy should be at the forefront of all prescription-filling activities. There are many medication error prevention strategies. Verification of patient information should be performed at every pharmacy visit. This practice is key in the reduction of allergic drug reactions and drug-drug interactions. There are various resources available on the Internet aimed at the prevention of medication errors. Pharmacies should also maintain an up-to-date library pertinent to the practice of pharmacy.

Advancements in pharmacy technology have made it possible to provide additional safety controls within the dispensing process. The order entry process can be automatically linked to the particular NDCs stocked on the pharmacy's shelves. As a result, the prescription label can be printed with a unique barcode linking it to a particular drug and patient profile. A barcode scanner can then be used to verify the correct medication is being used to fill an individual patient's prescription. In the hospital setting, barcodes can be incorporated into patient hospital bracelets, allowing hospital personnel to verify that the correct medication is being administered to the right patient at the correct time. The automation of pharmacy dispensing equipment has reduced medication errors.

The separation of a pharmacy's inventory by drug categories is another medication error prevention strategy. TJC mandates that external and internal medications are stored separately. The commission also requires separate storage of oncology medications and volatile or flammable substances. Oncology medications should be stored in a sealed protective outer bag to prevent potential leakage. Volatile or flammable substances should be stored in a cool environment with adequate ventilation. The storage area must be designed to minimize fire and explosive potential. Common look-alike and sound-alike medications should be stored in different areas of the pharmacy. Lastly, insulin brands should be stored separately from one another.

The prescription label should be compared with the original prescription by at least two pharmacy personnel. Electronic prescribing is favored over writing, telephoning, or faxing prescriptions to a pharmacy. Other medication error prevention strategies include questioning illegible handwriting, ambiguous orders, and uncommon or unfamiliar abbreviations. Prescriptions should utilize the metric system. Prescribers should always position a leading zero in decimal values less than one. Likewise, a trailing zero to the right of a decimal point should never be used. Mistakes with both leading and trailing zeroes may result in a dosage error of between a tenth-fold and ten-fold. It is advisable to double-count prescriptions of narcotics. Overall, a prescription order should be reviewed a minimum of three times by pharmacy personnel.

Certain medicines require additional oversight when being prescribed and processed.

Thalidomide
The program **S.T.E.P.S. (System for Thalidomide Education and Prescribing Safety)** is used for patients that are prescribed thalidomide. Mandatory counseling, pregnancy testing (if applicable), and

registration are required before patients can receive their first prescription. Continued regular pregnancy screenings and counseling are required for patients before refills can be dispensed.

Isotretinoin

The **iPledge program** is used to confine isotretinoin drug distribution. Before patients can receive their first prescription, they must register for the program, undergo pregnancy testing (if applicable), choose two types of birth control, and promise to keep all scheduled appointments. In order to refill subsequent prescriptions, female patients need to take monthly pregnancy tests, use the iPledge system to describe her methods of birth control, and answer questions about the iPledge program.

Clozapine

This prescription medication requires using a program to track the patient's white blood cell count and the absolute neutrophil count. There are different programs through each manufacturer; any of these programs are acceptable, as long as the pharmacist and prescriber can have access to the files to see how the patient is reacting to the medication.

Medication Processing

The Drug Enforcement Administration is responsible for ensuring pharmacies abide by the federal regulations covered in the **Combat Methamphetamine Epidemic Act**. Federal regulations state that all asthma and cold products containing the chemical ingredients ephedrine, pseudoephedrine, and phenylpropanolamine be kept secured behind the pharmacy counter or in a locked cabinet. The provisions in the CMEA restrict the total number of packages or grams a person can purchase of products containing these ingredients to 3.6 grams per day and no more than 9 grams in a thirty-day period. A purchaser must show a form of state or federal photo identification to purchase any product with the restricted chemical. The pharmacy is required to document the customer's name, address, date and time of sale, product name, quantity sold, and signature. The information from the sale of these products must be recorded electronically or in a physical logbook, and it must be readily accessible if requested by state or federal regulatory agencies.

For medications with serious risks that may outweigh their benefits, the FDA may require a **Risk Evaluation and Mitigation Strategy (REMS)**. The FDA's evaluation of a medication to determine whether a REMS is necessary considers several factors including serious risks, potential and known adverse effects of the drug within the afflicted population, and the seriousness of the condition being treated. The FDA also considers the size of the population expected to use the medication, the expected duration of treatment, the beneficial expectation of the drug, as well as other factors. It is the responsibility of the drug manufacturer to develop and implement the REMS for their drugs. The iPledge program is an example of a REMS for acne medications that contain isotretinoin. Isotretinoin is contraindicated in pregnancy and can cause serious birth defects.

The REMS outline the requirements of the prescriber, patient, and pharmacy to ensure safe and effective use. To obtain a prescription for isotretinoin, females who can bear children must register with the iPledge program and verify they are not currently pregnant with a urine or blood test performed by a certified laboratory. The physician is required to counsel patients regarding the risks associated with the medication as well as document which two forms of contraception the patient is taking and enter the information into the iPledge system. Once the information is entered in iPledge, including the results of a second pregnancy test, the patient has seven days to obtain the medication from the pharmacy. The pharmacy must also register with iPledge to be able to verify that all patient requirements have been

70

met. This requires entering the patient's iPledge ID and documenting the Risk Management Authorization (RMA) number on the prescription as well as the date it must be picked up by. If, however, the patient does not pick up the medication, then the RMA must be reversed in the iPledge system, and the drug must be returned to stock.

FDA Recall Requirements

MedWatch is the FDA program that allows healthcare professionals and consumers to report adverse reactions to and safety concerns regarding products regulated by the FDA. These products include medications, medical devices and supplies, and dietary supplements.

The FDA has several methods of intervening when it has been determined that a product poses a risk and should be taken off the market. The FDA can seize the product, obtain an injunction to halt production of the product, or it can issue a recall. A recall removes a product from the market. There are three classes of recalls (Class I, II, and III) that the Food and Drug Administration (FDA) uses to systematically address the severity of the recall:

- **Class I** is the most serious recall; drugs that fall under this class present risks for serious adverse health conditions or death.

- **Class II** is slightly less serious than Class I; drugs that fall under this class are unlikely to cause serious adverse health conditions or death, but the drugs can lead to temporary health problems.

- **Class III** is the least serious recall; this type is used when an FDA regulation has been violated but adverse health conditions are not likely to occur.

FDA Market Recalls are another type of warning issued for a drug, where minor violations need to be corrected or the drug needs to be removed from the market. Medical device recalls are part of FDA Medical Device Safety Alerts.

A **market withdrawal** is initiated when a product has an issue that would not be subject to legal action, and the manufacturer voluntarily removes the product. A **medical device safety alert** is issued when a medical device poses a substantial risk of harm. Pharmacies will receive notification when a product has been recalled either by letter or fax. When a pharmacy receives notification that a product has been recalled, the pharmacy must immediately cease distribution of the product. Any remaining stock of medication should be isolated from other medications.

All patients who have received the product should be contacted. Medications should be returned to the pharmacy in exchange for a refund or substitution if available. The recall notification will include instructions for returning the product to the manufacturer as well as a response card to be returned that indicates the pharmacy has followed instructions for administering the recall. A pharmacy representative should also notify prescribing physicians that medications have been recalled. While conducting a recall of medication, pharmacies must document the following things: the number of customers affected, the dates the customers were notified, the number of customers that responded to the notification, and the amount of medication that was returned as a result of the recall.

Food and Drug Administration (FDA)

The **FDA** was formed by the 1906 Pure Food and Drugs Act and received its name in 1930. The FDA's purpose is to provide oversight for the production and safety of food and drugs in the United States. The main goal of the FDA is to safeguard and advance public health by overseeing and modulating the production of the following products:

- Food products
- Prescription medications
- Over-the-counter medications
- Tobacco products
- Dietary supplements
- Biological drug products
- Vaccines
- Blood transfusions
- Medical devices
- Cosmetics

The President appoints the director of the FDA, who is also the Commissioner of Food and Drugs. The FDA can examine and implement laws related to food and drug safety through the Office of Criminal Investigations. A majority of the laws that are of interest to, and affect, the operations of the FDA are found in the Food, Drug, and Cosmetic Act.

Federal Food, Drug, and Cosmetic Act (FD&C)

This act was put in place in 1938 after over 100 people died from taking a medication that had traces of diethylene glycol. As technology and manufacturing have evolved over the years, the Act continues to be amended to reflect current standards. This act gives the FDA supervision of the safety of the food, drug, and cosmetic industries.

There are ten sections, called subchapters, in the FD&C Act:

- Subchapter I – Short Title
- Subchapter II – Definitions
- Subchapter III – Prohibited Acts and Penalties
- Subchapter IV – Food
- Subchapter V – Drugs and Devices
- Subchapter VI – Cosmetics
- Subchapter VII – General Authority
- Subchapter VIII – Imports and Exports
- Subchapter IX – Tobacco Products
- Subchapter X – Miscellaneous
- The act also covers issues such as adulteration, including bottled water, and homeopathic preparations.

Glossary

Class I Recall	This is the most serious recall; drugs that fall under this class present risks for serious adverse health conditions or death.
Class II Recall	This slightly less serious than Class I; drugs that fall under this class are unlikely to cause serious adverse health conditions or death, but the drugs can lead to temporary health problems.
Class III Recall	This the least serious recall; this type is used when an FDA regulation has been violated but adverse health conditions are not likely to occur.
Combat Methamphetamine Epidemic Act	These are Federal regulations state that all asthma and cold products containing the chemical ingredients ephedrine, pseudoephedrine, and phenylpropanolamine be kept secured behind the pharmacy counter or in a locked cabinet.
Controlled Substances Act (CSA)	This includes every Federal law relating to the manufacture, regulation, and sale of certain controlled substances (narcotics as well) were made. Also, the CSA allowed for the creation of five controlled drug classes (Schedules I-V) and what criterion warrants the medications in each class.
DEA Form 222	This must be filled out, either electronically or on paper, by the pharmacy in order to transfer, order, or return Schedule II medications.
Drug Enforcement Administration (DEA)	This a governmental agency set up in 1973 to implement laws around drug use and to fight drug trafficking.
Drug Schedules	These arrange drugs into groups based on risk of abuse or harm. Under the CSA, drugs and other substances considered controlled substances are divided into five categories, schedule I to schedule V.
Environmental Protection Agency (EPA)	This regulates the proper disposal of pharmaceutical waste, including prescription medications.
FDA Market Recalls	These are another type of warning issued for a drug, where minor violations need to be corrected or the drug needs to be removed from the market.
Federal Food, Drug, and Cosmetic Act (FD&C)	This act was put in place in 1938 after over 100 people died from taking a medication that had traces of diethylene glycol. This act gives the FDA supervision of the safety of the food, drug, and cosmetic industries.
Food and Drug Administration (FDA)	This was formed by the 1906 Pure Food and Drugs Act and received its name in 1930. The FDA's purpose is to provide oversight for the production and safety of food and drugs in the United States.
Hazardous Waste	This is any substance or combination of substances that could produce harmful effects on the health and safety of a person.
Infectious Waste	This is blood, bodily fluids, blood products, sharps that are infectious, and waste from the laboratory.
iPledge Program	This is used to confine drug distribution. Before patients can receive their first prescription of Isotretinoin, they must register for the program, undergo pregnancy testing (if applicable), choose two types of birth control, and promise to keep all scheduled appointments.
Market Withdrawal	This is initiated when a product has an issue that would not be subject to legal action, and the manufacturer voluntarily removes the product.
Material Safety Data Sheets (MSDS)	These contain information about the materials and chemical compounds, including identifying physical features and what should be done in the case of a spill.
Medical Device Safety Alert	This is issued when a medical device poses a substantial risk of harm.
MedWatch	This is the FDA program that allows healthcare professionals and consumers to report adverse reactions to and safety concerns regarding products regulated by the FDA.
Nonhazardous Pharmaceutical Waste	This may include antibiotics, hormone medications, and OTC products.
Pharmacy Personnel	These are responsible for providing dependable, safe, and effective care, which includes implementing strategies focused on the reduction of medication errors.

Resource Conservation and Recovery Act (RCRA)	This was enacted to prevent the improper disposal of unused hazardous medications.
Risk Evaluation and Mitigation Strategy (REMS)	This is the FDA's evaluation of a medication to determine whether a REMS is necessary considers several factors including serious risks, potential and known adverse effects of the drug within the afflicted population, and the seriousness of the condition being treated.
Risk Management	This refers to systems that identify, assess, and implement procedures aimed at reducing medication errors.
S.T.E.P.S. (System for Thalidomide Education and Prescribing Safety)	This is used for patients that are prescribed Thalidomide. Mandatory counseling, pregnancy testing (if applicable), and registration are required before patients can receive their first prescription.
Schedule I	These substances have no currently accepted medical use, a lack of accepted safety for use under medical supervision, and a high potential for abuse.
Schedule II/IIN	These substances on this schedule have a high potential for abuse, which may lead to severe psychological or physical dependence.
Schedule III/IIIN	These substances have less potential for abuse than substances in Schedules I or II, and abuse may lead to moderate or low physical dependence or high psychological dependence.
Schedule IV	Controlled substances on this schedule have a low potential for abuse relative to substances on Schedule III.
Schedule V	These substances have a low potential for abuse relative to substances on Schedule IV and consist primarily of preparations containing limited quantities of certain narcotics.
Solid Waste	This includes all solid, liquid, and gaseous waste.
Waste Receptacles	These are waste-specific. There is usually a specified container for biohazards and sharps; it is typically a red/dark orange receptacle that is labeled "bio-hazard."

Practice Quiz

1. The following is a DEA registrants number: BJ6125341. What is the check digit and is the number valid?
   a. 1 and yes
   b. 4 and yes
   c. 1 and no
   d. 4 and no

2. What is needed to order Schedule II narcotics from a wholesale warehouse?
   a. Approval from the FDA
   b. A prescription from a physician
   c. Form 222 must be filled out on paper or electronically
   d. The perpetual inventory shows the Schedule II narcotics are fully stocked

3. When the laws differ between the state and federal level, which laws should be followed?
   a. The most lenient law should be followed
   b. Both sets of laws should be followed to the fullest extent possible
   c. Neither set of laws should be followed because they are different
   d. The strictest law should be followed

4. Which Act below designates five controlled drug classes (Schedules I-V) and specifies the type of medications that are controlled under each class?
   a. Prescription Drug Marketing Act
   b. Controlled Substances Act
   c. Federal Food, Drug, and Cosmetic Act
   d. Poison Prevention Packaging Act

5. How long should dispensed prescriptions be kept on file and should Schedule II prescriptions be kept with other medications that have been dispensed?
   a. Forever; keep everything together
   b. 2 years; keep Schedule II prescriptions separate from other medications
   c. 5 years; keep Schedule II prescriptions separate from other medications
   d. Until the prescription is filled; keep everything together

See answers on the next page.

Answer Explanations

1. A: Applying the DEA number formula, the individual should find the check digit and validate it is the same. The formula is to add digits 1,3, and 5 which is SUM1, and then add digits 2,4, and 6, which is SUM2. Then, SUM2 is multiplied by 2, resulting in Product 1. Next, SUM1 and Product 1 are added together. The check digit is the second digit in the answer.

2. C: Form 222 from the DEA must be filled out on paper or electronically to order Schedule II medications from a wholesale warehouse, to transfer Schedule II medications between locations, or to return Schedule II medications to the wholesaler. Approval from the FDA is required for a medication to be marketed. A prescription from the physician is required for the patient to obtain the medication. The perpetual inventory needs to be maintained at all times. However, if all of the Schedule II medications are fully stocked, it is unlikely that the pharmacy will need to order more.

3. D: The strictest law should be followed. If the state has more requirements than the federal government, then the state laws and requirements should be followed. Due diligence should be given to understanding both state and federal laws pertaining to the pharmacy and, if there are questions, follow-up with the appropriate agencies and authorities is required.

4. B: The Controlled Substances Act classifies drugs into five controlled categories. The Prescription Drug Marketing Act ensures that all drugs marketed to the public are safe and effective and do not introduce risk from alterations. The Federal Food, Drug, and Cosmetic Act grants the FDA oversight of the safety of the food, drug, and cosmetic industries. The Poison Prevention Packaging Act requires the use of child-resistant caps on medication bottles.

5. B: Prescriptions should be kept on file for a minimum of two years and Schedule II medication prescriptions must be filed separately from other prescriptions. All prescriptions that were filled, need to be readily accessible during an inspection or visit from authorities. The other answer options are not correct due to 1) not maintaining the prescription file for appropriate length of time, 2) not separating controlled substance prescriptions from regular prescriptions, and 3) discarding the prescription after it has been filled.

Patient Safety and Quality Assurance

High-Alert/Risk Medications and Look-Alike/Sound-Alike (LASA) Medications

High-Alert/Risk Medications

High alert/risk medications refer to those medications that can cause significant harm to the patient when administered incorrectly or used in error. These medications generally have a narrow window of safety. Errors associated with high-risk medications result in devastating consequences to the patient and cause practitioners to suffer immense anxiety and guilt.

Here are some examples of high-alert medications:

- **Benzodiazepines**, primarily **midazolam**: used for sedation
- **Chemotherapeutic agents**: used for cancer treatment
- **Intravenous digoxin**: used to treat cardiac arrhythmia and heart failure
- **Dopamine, dobutamine**: used to treat depressed cardiac function
- **Heparin, warfarin**: used to prevent blood clots
- **Insulin**: used to control blood sugar
- **Lidocaine**: used to induce anesthesia
- **Opiate narcotics**: used for pain management
- **Neuromuscular blocking agents**: used as a muscle-relaxant or paralyzing agent
- **Electrolyte solutions**, e.g., intravenous sodium chloride, potassium chloride (or potassium phosphate), and magnesium sulphate

Pharmacies can use the following strategies to aid in avoiding errors associated with high-alert medications:

- Remove high concentration electrolytes from dispensing areas
- Use a leading "0" before the decimal place
- Avoid using risky abbreviations like "u" for unit or a tailing "0" on the dosage (e.g., 1.0 mg)
- Review LASA medications
- Use "tall man" letters for LASA medications
- Use colored warning labels
- Double-check dosage calculation independently

It is also necessary to pay attention to medications that should not be crushed as doing so could lead to high-risk situations. There are several reasons why certain medications should not be crushed:

- Dosage form is slow-release
- Dosage form is extended-release
- Dosage form is enteric-coated
- Mucous membrane could be irritated
- Possible increased rate of absorption
- Tablet coating could release the drug over a set period of time
- Taste
- Can irritate the skin

- Medication is liquid filled
- Dosage form is sublingual
- Dosage form is coated with a film
- Tablet is effervescent
- Potential for birth defects, teratogenic effect
- Acts as local anesthetic on the oral mucosa

A few examples of some medications that should not be crushed are *Cymbalta, Depakote, Prilosec,* and *Wellbutrin (SR, XL).*

Look-Alike and Sound-Alike (LASA) Medications

Some drug names look like or sound like other drug names. These include both generic and brand names of medications. **LASA medications** are a common cause of medication errors. With the presence of thousands of medications in the market, errors due to confusing drug names are possible and can be significant.

Consider the following examples:

LASA Medications	
Drug name	**Often confused with**
amlodipine	aMILoride
acetazolamide	acetoHEXAMIDE
ARIPiprazole	RABEprazole
chlorpropamide	chlorproMAZINE
ClobaZAM	ClonazePAM

Pharmacies can adopt the following strategies to prevent or reduce errors associated with LASA medications:

- Printing both the brand name and the generic name on prescriptions and pharmacy labels

- Adding the indication of each medication on a prescription

- Designing clinic-office/pharmacy software in a way that prevents LASA medications from appearing concurrently

- Changing the appearance of LASA medications to attract attention to their dissimilarities

- Implementing independent double-checks throughout the entire pharmacy workflow

- Storing LASA medications in separate locations on the shelves

- Reading back prescriptions, spelling out the name of medications, and providing the indication of the medication, when receiving a verbal prescription from the prescriber

- Emphasizing the use of methods such as "tall man lettering" to differentiate drug names

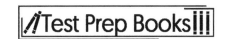

Error Prevention Strategies

Medication dispensing errors can be prevented or minimized by adopting systematic approaches in workflow.

1. Collect adequate information about the patient and the prescription.

   a. Verify the patient's information with the information written on the prescription— e.g., name, address, and date of birth. In the case of a patient with hearing or visual impairment, find an alternative means to communicate with the patient to verify the information.

   b. For existing patients, find the patient's profile by entering the patient's date of birth, and then verify by matching two unique identifiers on the pharmacy profile and the prescription.

   c. For new patients, verify two unique identifiers (e.g., date of birth and address) between the prescription and the newly-entered pharmacy profile before entering the prescription.

   d. If any part of the prescription information is missing, incomplete, or unclear, contact the corresponding physician to reconfirm the information.

   e. Be cautious when dispensing look-alike or sound-alike drugs. It's important to be careful about zeros, decimal points, and abbreviations.

   f. Incorporate an IVR (interactive voice response) that prompts physicians to leave thorough details about the prescription. The message should require that they provide details about the prescriber (prescriber's name, license number, phone number), details about the patient (patient's name, date of birth, phone number), and details about the medication (name, strength, direction of use, duration of treatment, and number of repeats/refills).

   g. Verify the "therapeutic use of the medication" with the patient to confirm that the treatment is appropriate for the patient's condition.

   h. If a verbal prescription is received through an IVR or direct communication, collect all necessary information and always reconfirm by reading back the prescription.

   i. Pharmacy prescription entry load can be reduced through electronic prescriptions.

2. Provide an environment that reinforces accurate prescription entry.

3. Provide supportive measures that assist in accurate information entry for filling out the prescription. Consider integrating the following at the prescription entry/drop-off station/counter:

   - A scanner with a re-sizable prescription imaging system on the screen
   - A stand to hold the prescription at eye level
   - Image magnification and zooming software
   - Adequate light and counter space

4. Allow entry of only one patient's prescriptions at a time. Keep other prescriptions away to avoid possible mix-up. Distractions should be reduced as much as possible.

5. Always use "baskets" to keep individual patient's prescriptions separate. This strategy significantly decreases dispensing errors and allows better tracking of patients to be served (in order according to drop-off or requested pick-up time).

6. Provide facilities that allow remote prescription entry during peak hours.

7. Patients should be encouraged to place orders in advance through the IVR, online, or email to reduce the workload at peak hours.

8. The technicians' shifts should be planned efficiently so that adequate staff is available during busy hours (or predicted busy days).

9. Employ additional staff and/or utilize automated processes to identify and correct errors.

    a. If feasible, provide additional employees to cross-check the prescription entry before it reaches the pharmacist for the final check.

    b. Design the pharmacy software in a way that requires action by the staff to enter a patient's information completely prior to processing the prescription.

    c. Keep the hard copy and/or scanned image of the prescription available for the pharmacist for the final check.

A pharmacy should adopt and implement suitable strategies to prevent medication-dispensing errors. The following are some examples that can minimize medication-dispensing errors in a pharmacy.

Tall Man Lettering

Tall man lettering refers to the practice of using mixed case letters (uppercase and lowercase) to bring attention to the dissimilarities in LASA medication names. The **Institute for Safe Medication Practices (ISMP)** and the FDA encourage use of tall man lettering to decrease possible mix-ups of LASA medications.

Examples of Tall Man Lettering	
acetaZOLAMIDE	acetoHEXAMIDE
Chlorpromazine	chlorproPAMIDE
DAUNOrubicin	DOXOrubicin
Dimenhydrinate	diphenhydrAMINE
DOBUTamine	DOPamine

Separating Inventory

Dispensing errors can happen from mix-ups of the medications that are LASA or from medications that are packaged in similar ways. Mix-up errors can also happen from a medication with different strengths.

The following inventory management strategies can be implemented to minimize such errors:

- Label medications with both the brand name and generic name
- Use separate shelving for LASA medications
- Tag warning labels on high-alert medications
- Incorporate provisions in pharmacy software to alert users of LASA or high-alert medications

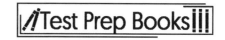
Understanding Leading and Trailing Zeros

A decimal point could be misplaced and lead to misinterpretation. The following strategies should be followed to avoid errors:

- **Leading zero**: A decimal point (a dose less than 1) should never be left "naked" and should carry a leading zero. It is often missed in fax prescriptions due to "fax noise." For example, without a leading zero, *.5 mg* of haloperidol could be misinterpreted as *5 mg* and cause overdosing.

- **Trailing zero**: A whole number should never be followed by a decimal point and a trailing zero. For example, with a trailing zero, *1.0 mg* warfarin could be misinterpreted as *10 mg* and cause ten-fold overdosing.

Bar Code and Automation Usage

Automation of pharmacies has increased both pharmacy productivity and efficiency with fewer medication errors. Automation to improve these processes may include barcode scanners, automated filling cabinets (e.g., ScriptPro or Omnicell®), and electronic pill counters. **Barcodes** are used to detect a drug's dosage form and strength.

Barcode advantages	Barcode disadvantages
Because the barcode is portable, it can be used during prescription filling and examining at any location. The handheld device scans the NDC number on the barcode of the patient's label or receipt and confirms it with the scanned NDC number of the barcode on the stock medication container from which the prescription was filled.	Not all drugs are linked or barcoded to the dose.
	Not every medicine has a barcode, as there are numerous dosage types.
The nurse can scan the barcode on the patient's wristband before administering a drug in a hospital. Directly after, the software compares information with the doctor's request to ensure the correct drug and dosage were dispensed to the right patient at the right time.	Installation of barcoding is costly.
This system establishes greater relations with the patient and care provider.	

In pharmacy, **robotics** encompasses a centralized system of using barcode technology. It contains a chain of computers working cohesively. In this system of conveyors, robots are capable of choosing drugs from a patient's file, as well as putting the medicine in the right drawer for the given patient.

Limiting Use of Error-Prone Abbreviations

Some abbreviations could be misinterpreted and cause medication dispensing errors. It is recommended that pharmacies minimize the use of the following abbreviations in prescriptions, labels, and medication administration records:

Common Error-Prone Abbreviations			
Abbreviation	**Intended Meaning**	**Misinterpretation**	**Suggested Correction**
AD, AS, AU	Right ear, left ear, each ear	OD, OS, OU (right eye, left eye, each eye)	Use the written words instead (i.e., "right ear")
BT	Bedtime	BID (twice daily)	Use "bedtime"
cc	Cubic centimeters	"u" (units)	Use "mL"
IU	International unit	10 (ten) or IV	Use "unit"
IJ	Injection	IV (intravenous)	Use "injection"
o.d. or OD	Once daily	OD (right eye)	Use "daily"
qhs	Nightly at bedtime	qhr (every hour")	Use "nightly"
UD	"ut dictum" (as directed)	Unit dose	Use " as directed"

Issues that Require Pharmacist Intervention

There are certain activities in pharmacy operations that require pharmacist intervention in order to ensure safe and effective use of medications by patients. A pharmacist needs to utilize various resources, professional judgement, and/or consultation with the prescriber and patient to make a decision under those circumstances. Provided below are examples of situations where a technician should seek the pharmacist's attention for guidance and the appropriate intervention.

Drug Utilization Review (DUR)

A **DUR** is an authorized, systematic, and ongoing review about the prescribing, dispensing, and use of a medication in respect to a specific patient's condition(s). It incorporates a comprehensive review of the patient's health history and medication profile for the purpose of making an appropriate decision prior to dispensing a medication.

A pharmacist intervention in a DUR improves the quality of patient care by preventing adverse drug reactions and minimizing inappropriate drug therapies. Pharmacy software generally picks up on various issues that require a DUR intervention. When a DUR conflict arises, the pharmacist needs to use an appropriate intervention code to fill, or reject to fill, the prescription.

Here are some examples:

- **Drug-drug interactions**: patient taking two or more medications that could interact and alter the intended therapeutic effects and/or cause some adverse effects

- **Drug-disease interactions**: patient receives a prescription for a medication that is contraindicated in the patient's disease condition

- **Drug-patient precaution**: medication that could be inappropriate for a patient in respect to the patient's age, gender, allergies, pregnancy, or other factors

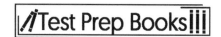

- Inappropriate treatment duration

- Medication overuse/misuse/abuse or under-utilization

- Drug dosage modification

- *Formulary substitutions* (e.g., therapeutic interchange, generic substitution)

Scenario for a DUR: A patient is on warfarin as a blood thinner for prevention of cardiovascular events. The patient receives a prescription for naproxen 500 mg (non-steroidal anti-inflammatory medication) for treatment of his tendinitis. This situation will result in a DUR conflict for drug-drug interaction requiring pharmacist intervention. The pharmacist needs to consult with the prescriber to change the therapy as naproxen could augment the effect of warfarin and cause internal hemorrhage (bleeding).

Adverse Drug Event (ADE)
An **ADE** refers to an unwanted effect of a medication that could cause injury to the patient. If untreated, an ADE could lead to organ damage, disability, hospitalization, and even fatality. A pharmacist should appropriately intervene in a situation of an ADE to ensure the best patient outcome.

An ADE can result from augmented pharmacological effects, which are mostly dose-dependent. It is more prevalent with medications that have a narrow therapeutic index (i.e., dose margin). For example, warfarin is an anticoagulant that has a narrow therapeutic index. The dose of warfarin is determined and adjusted based on routine blood work. An augmented effect of warfarin from a high dose or interaction with other medications can cause an ADE, i.e., an internal hemorrhage.

An ADE may also result with a medication for which a patient has medical allergies. For example, a patient allergic to penicillin can experience anaphylactic reactions from amoxicillin.

Over-the-Counter (OTC) Recommendations
Patients often seek OTC recommendations for the treatment of minor ailments. However, the pharmacist should assess the patient's condition(s), including the disease and concurrent use of other medications, prior to giving any recommendation. Pharmacist intervention is crucial in OTC recommendations to ensure the patient's safety and benefit. Before recommending an OTC medication, a pharmacist should rule out any alarm symptoms that might require an emergency or physician intervention.

Scenario for OTC Recommendation: A patient comes to the pharmacy counter asking the technician for an OTC pain reliever for his neck and chest pain. When the pharmacist collects the patient's information, the description of his pain (pain radiating to the left side of the body) strongly resembles symptoms of ischemic heart disease. The patient should be immediately referred to a hospital without any OTC medication recommended.

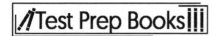

Miscellaneous Interventions

There are certain other situations that require pharmacist intervention. Technicians should be advised to always seek the pharmacist's attention while dealing with these issues:

- **Formulary substitution**: Therapeutic and generic substitutions often require an intervention by the pharmacist for the best treatment outcome. A pharmacist might contact the prescriber if drug-drug/drug-disease interactions or allergies warrant a therapeutic substitution.

- **Misuse/overuse**: Certain medications, including narcotics, controlled substances, stimulants, and psychotomimetic agents, may be misused or overused. A pharmacist should intervene appropriately to limit the use of those medications by the patient. The pharmacist can educate the patient and consult with the prescriber when he or she suspects medication overuse.

- **Missed dose**: Patients often seek advice regarding missed doses. The recommendations for a missing dose vary significantly for different medication types, including maintenance medications (e.g., for hypertension, diabetes), antibiotics, and oral contraceptives. A pharmacist can appropriately intervene in such situations to find solutions and offer the best advice to the patient.

Compliance

Compliance with a medication refers to adherence of the patient to the prescribed medication as directed by the prescriber. Non-compliance is one of the major causes for discontinuation of a medication.

The following are examples of non-compliance:

- Not taking the full dose of the medication (i.e., taking a smaller dose than what was prescribed)
- Not taking medication for the full length of time (i.e., stopping early)
- Not adhering to the time of day to take the medication (i.e., night vs. morning)
- Discontinuation of treatment
- Taking expired medications

Non-compliance with a medication can impose significant harm to the patient. There are many reasons for non-compliance, such as physical issues, cognitive problems, misunderstandings, and fear of or experience with side effects. Pharmacies have systems to help keep track of refills and reminders (calls, texts, and emails) for patients to promote compliance. The physician's office can send notifications to the patient and their physician when the patient is not compliant with treatment.

How to Identify a Forged Prescription

Individuals who falsify or change prescriptions frequently make common mistakes that are easy to recognize. It is important to review new prescriptions for these "tell signs" or mistakes:

- Personal information on the prescription is conflicting.

- The type of doctor who "wrote" the prescription would not usually prescribe the specified type of medication, for example, certain specialists or cardiologists. This "tell sign" could hint that the prescription blanks were stolen.

- Mistakes in the dosing instructions or abbreviations are hints, such as an unusual dose for the specified medication or mistakes using the codes.

- Glaring changes on quantity to be dispensed or number of refills. Sometimes erasing happens by the prescriber, but in such cases, the prescriber should be contacted to confirm the numbers.

- Varying types of ink on the prescription can indicate that changes have been made to a previously valid prescription.

- Usually no refills are provided on Schedule II prescriptions; if there are refills requested, check with the prescriber to make sure it was not in error.

- Observe the quantity prescribed closely.

Post-Immunization Follow-Up

The vaccines commonly administered by pharmacists include pneumococcal for pneumonia, the herpes zoster series for shingles, and influenza for flu. Protocols govern which vaccines pharmacists may administer and the age groups they can administer vaccines to. Protocols also govern required licensing, training, and vaccine reporting procedures, which vary by state. Pharmacists are trained to recognize adverse reactions following immunizations, educate patients on potential side effects after receiving a vaccination, and report adverse reactions and side effects when they happen. Adverse vaccine reactions should be reported using the Vaccine Adverse Event Reporting System (VAERS). VAERS operates under the guidance of the Centers for Disease Control (CDC) and the Food and Drug Administration (FDA). The CDC and FDA are responsible for the collection and surveillance of adverse event information across the United States.

Patient education is perhaps one of the most important responsibilities of a pharmacist regarding vaccinations. Pharmacists should understand current vaccination schedules in order to properly counsel patients on which vaccines are recommended and when to receive them. Vaccine schedules are important to make sure patients are fully protected. This is especially true of vaccines that are given in series. For example, the herpes zoster vaccine Shingrix is a series of two vaccines typically administered two to six months apart. Pharmacist follow-up will help to not only ensure patients receiving the initial vaccine in the series also receive the second in the series but that the vaccines are also administered within the recommended time frame.

Event Reporting Procedures

Medication error documentation may be accomplished with incident reports. Medication errors are numerous and varied, ranging from issues in filling the quantity or type of medication dispensed, errors reading a prescription or label, failing to verify a patient's medical conditions and any contraindications for a prescription, or dispensing a different patient's prescription to the wrong recipient. The individual staff member observing or initially informed of the incident should complete the incident report and turn it in to the supervisor on duty. Incident reports should contain the following information: specifics of the individuals involved in the incident (name, contact information, whether employee or patient), date, time, and location of incident, description of occurrence, type of injury, treatment provided (if applicable), name and signature of individual filing the report, and the date report was filed.

The MedWatch Program is overseen by the FDA and provides an online voluntary reporting form. MedWatch also furnishes safety alerts for drugs, medical devices, biologics, cosmetics, and nutritional supplements. It is the FDA's "gateway for clinically important safety information and reporting serious problems with human medical products." The FDA also administers the Adverse Event Reporting System (FAERS) containing information on medication error reports and adverse events. The FDA also oversees the **Vaccine Adverse Reporting System (VAERS)**, which is a national vaccine safety surveillance database.

The **Institute of Safe Medication Practices (ISMP)** provides impartial, timely, and accurate drug safety information. The ISMP provides pharmacy resources such as "do not crush" lists, black box warnings, error-prone abbreviations lists, confused drug names lists, high alert medications, and tall man letters. The ISMP also manages the **National Medication Errors Reporting Program (MERP)** and the National **Vaccine Errors Reporting Program (VERP)**. Currently, the ISMP is the only national nonprofit body concentrating on the prevention of medication errors.

An adverse effect or reaction to a medication is usually an unexpected event and can often be harmful. An allergic reaction to a medication such as a severe rash is an example of an adverse effect. It is important to report to MedWatch adverse events when they happen. The Food and Drug Administration's **Adverse Event Reporting System**, or **FAERS**, is an information database that compiles incident reports which have been submitted to MedWatch regarding adverse medication effects, product integrity, and medication errors. The reports in the database are evaluated to identify possible safety concerns that have arisen after products have gone to market. MedWatch is a useful tool used by clinicians to look for trends regarding product safety and provide the FDA with information for issuing safety warnings when necessary. Anyone can voluntarily submit a report to the FDA concerning an adverse event. The FDA, however, requires the manufacturer of a product to forward any adverse effects that are reported directly to them by a healthcare professional or consumer.

Product integrity concerns might include an adulterated product, misbranded drugs, counterfeit products, or an improperly labeled product. The sudden increase in the number of recalled counterfeit medications entering the market led to legislation to protect supply chains. In 2013, the **Drug Supply Chain Security Act (DSCSA)** was enacted to help establish guidelines for the tracing of prescription medications within the supply chain. The Drug Supply Chain Security Act requires wholesale distributers and their third-party logistic providers to obtain national licensure with the FDA in order to ensure a prescription medication's chain of custody remains unbroken within the supply chain.

Most medication errors are reported and reviewed internally utilizing established pharmacy or hospital protocols. Internal medication reporting practices allow for the immediate review of an error within the environment in which it occurred. MedWatch can be used to report all types of medication errors in addition to reporting adverse events and product integrity concerns. A near miss is a type of medication error that has the potential to do harm but does not because it does not reach the patient, or the medication does reach the patient but by mere chance, no harm was done. Reporting medication errors is important because it allows a systemic procedural review to determine how the error occurred. Knowing what led to the error can be useful in creating an action plan to prevent it from happening again.

Root cause analysis is a method of reviewing the underlying factors that can lead to a medication error rather than seeking to place blame on an individual or individuals. Root cause analysis examines the current pharmacy procedures and helps to identify systemic failures that led to the error. Conducting a

root cause analysis requires establishing an investigation team, collecting data, analyzing the incident, and identifying risk factors and causal pathways. After evaluating all the information, the team will create an action plan for corrections, finalize the report, and share the action plan with the entire pharmaceutical team.

Types of Prescription Errors

Medication dispensing errors refers to the deviations in a medication dispensed to a patient from that which was written in a prescription order.

An error might fall into one of these categories:

- Incorrect medication
- Incorrect dose
- Incorrect dosage form
- Incorrect quantity
- Incorrect or confusing direction
- Incorrect or inadequate labeling
- Incorrect patient
- Incorrect preparation etc.

Certain situations can increase the chance of medication dispensing errors:

- Unorganized work flow
- Work interruptions and distractions
- Poor handwriting and inadequate/incorrect information on prescriptions
- Excessive workload and stress
- Long shifts (fatigue)
- Ineffective communication with physicians and patients
- Lack of skilled personnel
- Inadequate staffing

Pharmacy technicians routinely handle refills of prescription medication. Some refill situations require special attention, including:

- **Early refill**: Medication dosage may have changed, or a patient may need a vacation fill. In some cases, insurance carriers have to be contacted.

- **No refills**: Generally, the prescriber must be contacted for a refill authorization. In some instances, the prescription may be greater than a year old, making it invalid.

- **Controlled substances**: Schedule II controlled substances cannot be refilled. Schedule III and IV controlled substances can only be refilled five times within a six-month period.

Medication error is a leading cause of death in the United States. Dispensing errors account for 21% of all medication errors. Examples of dispensing errors include dispensing the incorrect drug, quantity, dose, labeling, or dosage form.

There are many strategies to minimize dispensing errors, including:

- Correctly enter the prescription: Transcription errors (such as omissions and inaccuracies) account for approximately 15% of dispensing errors. These errors may be reduced by consistently using reliable methods of verification while entering a prescription order into the computer.

- Confirm the prescription is accurate and complete: Pharmacy personnel should not second-guess ambiguous or illegible prescriptions. Other causes of medication error include the use of acronyms, nonstandard abbreviations, decimals, and call-in prescriptions. The prescriber should be contacted for clarification.

- Be aware of sound-alike and look-alike medications: Similar medication names account for 33% of medication errors. One example would be dispensing methadone instead of methylphenidate. Occasionally, these errors are fatal.

- Be careful with zeros and abbreviations: Misplaced decimal points or zeros and faulty units are frequent causes of medication error and are typically the result of misinterpretation. Misplacing a decimal point or zero may result in the patient receiving at least 10 times more medication than originally indicated. Stocking a single strength of a particular medication, computer alerts, and reviewing label instructions during patient medication counseling may reduce these errors.

- Keep workplace organized: In clinical trials, organization (e.g., work environment, workspace, and workflow) has been shown to markedly reduce medication dispensing errors. Examples of organization include adequate workspace and appropriate lighting. Pharmacy technicians should develop a routine for entering, filling, and checking pharmacy prescriptions.

- Reduce distraction: Distraction while working and multitasking are leading causes of dispensing errors. Automatic refill requests may reduce distractions. Factors that may influence work environments include window services, design of workflow, and automatic dispensing.

- Balance heavy workloads and reduce stress: Increased workloads have often been noted as contributing to dispensing errors. Sufficient staffing with appropriate workload assignments may help to reduce dispensing errors. These measures should also reduce stress, which may limit medication errors.

- Store drugs properly: Storing look-alike/sound-alike medications away from each other on the shelves can decrease dispensing errors. Always store stock medication with the container label facing forward. Locked storage for medications with a high potential for inducing errors is advisable.

- Thoroughly check all prescriptions: Checks and counterchecks of medication labels may reduce dispensing errors. For instance, check the written prescription against the NDC in the computer, the printed medication label, and the drug being filled/dispensed.

- Always provide medication counseling to patients: The vast majority of dispensing errors (83%) are identified during medication counseling sessions between the patient and pharmacist. These errors may be corrected before the patient leaves the pharmacy. Directions for use of

medications should be covered during the counseling session, as misunderstood directions for use account for a significant portion of dispensing errors.

Prescription Interpretation

After intake, the pharmacy staff is obligated to understand and fill the patient's prescription. Prescription interpretation requires knowledge of medical abbreviations and may also require calculations to ensure that the proper quantity of medication is dispensed.

Prescription interpretation is ideal when the following elements are provided:

- Name, strength, dosage form, and quantity of medication to be dispensed

- Route of administration

- Frequency of administration

- Indication of whether a generic medication may be dispensed

- Number of refills: In the event the prescriber doesn't indicate the number of refills, it's assumed no refills will be permitted.

- If doubt exists when interpreting a particular prescription interpretation, a pharmacist should be asked to clarify.

- If the pharmacist cannot clarify, the prescriber should be contacted for clarification.

The following table illustrates some common dispensing errors:

Prescriber's Intention	Misinterpretation
AD, AS, AU *right ear, left ear, each ear*	OD, OS, OU *right eye, left eye, each eye*
qod *every other day*	qd or qid *daily 4 times a day*
U or u *units*	Zero, causing a 10-fold increase in dose *eg, 4U to 40*
Trailing zero *1.0 mg*	1.0 mg mistaken as 10 mg
Naked decimal point *.5 mg*	.5 mg mistaken as 5 mg
Drug name and dose run together *Inderal40*	Mistaken as Inderal 140
Large dose without properly placed commas	100000 units mistaken as 10,000 units
AZT *zidovudine*	Mistaken as azathioprine or aztreonam

There are several types of prescription medication orders: STAT, ASAP, PRN, and standing. **STAT** refers to a medication order that must be filled within 15 minutes of receiving it in a hospital. **ASAP** refers to a medication order that doesn't have the priority of a STAT order but needs to be processed as soon as possible. **PRN** refers to a medication order that may be filled or administered per patient request, but there are parameters set forth by the prescriber. **Standing** refers to a medication order that a patient receives at regularly scheduled intervals (e.g., one capsule every 6 hours).

Abnormal Doses

It is important for pharmacy technicians and pharmacists to understand the normal dosing for a medication in order to better identify abnormal dosing regimens. A prescription with directions that do not reflect the typical dosing regimen for the drug being prescribed could be due to an off-label or unapproved use of the medication. **Off label use** of a medication is when a medication is used to address a specific health issue that it was not initially approved to treat. It is therefore best to consult with the prescribing practitioner to clarify if it is simply off-label usage or a serious medication error. Abnormal dosing patterns are seen often with the blood thinner Warfarin, where patients might take different strengths of the medication on different days of the week. It is best to evaluate the written order for irregularities, for example, recognition of an adult dose of the NSAID Prednisone that is written for a small child. Prescription errors related to abnormal dosing of a medication can be avoided with attention to detail and some due diligence.

Hygiene and Cleaning Standards

In a pharmaceutical compounding practice, personnel are accountable for providing safe and ethical services to patients by strictly following the guidelines of infection control and hygiene and cleaning standards. It is recommended that all personnel adhere to the current infection control programs.

The infection control guidelines should be practiced in the following terms:

- Personal safety and prevention of spreading disease
- Prevention of an infection spread caused from compounding tools and equipment
- Prevention of an infection spread from materials and sources in the compounding environment

To prevent infections, the following routine practices must be employed:

- Hand washing or hand hygiene
- Use of additional barrier precautions, i.e., use of Personal Protective Equipment (PPE)
- Appropriate handling of workplace equipment
- Cleaning of the premises, equipment, and environment
- Appropriate method for handling waste
- Personal care for disease prevention, e.g., immunization

Hand Washing

Hand washing is the simplest and most cost-effective means of preventing the spread of infections. Bar or liquid soaps are recommended for routine hand washing. Antiseptic gels, rinses, and rubs can also be used. The most common antimicrobial agents used in healthcare practices for hand washing are alcohol (70-90%), aqueous chlorhexidine (2% or 4%) solutions, and iodine compounds.

Following the standard, proper, hand washing technique is important in preventing the spread of infection and should include the following steps:

1. Remove rings, watches and other jewelry.
2. Wet hands with warm water.
3. Apply soap or disinfectant preparation.
4. Vigorously rub all areas of hands including the back of hands, palms, fingers, nails and wrists.
5. Continue rubbing for at least 10 to 20 seconds (time varies according to different guidelines).
6. Rinse hands and dry properly using a paper towel.
7. Turn off the tap with the paper towel used to dry hands, and discard the towel.
8. After drying, apply lotions to keep hands moist and healthy.

Standard Hand Washing Technique

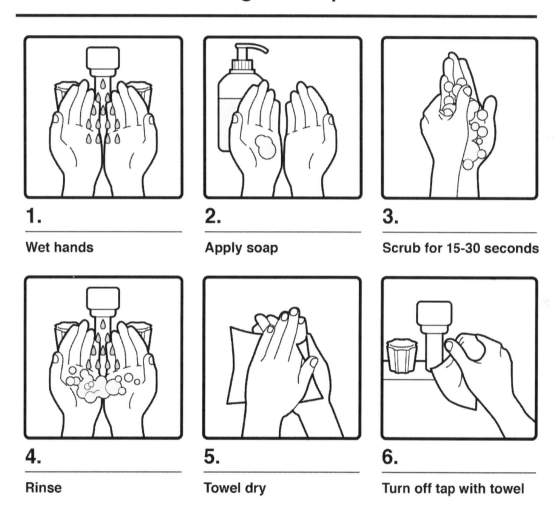

1. Wet hands
2. Apply soap
3. Scrub for 15-30 seconds
4. Rinse
5. Towel dry
6. Turn off tap with towel

Personal Protective Equipment (PPE)

The pharmacy staff should use PPE appropriate to the nature of the contaminating agents. The PPE most commonly used in healthcare facilities are gloves, masks, gowns, head covers, shoe covers, and eye protection. Note that the use of PPE does not eliminate the need for proper hand washing. When used properly, PPE can significantly reduce the risk of infection spread; however, PPE cannot completely

eliminate the risk. Staff should never share PPE. PPE should be completely changed after a task, and used PPE should be disposed of appropriately. Hand washing should be done every time after disposal of the PPE and before attending to another duty.

Gloves are routinely used in compounding practice to prevent contamination and the spread of infection. Their use also helps personnel reduce contamination while performing procedures.

The following considerations should be kept in mind for best use of gloves in practice:

- Gloves should be removed carefully to prevent skin contamination.
- Hands should be washed each time after removing gloves.
- Single-use gloves should not be reused and should be discarded.
- Gloves should be changed after contact with contaminated items, such as linens or wastes.
- Gloves should be purchased from manufacturers that meet the regulatory board standards.

Masks provide respiratory protection from airborne solid particles and droplets. Droplets refers to liquid particles larger than 5μm in size. The symbol μ means one millionth. So, 1 μm is equivalent to one millionth of a meter. Droplets do not stay suspended in air for very long. and instead fall on various surfaces. N-95 masks are widely used in health practice. The "N" means "not resistant to oil" and "95" indicates that it has 95% efficacy for filtering particles of 0.3 μm size. The National Institute for Occupational Safety and Health (NIOSH) in the U.S. certified that N-95 masks provide adequate protection against airborne particles, but not against gas or vapor. They also provide little protection against direct liquid splashes.

The following considerations need to be considered for proper use of masks in practice:

- Gloves should be removed first, and hands should be washed prior to removing the mask.

- The mask should be removed carefully to prevent contamination to airway or skin.

- Hold the mask, remove ties, and pull mask away from the face. Do not drag the mask over the face.

- Discard gloves and mask, and wash hands afterward.

Medical personnel should know the proper sequence for putting on and removing PPE. For example, pharmacy staff must adhere to guidelines set forth in USP <797>, a chapter on pharmaceutical sterile preparations in the USP National Formulary, when compounding sterile preparations. First, staff should remove all unnecessary outer garments and jewelry. Next, staff should put on shoe, facial, and hair covers, facemasks, and optional face shields. Then, staff should perform mandatory hand hygiene. USP <797> specifies:

"...personnel perform a thorough hand-cleansing procedure by removing debris from under fingernails using a nail cleaner under running warm water followed by vigorous hand and arm washing to the elbows for at least 30 seconds with either nonantimicrobial or antimicrobial soap and water."

After performing hand hygiene, staff should put on a gown with sleeves fitting snugly around the wrists. Upon advancing to the buffer area (a clean, sterile area), a waterless alcohol-based scrub should be carried out. Lastly, sterile gloves should be put on prior to compounding sterile preparations.

92

Infection Control of Environment and Equipment

Environmental surfaces should be cleaned daily and when visibly dirty. These surfaces generally need a low level of disinfectant similar to general housekeeping. The places requiring cleaning include tables, counter tops, floors, bathrooms, doorknobs, sinks, and waiting room chairs. Disinfectants used in daily cleaning are toxic and hazardous and, therefore, should be properly labeled, handled, and stored. The most common disinfectants include alcohols, 3% hydrogen peroxide-based products, phenolic compounds, and household bleach.

The type of disinfectants to be used for cleaning tools and equipment depends on the purpose and level of disinfection required. Here are some examples of routinely-used disinfectants in clinical practice:

Low-Level Disinfectants
- Phenolic compounds
- Quaternary ammonium compounds
- 3% hydrogen peroxide
- Hypochlorite household bleach

Intermediate-Level Disinfectants
- Alcohols (70-90%)
- Hypochlorite household bleach
- Iodines and iodophor (e.g., povidone-iodine)
- Boiling item for more than 20 minutes
- Ortho-phthalaldehyde
- Glutaraldehyde for 20 minutes
- 6% hydrogen peroxide soak for 5 minutes

High-Level Disinfectants
- Sterilization
- Exposure to steam at a high temperature and pressure (autoclave)
- Glutaraldehyde for 10 hours
- Gas sterilization (ethylene oxide)
- Dry heat sterilization

The goal of infection control is the prevention of healthcare-associated infections. These types of infections may be acquired in hospitals, outpatient clinics, rehabilitation facilities, nursing homes, or other clinical settings. The infections may spread from medical staff to patients, from patients to medical staff, from patient-to-patient, or among medical staff.

Laminar Flow Hood

A **laminar flow hood** is an air filtration system designed to ensure that the space in a pharmacy used for compounding sterile preparations does not have any contaminants or particulates. It pulls air through a **High Efficiency Particulate Arresting (HEPA) filter** and then blows it toward the person making the sterile compound, providing a constant stream of filtered air over all of the compounding materials and tools within the hood. Laminar flow hoods come in both vertical and horizontal designs, as well as additional airflow patterns needed for particular systems or uses. Manufacturers will provide specifications for maintenance; these must be followed carefully and the laminar flow hood must be thoroughly cleaned prior to each use to avoid spreading contaminants into sterile compounds.

Cleaning the laminar flow hood requires the use of a proper technique:

1. Collect your cleaning equipment: 70% ethanol or other disinfectant, sterile gauze or other laboratory grade wipes.

2. Dress in personal protective equipment, including gloves, mask, goggles, foot coverings, and a gown.

3. Turn the hood on, and allow the hood to run for five to twenty minutes before cleaning, depending on the hood manufacturer's manual. The hood should run for at least thirty minutes before use.

4. Remove any items that do not belong in the hood.

5. Spray the internal surfaces with the disinfectant, and clean with sterile wipes using a sweeping back and forth motion. Do not spray disinfectant into the HEPA filter.

6. Allow the hood to air dry.

Cleaning Items and Equipment Used to Count Medication

Throughout the pharmacy, there are tools and equipment used in the preparation of medications (measuring, counting and pouring) that become dirty or tainted with dust from the medications. At least once a day, these tools and equipment (counting trays and spatulas, etc.) should be washed with hot soapy water. It is also recommended to keep cleaning wipes readily accessible to wipe down counting trays throughout the day. Most pharmacies have separate tools for preparing prescriptions that are often known to cause allergies (sulfa antibiotics and penicillin are examples). In theory, the powder from these medications can be transferred to other medications if counted on the same trays and equipment, leading to an allergic reaction. Any tools used to pour or scoop liquid and cream medications should be cleaned directly after use.

Areas of the Pharmacy to be Cleaned Each Day

Pharmacy Technicians are responsible for keeping the pharmacy as clean as possible on a daily basis. In order to keep the pharmacy clean, dusting should be performed regularly. Below are the daily cleaning tasks that a pharmacy technician should perform:

- Washing off the counter and all surface areas
- Rinsing all tools from medication dispensing
- Washing off keyboards and all phone surfaces
- Taking out the trash from the pharmacy
- Cleaning the floor of the pharmacy using a broom or a vacuum
- Using a wet mop with disinfectant on the pharmacy floor
- Disinfecting the waiting area or lobby of the pharmacy

Glossary

Adverse Drug Event (ADE)	This refers to an unwanted effect of a medication that could cause injury to the patient.
Adverse Event Reporting System (FAERS)	This is an information database that compiles incident reports which have been submitted to MedWatch regarding adverse medication effects, product integrity, and medication errors.
ASAP	This refers to a medication order that doesn't have the priority of a STAT order but needs to be processed as soon as possible.
Barcodes	These are used to detect a drug's dosage form and strength.
Compliance	This refers to adherence of the patient to the prescribed medication as directed by the prescriber.
Controlled Substances	Schedule II controlled substances cannot be refilled. Schedule III and IV controlled substances can only be refilled five times within a six-month period.
Drug Supply Chain Security Act (DSCSA)	This was enacted to help establish guidelines for the tracing of prescription medications within the supply chain.
Drug Utilization Review (DUR)	This is an authorized, systematic, and ongoing review about the prescribing, dispensing, and use of a medication in respect to a specific patient's condition(s).
Drug-Disease Interactions	The patient receives a prescription for a medication that is contraindicated in the patient's disease condition
Drug-Drug Interactions	The patient is taking two or more medications that could interact and alter the intended therapeutic effects and/or cause some adverse effects
Drug-Patient Precaution	This is medication that could be inappropriate for a patient in respect to the patient's age, gender, allergies, pregnancy, or other factors
Early Refill	This medication dosage may have changed, or a patient may need a vacation fill. In some cases, insurance carriers have to be contacted.
Formulary Substitution	These are therapeutic and generic substitutions often require an intervention by the pharmacist for the best treatment outcome.
Hand Washing	This is the simplest and most cost-effective means of preventing the spread of infections.
High Alert/Risk Medications	These refer to those medications that can cause significant harm to the patient when administered incorrectly or used in error.
High Efficiency Particulate Arresting (HEPA)	This is when air from the room is drawn through a HEPA filter and blown back toward the user to keep a steady stream of filtered air flowing over the items in the hood.
Institute of Safe Medication Practices (ISMP)	This provides impartial, timely, and accurate drug safety information. Manages the National Medication Errors Reporting Program (MERP) and Vaccine Errors Reporting Program (VERP)
Laminar Flow Hood	This is designed to provide a space in pharmacy that is free of contaminants and particulates for the purpose of compounding sterile preparations.
Leading Zero	This is when a decimal point (a dose less than 1) should never be left "naked" and should carry a leading zero.
Look-Alike and Sound-Alike (LASA) Medications	These are a common cause of medication errors. With the presence of thousands of medications in the market, errors due to confusing drug names are possible and can be significant.
Medication Dispensing Errors	This refers to the deviations in a medication dispensed to a patient from that which was written in a prescription order.
Missed Dose	This is when patients often seek advice regarding missed doses. The recommendations for a missing dose vary significantly for different medication types.
Misuse/Overuse	There is concern that certain medications, including narcotics, controlled substances, stimulants, and psychotomimetic agents, may be misused or overused.
No Refills	Generally, the prescriber must be contacted for a refill authorization. In some instances, the prescription may be greater than a year old, making it invalid.
Off Label Use	This is when a medication is used to address a specific health issue that it was not initially approved to treat.

PRN	This refers to a medication order that may be filled or administered per patient request, but there are parameters set forth by the prescriber.
Robotics	This encompasses a centralized system of using barcode technology.
Root Cause Analysis	This is a method of reviewing the underlying factors that can lead to a medication error rather than seeking to place blame on an individual or individuals.
Standing	This refers to a medication order that a patient receives at regularly scheduled intervals (e.g., one capsule every 6 hours).
STAT	This refers to a medication order that must be filled within 15 minutes of receiving it in a hospital.
Tall Man Lettering	This refers to the practice of using mixed case letters (uppercase and lowercase) to bring attention to the dissimilarities in LASA medication names.
Trailing Zero	A whole number should never be followed by a decimal point and a trailing zero.
Vaccine Adverse Reporting System (VAERS)	This is a national vaccine safety surveillance database.

Practice Questions

1. Which of the following could contribute to infection spread in a compounding pharmacy?
   I. Droplet transmission
   II. Contact transmission
   III. Airborne transmission
   a. I and II
   b. I and III
   c. II and III
   d. I, II, and III

2. Which of the following explains why separate spatulas and counting trays should be used for medications that are likely to cause allergies?
   a. Each medication should have its own spatula and counting tray
   b. Separate tools are not required, but frequent washing is needed for these medications
   c. The powders of potentially allergen-inducing medications can cross-contaminate other prescriptions
   d. It is unrealistic to keep track of which spatula and counting tray was used for a particular medicine, but pharmacists and technicians should be careful about contamination

3. Which of the following is a sign that a prescription might be forged?
   a. The number of refills appears to have been altered
   b. The patient is a first-time customer of the pharmacy
   c. No refills are given for a Schedule II medication
   d. The prescription is phoned in by the physician

4. Which of the following medications should not be combined with Warfarin?
   I. Aspirin
   II. Diclofenac
   III. Celecoxib
   a. I and II
   b. I and III
   c. II and III
   d. All of the above

5. Which is NOT an effective strategy for preventing errors when receiving a verbal prescription?
   a. Collecting treatment indication
   b. Reading back prescription
   c. Spelling the drug's name
   d. Using abbreviations

See answers on the next page.

Answer Explanations

1. D: All of the provided choices are potential causes of transmission.

2. B: It is essential to keep track of tools that were used to dispense medications that could potentially lead to allergic reactions and to only use the tools to dispense the particular medication (i.e. penicillin). Powders from medications can easily get on other pills that are being dispensed with the same tools. The best practice is to wipe down the tools after use and to mark tools used for certain medications that have higher allergen potentials.

3. A: It's possible that the doctor made a mistake or changed their mind when writing the number of refills; however, it's still suspicious if the number of refills has been altered. You should contact the physician by looking up the number to their office (rather than using the number on the prescription pad), and ask them to confirm the number of refills they are prescribing. People must be a first-time customer of a pharmacy at some point, and people often relocate, so it's not necessarily suspicious. Schedule II medications typically do not have refills associated with the prescription. In emergency situations, a physician can call in a prescription as a verbal order, which must then be followed up with a paper version within seven days.

4. D: All of the listed medications impose a risk when taken with Warfarin, as they increase the blood-thinning activity and can lead to the blood becoming too thin.

5. D: Using abbreviations increases the chance of errors due to misinterpretation. For example, some abbreviations are particularly risky like writing "u" for unit or adding a tailing "0" on the dosage (e.g., 1.0 mg).

Order Entry and Processing

During the order-entry and prescription-filling process, a pharmacy technician may be required to carry out a broad array of tasks, such as:

- Accepting new prescriptions
- Receiving prescription refills
- Asking prescribers for refill authorizations
- Gathering patient data
- Initiating and maintaining an electronic patient profile
- Entering pertinent information into the pharmacy management software system
- Interpreting prescriptions
- Billing prescriptions to third-party pharmacy benefit providers
- Counting and pouring medications
- Labeling prescription containers
- Returning medication stock to pharmacy shelves
- Repackaging medications
- Preparing unit dose medications

Under no circumstances should pharmacy technicians provide medical advice to patients. It is essential for pharmacy technicians to maintain current awareness of medications and healthcare information. This equips them to be better able to recognize possible mistakes and other issues so they can notify the pharmacist.

Every pharmacy should have a standardized book outlining their particular policies and procedures, including a **mission statement** stating the goals and purpose of an organization. A book of policies and procedures is mandatory per regulatory and professional bodies (e.g., the American Pharmacists Association [APhA], the Joint Commission, and the American Society of Health System Pharmacists [ASHP]). Manuals for policies and procedures may be used as reference tools as well as for the promotion of workplace safety.

Per federal law, a pharmacy may receive a prescription order via one of the following methods:

- Written: The patient hands the original prescription to a pharmacy technician.

- Telephone: Also called a verbal order

- If the original prescription is for a non-scheduled II is a controlled substance, it may be telephoned in by prescribers or their representatives (e.g., a nurse).

- The patient may call in a refill for a prescription.

- Electronic or E-prescription: Transmitted electronically

- Fax

It's becoming common practice for Medicaid, Medicare, and private insurers to track prescriptions using a prescription origin code (POC). The codes are usually entered into the pharmacy management software system and signify the following:

- 0 = Unknown (e.g., a transferred prescription)
- 1 = Written prescription
- 2 = Telephone prescription
- 3 = Electronic prescription
- 4 = Fax prescription

Compounding Non-Sterile Products

Pharmaceutical compounding refers to the formulation of a product in a pharmacy, distinct from one supplied by a commercial manufacturer, in order to meet the unique needs of a patient as specified by the physician. The reasons for pharmaceutical compounding vary:

- The product might not be available commercially.

- The product may be in short supply (e.g., a product on back-order).

- There may be a change in the dosage form (e.g., formulation of a liquid dosage form from solid tablets or capsules).

- The patient may have an allergy to an excipient (filler) in a product.

- There may be a need for large-scale intravenous or parenteral medications for hospital supply.

- There may be a need to improve compliance by altering the taste and texture of an otherwise unfavorable formulation.

Certain considerations should be considered to ensure the safety and efficacy of a pharmaceutical admixture:

- **Personnel**: It is crucial to delegate the responsibility of compounding a formulation to a person who has the requisite knowledge and expertise in pharmaceutical compounding. If a pharmacy is unable to compound an item, the patient should be referred to another pharmacy that has the ability to formulate it as specified. The designated personnel should have adequate knowledge in the following areas:

    - Physical and chemical properties of the ingredients
    - Physical and chemical compatibilities between ingredients and excipients (fillers)
    - Pharmaceutical calculations
    - Use of appropriate methods
    - Use of appropriate equipment

- **Premises and environment**: Compounding should be performed in a designated area that ensures an appropriate environment in terms of space, storage, and lighting. The assigned area for compounding should be clean, orderly, and sanitary. The compounding area might maintain a written protocol addressing various issues, such as hand washing, equipment cleaning, and

managing staff injuries that result from compounding. The compounding area should have access to water for cleaning hands, equipment, floor, and surfaces.

- **Equipment and supplies**: The pharmacy should have appropriate equipment and supplies in order to formulate pharmaceutical admixtures per the specified standards. Equipment should be routinely cleaned and kept dry to minimize contamination with the formulation ingredients and extraneous materials. Pharmaceutical compounding generally requires the following equipment and auxiliary supplies, in addition to therapeutic ingredients, to formulate a compound:

  - Class A prescription balance or analytical balance to weigh the ingredients
  - Weighing papers, wax papers, or measuring boats
  - Spatula to transfer ingredients
  - Mortar and pestle for grinding and mixing
  - Graduated cylinders (10 ml and 100 ml)
  - Ointment slab
  - Cream or ointment base
  - Wetting or levigating agent to reduce particle size
  - Personal protective equipment (PPE)

- **Resources**: A compounding pharmacy should have adequate resources available to render the intended service. The pharmacist should gather information from peer-reviewed sources, such as academic journals, to formulate a product. If the formula is not available for the intended preparation, it should be prepared utilizing the knowledge of physical and chemical properties of the ingredients, pharmacology, and pharmaceutical science.

The following considerations should be considered when selecting tools and equipment for compounding practice:

- Equipment and utensils used in pharmaceutical compounding should have a suitable design and capacity that will allow for effective admixing. The type and size of the equipment to be utilized depends on the intended purpose of compounding, the dosage form, and the volume/amount to be compounded.

- The surface of the equipment should be chemically inert and should not alter the admixture through chemical reaction, addition, or absorption.

- Tools and equipment should be routinely cleaned and properly stored to avoid contamination.

- All electronic, automated, mechanical, and other instruments used in preparing or testing admixtures should be routinely calibrated and inspected.

- The cleaning of equipment should include extra care and caution when the preparation includes cytotoxic agents, antibiotics, and hazardous materials.

- When possible, equipment can be dedicated for a specific job that involves hazardous chemicals or requires high precision. Disposable equipment should be used to reduce the bio-burden and cross-contamination.

101

- The ingredients used in pharmaceutical compounding should be carefully selected to ensure acceptable strength, quality, purity, and stability in the final formulation. In the selection and use of ingredients, the following measures should be taken:

  o The compounding ingredients should be collected primarily from a preferred source that meets United States Pharmacopeia (USP) and National Formulary (NF) grades. If not available, another source that ensures high quality grade, e.g., Analytical Reagent (AR), American Chemical Society (ACS), and/or Food Chemicals Codex (FCC) can be used.

  o Components produced in an FDA-registered manufacturing facility should be used first. If that's not possible, the purity and safety of the ingredients should be ensured by reasonable means, which includes obtaining a Certificate of Analysis (C of A), determining the reputation of the manufacturer, and determining the reliability of the source. The C of A should be maintained in record for future reference.

  o Pharmaceutical products such as tablets, capsules, and injectables are often used as sources for active ingredients. Staff should make sure that the pharmaceutical products used in compounding are collected from bottles labelled with a batch control number and expiration date.

  o If the manufacturer does not assign an expiration date to any of the ingredients, then the container should be labeled with the date of the receipt. A conservative expiration date should be assigned, based on the nature of the chemical, its degradation pattern, and the storage condition.

  o To ensure safety and avoid toxicity when compounding a formulation for human use, it is important to check that the required medication is not on the FDA list of drugs withdrawn from the market.

  o To ensure consistency and quality of the formulation, it is important to receive an ingredient from the same supplier every time. Ingredients from different suppliers may have a variation in physicochemical properties, resulting in an alternative drug response of the final formulation.

- Ingredients and excipients utilized in a particular formulation should be selected based the following criteria:

  o Physical properties
  o Compatibility
  o Patient conditions (allergy, disease state, use of other medications)
  o Intended use
  o Possible duration of treatment
  o Possible drug-drug and drug-excipient interactions
  o Route and frequency of administration

There are several general considerations to take into account before initiating pharmaceutical compounding of non-sterile products (these also apply to sterile compounding):

- The physical and chemical properties of active ingredient(s)

102

- The pharmaceutical and therapeutic uses of active ingredient(s)

- Analysis of whether the admixture will provide adequate topical or systemic absorption

- Assessment of whether any components of the admixture will render unexpected allergic, toxic, or undesirable reactions

- A dedicated clean and sanitized area is available for compounding

- Compounds are performed one at a time in that dedicated area

- For orally-administered admixtures: an assessment of what the possible effects of gastro-intestinal pH and hepatic metabolism on the bioavailability for active ingredient(s) would be

The compounding process (sterile and non-sterile) involves five distinct steps:

1. Preparing

- Review the prescription and determine whether the preparation would be safe and would fulfill the intended purpose.
- Make a list of chemical ingredients and excipients required for the formulation.
- Perform calculations to determine the amount of active ingredients and excipients required to compound the admixture.
- Select suitable equipment, ensuring that it is clean.
- Wash hands and wear appropriate PPE.
- Arrange necessary ingredients and equipment to perform compounding.

2. Compounding

- Perform the admixing according to the formulary and directions in the prescription.
- The admixing should utilize the art and science of pharmaceutical compounding.

3. Checking

- Check certain physical parameters of the admixture, including color, odor, consistency, and pH.
- Enter the information in the compounding log.
- Label the compound.

4. Recording and signing: All information should be entered and signed by a pharmacist, confirming that the assigned procedure was carried out properly (to ensure quality and to serve the intended purpose) as specified in the prescription.

5. Cleaning

- Clean the equipment and compounding areas.
- Dispose of waste and PPE.
- Wash hands.

Techniques Used in Non-Sterile Compounding

- **Blending**: mixing two substances together

- **Communition**: making a substance into small, fine particles

- **Geometric dilution**: mixing two different ingredients together of unequal quantities, starting with the ingredient of smallest quantity and adding the same quantity of the other ingredient (of larger amount), continuing to repeat until all the ingredients are used

- **Levigation**: the use of water or another solvent to carry an insoluble drug powder through the process

- Powder can turn into a thin paste with use of less water

- **Pulverization by intervention**: for powders that do not crush easily, a solvent (usually an alcohol) dissolves the powder can be used to intervene.

- Mixing dissolved powder on an ointment slab or in a mortar helps the solvent evaporate, and the powder will come out in finer particles.

Documentation

Documentation helps in systematically tracing, evaluating, and replicating the steps that were involved in a compounding process. Compounding pharmacies should maintain four sets of records:

1. Master formulation records

- Official name, strength, and dosage form of the compounded product
- Calculations used to determine and check quantities of components and doses
- Description of all ingredients and the individual quantities
- Compatibility and stability information (including available references)
- The equipment used/needed to make the preparation (when relevant)
- Instructions for mixing
- Order the ingredients were mixed
- Temperature during mixing or other environmental settings
- Amount of time of mixing
- Other relevant factors for repeating the preparation as compounded
- Sample label information, including legally required information as well as the following:
  - The generic name and the amount of each active ingredient
  - The Beyond Use Date (BUD) that was given
  - Required storage conditions
  - The number for the prescription
  - The container that was used to dispense the product
  - Requirements for packaging and storage of the product
  - Final preparation description
- Procedures used for quality control and expected results

2. Compounding records describe what happens while the formulation is being compounded
3. Standard operating procedures (SOPs), including equipment maintenance records

4. Ingredients' records, including Certificates of Analysis (C of A) and Material Safety Data Sheets

Documentation should be preserved for the period of time specified by state laws. Records should be available in the pharmacy during the retention period for auditing purposes. Proper documentation is important to ensure consistency in batch-to-batch preparations. Records of complaints by patients and of serious harmful events due to compounded medications should be kept on record for at least two years from the day the prescription was dispensed. Follow-up investigations on the complaints should be included in the records. Calculations of the quantity of each component in the compounded medication should also be documented.

Master Formulation Record (Compound Formula)

Name of compound: _____

Strength: _____ Dosage form: _____ Total quantity: _____

Ingredients	Manufacturer	DIN	Quantity

Preparation instructions: _____

_____

_____

_____

Prepared by: _____

Reference: _____

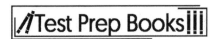

Compounding Record

<table>
<tr><td colspan="2" align="center">Affix Rx label</td><td>Source of formula: _____</td></tr>
<tr><td colspan="2">Compound name: _____</td><td>Beyond-use date: _____</td></tr>
<tr><td colspan="2">Strength: _____</td><td>Deviation from master formula: _____</td></tr>
<tr><td colspan="2">Dosage form: _____</td><td>_____</td></tr>
<tr><td colspan="2">Quantity: _____</td><td>_____</td></tr>
<tr><td colspan="2">Batch: _____</td><td>Deviation approved by: _____</td></tr>
<tr><td colspan="2">Date prepared: _____</td><td></td></tr>
</table>

Ingredients	MFR	DIN	Lot #	EXP date	Quantity	Measured by	Verified by

Calculation: _____

_____

_____

Calculated by: _____ Verified by: _____

Formulation prepared by: _____

Signing off (Pharmacist): _____

Emulsions and Enemas

Nonsterile emulsions are thermodynamically unstable mixtures composed of at least two liquids that are immiscible—liquids that are insoluble in one another and do not mix easily. The procedure for compounding these types of nonsterile formulations depends on the type of emulsion being prepared. Simple emulsions can either be oil in water or water in oil, while more complicated emulsions include water in oil in water and oil in water in oil. An emulsion consists of two phases; the dispersed liquid makes up the **internal phase**, while the medium which it is dispersed in composes the **external phase**. **Emulsifying agents**, which have chemical properties that make them both water and oil soluble, or amphiphilic, are used to stabilize the emulsion. The emulsifying agent acts by creating a barrier between the two phases. The Dry Gum Method and the Wet Gum Method of emulsion preparation involve the same ratio of 4:2:1, or four parts oil, two parts water, and one part emulsifying agent, but the order of application differs.

The nonsterile preparation of compounded enema solutions involves dissolving the active pharmaceutical ingredients in purified water, titrating to the necessary pH, and packaging the solution in individual bottles for dispensing. Referring to a master formulation, the procedure to compound would be to first weigh out the active pharmaceutical ingredient (API). The weighed API or solute is added to a

solvent. When adding the API to a solvent, it is important to consider the displacement of the solvent by the API. It is generally best to add the API to a percentage of the final volume, which is typically specified in the master formula. A magnetic stirring rod should be used to thoroughly dissolve the API to achieve a homogenous mixture. The pH of the solution should be verified to make sure it is within the specified range for the specific enema being made. Then the solution should be brought to its final volume, and its pH checked again. If necessary, the pH can be adjusted to meet the specific range required in the quality assurance portion of the formula. The solution can then be poured into individual enema bottles and labeled appropriately.

Formulas/Calculations

Converting Liquid Measurements

Converting Between Teaspoons, Tablespoons, and mL

It is important for patients to measure the dose when prescribed liquid medications that require a spoon or an oral syringe. One teaspoon is equal to 4.929 mL, and one tablespoon is equal to 14.79 mL.

Some examples of equivalent liquid measurements are shown below:

1.5 tsp.	7.394 mL
2 tbsp.	29.58 mL
10 mL	2.029 tsp.
0.5 tbsp.	7.40 mL
2.5 mL	0.507 mL

Converting Between mL and Ounces

It is important to use a graduated cylinder when measuring a liquid drug, and to pour with caution to measure the exact amount. A liquid ounce is equal to 29.57 mL. Below are some examples of equivalent measurements:

270 mL	9.130 ounces
3 ounces	88.72 mL
12 ounces	354.88 mL
240 mL	8.12 ounces

Converting Between Cups, Pints, Quarts, and Gallons

The following allow for conversions between the above-mentioned measurements:

2 cups	1 pint
2 pints	1 quart
4 quarts	1 gallon
1 cup	8 ounces
1 pint	16 ounces
1 quart	32 ounces
1 gallon	128 ounces

Converting Between Grams, Pounds, and Kilograms
The following examples show conversions between grams, kilograms, and pounds:

1 kilogram	1000 grams
1 kilogram	2.205 pounds
1 pound	453.6 grams
2 pounds	907.2 grams
227 grams	0.500 pounds
681 grams	1.501 pounds

Converting Between Grams and Ounces
One ounce is equal to 28.35 grams. The following examples convert ounces and grams:

0.5 ounces	14.18 grams
85 grams	2.998 ounces
1.5 ounces	42.53 grams
4 ounces	113.40 grams

Converting Between Drops and mL
One mL has 12 drops. "gtt" stands for drops.

2 gtt ou bid x 10 days (2 drops in each eye twice daily for 10 days)	40 gtt	3.33 mL
4 gtt sl q4h x 7 days (4 drops sublingually every 4 hours for 7 days)	168 gtt	14 mL
5 gtt os qd x 15 days (5 drops in the left eye every day for 15 days)	75 gtt	6.25 mL

Most medications that are dispensed in drops come in 5mL, 10 mL, or 15 mL bottles. It is standard practice to dispense the whole bottle, although it may be more than what is needed for the duration of treatment. Calculating the total quantity needed for the duration of treatment is required for insurance purposes, and to figure out how many or which size bottle is needed to cover the treatment.

Converting Between Grains and Milligrams
Each grain is equal to 64.80 milligrams.

3 grains	194.4 mg
1.5 grains	97.2 mg
650 mg	10.03 grains
162.5 mg	2.51 grains

Converting Between Celsius and Fahrenheit
The following is the formula used to convert degrees Fahrenheit to Celsius:

$$°C = (°F - 32) \times \frac{5}{9}$$

The following is the formula used to convert Celsius to Fahrenheit:

$$°F = \left(°C \times \frac{9}{5}\right) + 32$$

The following table gives examples of temperature conversions:

32 °F	0 °C
40 °F	4.45 °C
20 °C	68 °F
60 °C	140 °F

Pediatric Dosage Rules

It is important to check and compare the dosage for children relative to that of adults, as the physician may request a dose that a manufacturer does not supply.

The following formula is used to calculate pediatric doses:

1. Dose calculation related to age:

- **Young's Rule**: This formula depends on age to calculate the dose, and is preferably used for children between 1-12 years of age:

    - $Child\ dose = Adult\ dose \times \frac{Age\ in\ years}{(Age+12)}$

    Example: A child is 12 years old and the adult dose of the medicine is 500 mg:

    - $Child\ dose = 500\ mg \times \frac{12}{(12+12)} = 250\ mg$

- **Dilling's Rule**: This formula uses the age of the child expressed in years:

    - $Child\ dose = Adult\ dose \times \frac{Age\ in\ years}{(20)}$

    Example: A child is 10 years old and the adult dose of the medicine is 750 mg:

    - $Child\ dose = 750\ mg \times \frac{10}{(20)} = 375\ mg$

- **Fried's Rule**: This formula is better to use in infants until 2 years of age, and the age of the child is expressed in months:

    - $Child\ dose = Adult\ dose \times \frac{Age\ in\ months}{(150)}$

    Example: A child is 8 months old and the adult dose is 250 mg:

    - $Child\ dose = 250\ mg \times \frac{8}{(150)} = 13.33\ mg$

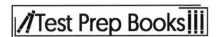

2. Dose calculation related to body weight:

- **Clark's Rule**: This is based on weight in pounds (not kg) and can be calculated with the formula below:
    - $Child\ dose = Adult\ dose \times \dfrac{Body\ weight\ in\ lb}{(150)}$

    Example: A child weighs 80 pounds and the adult dose is 500 mg:

    - $Child\ dose = 500\ mg \times \dfrac{80}{(150)} = 266.7\ mg$

3. Dose calculation related to body surface area:

A child's dose can also be calculated relative to **body surface area (BSA)**. This approach is distinguished by obtaining a more representative measure of metabolic mass instead of body weight, as it is not affected as much by unusual amounts of fat. Note that an average adult with a weight of 70 kg and a height 175 cm has a body surface area of approximately 1.85 m^2.

- $Child\ dose = Adult\ dose \times \dfrac{Child's\ BSA}{Average\ adult's\ BSA}$

Body surface area (BSA) can be calculated using **Mosteller's equation** as follows.

$$BSA\ (m^2) = \sqrt{\dfrac{\left(Height\ (cm) \times Weight\ (kg)\right)}{3600}}$$

For example, a prescription comes as 600 mg/m^2 of drug "X" for a 32-month old boy. The boy weighs 30 lbs (13.6 kg) and is 30 inches (76.2 cm) tall. What dosage should the boy receive?

$$BSA\ (m^2) = \sqrt{\dfrac{(76.2\ cm \times 13.6\ kg)}{3600}} = \sqrt{.288} = 0.537\ m^2$$

Therefore, the child's dose $= 600\ mg \times 0.537 = 322\ mg$

Proportional Calculations

Proportional calculations are often used in the pharmacy to determine how much of a medication should be dispensed, to calculate a dose, or to measure the amount in compounding.

Proportional calculations are usually conducted as follows:

$$\dfrac{A}{B} = \dfrac{X}{C}$$

For example, the following prescription may be received: Amoxicillin suspension, 300 mg bid x 10 days. When checking the shelf, the only amoxicillin suspension concentration available is 5 mL/200 mg. To find the dose, the equation should be set up as:

$$\frac{5 \text{ mL}}{200 \text{ mg}} = \frac{X}{300 \text{ mg}}$$

$$X = \frac{5 \text{ mL} \times 300 \text{ mg}}{200 \text{ mg}} = 7.5 \text{ mL}$$

This set up allows you to apply the same concentration to a different quantity.

Proportion Technique

The following steps should be used to solve a dilution problem while using the proportional technique:

- Set up the proportion equation
- Solve for x, which is the total number of units of active ingredient in the solution
- Calculate the amount of diluted solution that should be made using proportions
- Calculate x to obtain the total amount of diluted solution that can be made

To find how much diluent to add, the technician needs to subtract the original amount of solution from the total amount of diluted solution.

Example: You have 1L of 70% alcohol solution. How much sterile water and how much 70% solution will you need to get 1L of 40% alcohol solution?

Set up the proportional equation and solve for x to get the amount of 70% alcohol solution you need:

$$\frac{70\%}{1,000 \text{ mL}} = \frac{40\%}{X}$$

$$X = \frac{1000 \text{ mL} \times 40\%}{70\%} = 571.4 \text{ mL}$$

Subtract the amount of 70% solution from the desired total solution (1L) to find the amount of diluent:

$$1000 \text{ mL} - 571.4 \text{ mL} = 428.6 \text{ mL of sterile water}$$

Finally, add the total diluent to the total original solution to get the correct amount of the desired solution:

$$428.6 \text{ mL sterile water} + 571.4 \text{ mL of 70\% solution} = 1 \text{ L of 40\% alcohol solution}$$

You will use 571.5 mL of 70% alcohol solution and 428.6 mL of sterile water to get 1L of 40% alcohol solution.

V/V, W/W and W/V Concentrations

There are different ways that concentrations can be expressed, for example, as a ratio of weight, volume, or percentage. The following ratios are used to present a concentration: V/V, W/W, and W/V. The unit for a **V/V** ratio is mL, as this represents a **volume/volume ratio**. The unit for a **W/W** ratio is

111

grams, as this represents a **weight/weight ratio**. The measurement unit for **W/V** is grams/mL, as this represents **weight/volume ratio**.

Examples are:

- $V/V = 1:500 = 1 \text{ mL}/500 \text{ mL} = 0.2\%$
- $W/W = 5:100 = 5 \text{ grams}/100 \text{ grams} = 5\%$
- $W/V = 10/100 = 10 \text{ grams}/100 \text{ mL} = 10\%$

Alligation Method

This method is commonly called the **Tic-Tac-Toe method**, because it uses a grid that looks similar to a tic-tac-toe grid. The problem is set up by placing the desired concentration in the middle box, the higher concentration in the upper left-hand corner, and lower concentration in the lower left-hand corner. The process begins in the lower left-hand corner and moves towards the upper right-hand corner. The difference between the number in the lower left-hand corner and that in the middle box goes in the upper right-hand corner. Then, the difference between the upper left corner and the number in the middle is put in the lower right-hand corner. On the right, the number represents the parts of the concentration on the left that are used to make the needed concentration. By using proportion math, the volume of each can be calculated.

A figure and an example follow:

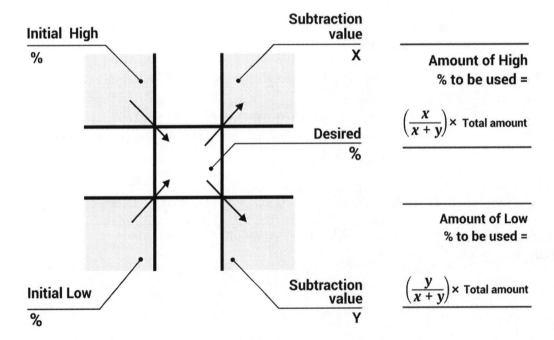

For example, how many grams of 1% hydrocortisone cream should be mixed with an appropriate quantity of 2.5% hydrocortisone cream to make 250 grams of 1.5% hydrocortisone cream?

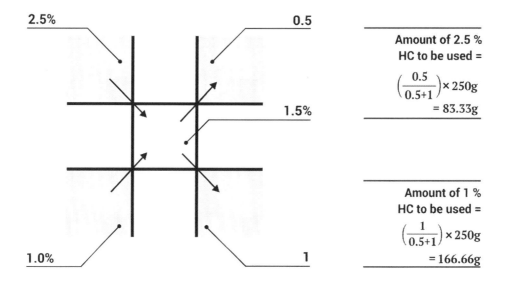

Amount of 2.5 % HC to be used =

$$\left(\frac{0.5}{0.5+1}\right) \times 250g$$
$$= 83.33g$$

Amount of 1 % HC to be used =

$$\left(\frac{1}{0.5+1}\right) \times 250g$$
$$= 166.66g$$

Therefore, 166.66 g of 1% hydrocortisone cream should be mixed with 83.33 g of 2.5% hydrocortisone cream to make 250 g of 1.5% hydrocortisone cream.

Calculating Doses Required

Since physicians usually don't know how long a prescription will last, a pharmacy technician must be adept at an assortment of calculations. The first thing to master is the calculation of the days' supply of medication, which indicates how long a prescription will last. It must be calculated not only for tablets and capsules, but also for injectables, liquid medications, inhalers, and nasal sprays, as well as for PRN (as needed) lotions, ointments, creams, and drops. Other tasks requiring calculations are adjusting refills and short-fills.

Days' Supply for Tablets, Capsules, and Liquid Medications
The most straightforward calculations for days' supply are for tablets, capsules, and liquid medications.

Example: Calculate the days' supply for a prescription written for penicillin VK 500 mg tablets #40 i tab PO q.i.d.

$$Days'\ supply = \frac{Quantity\ Dispensed}{(Dose \times Frequency)}$$

$$Days'\ supply = \frac{40\ tabs}{(1\ tab \times 4\ times\ per\ day)} = 10\ days$$

Example: Calculate the days' supply for a prescription written for penicillin VK 500 mg/5 mL 200 mL i tsp PO q.i.d.

$$Days'\ supply = \frac{200\ mL}{(5\ mL \times 4\ times\ per\ day)} = 10\ days$$

113

Calculations for PRN (as needed) tablets, capsules, and liquid medications are more complicated due to the variability of doses and their frequencies. In general, the calculation should be made using the highest dose with the shortest interval.

Example: Calculate the days' supply for a prescription written for alprazolam (Xanax®) 0.5 mg #60 i-ii tabs PO q4-6h PRN anxiety.

$$Days'\ supply = \frac{60\ tabs}{2\ tabs \times \dfrac{24\ hours\ per\ day}{4\ hours}}$$

$$\frac{60\ tabs}{(2\ tabs \times 6\ per\ day)} = 5\ days$$

The results in the calculations above are even numbers. If the calculation yields a decimal, it's usually appropriate to drop the decimal.

Days' Supply for Insulins

The majority of insulins contain 100 units per mL, and insulin vials are typically packaged as either 10 mL vials or boxes of 5 syringes containing 3 mL per syringe for a total of 15 mL per box. Insulin vials should be kept no longer than 30 days after being opened.

Example: Calculate the days' supply for a prescription written for insulin glargine (Lantus®) 10 mL 40 units SC daily.

$$Days'\ supply = \frac{10\ mL \times 100\ units}{40\ units\ per\ day} = 25\ days$$

This calculation does not account for the small amount lost per injection by priming a needle, however. If the wastage is accounted for, the calculated days' supply will be lower. In the case of insulin pens, up to approximately 2 units per injection may be lost by priming the needle before use.

Example: Calculate the days' supply for insulin glargine (Lantus®) 15 mL 50 units SC daily.

$$Days'\ supply = \frac{15\ mL \times 100\ units}{(50\ units\ per\ day) + (2\ units)} = 28.8\ days = 28\ days$$

Days' Supply for Inhalers and Sprays

With inhalers and sprays, it's important to observe on the packaging how many metered inhalations or sprays are actually in a container.

Example: Calculate the days' supply for a prescription written for a fluticasone (Flovent® HFA) 44 mcg inhaler ii puffs b.i.d. Each container is labeled as containing 200 metered inhalations.

$$Days'\ supply = \frac{200\ puffs}{(2\ puffs \times 2\ times\ a\ day)} = 50\ days$$

Days' Supply for Ointments and Creams

Calculations for ointments and creams are more complicated, because exactly how much is used per dose is unknown. Other complicating factors include the size of the area affected and the number of areas treated. In general, the directions are to use 1 gram (1000 mg) per dose per affected area.

Example: Calculate the days' supply for Kenalog® cream 15g apply b.i.d. to affected area(s).

$$Days'\ supply = \frac{15\ g}{(1\ g \times 2\ times\ per\ day)} = 7.5\ days = 7\ days\ (after\ dropping\ the\ decimal)$$

Days' Supply for Ophthalmic and Otic Medications

To determine the days' supply for ophthalmic and otic medications, use a conversion factor to convert milliliters (mL) to drops (gtt). The agreed-upon factor is 20 gtt/mL. For ophthalmic ointments, a dose equals 100 mg.

Example: Calculate the days' supply for pilocarpine 2% solution 15 mL ii gtt OU tid.

$$Days'\ supply = \frac{15\ mL \times \dfrac{20\ gtt}{mL}}{(4\ gtt \times 3\ doses\ per\ day)} = \frac{300\ gtt}{12\ gtt\ per\ day} = 25\ days$$

Example: Calculate the days' supply for Neosporin® ophthalmic ointment 3.5 g apply OU q3-4h while awake.

$$Days'\ supply = \frac{3.5\ g \times \dfrac{1000\ g}{mg}}{(200\ mg \times 5\ doses\ per\ day)} = 3.5\ days = 3\ days\ (after\ dropping\ the\ decimal)$$

The assumption, in this case, is that a patient sleeps 8 hours per day and is awake 16 hours per day. Using the shortest interval of dosing (every 3 hours while awake), the patient should apply approximately 5 doses per day.

Adjusting Refills and Short-Fills

Third-party prescription insurance providers often have dispensing limitations restricting the quantity of a medication that can be filled by a pharmacy. As a result, pharmacy technicians may have to adjust refills. The adjustment of refills oftentimes leads to short-filled prescriptions, or short-fills.

Example: A prescription is written for Celebrex® 100 mg caps #50 Ť PO cap daily with 1 refill. The patient's insurance plan has a 30-day supply limitation. Calculate the number of refills and short-fills (if any) for the adjusted quantity.

First, calculate the total number of capsules over the life of the prescription:

$$50\ capsules \times 2\ total\ fills = 100\ capsules$$

Next, calculate how many capsules needed per fill:

$$Capsules\ per\ fill = \frac{1\ cap}{dose} \times \frac{1\ dose}{day} \times \frac{30\ days}{fill} = 30\ caps/fill$$

115

Next, calculate how many fills are needed to dispense the quantity as specified by the prescriber:

$$Fills = \frac{100 \text{ caps}}{(30 \text{ caps/fill})} = 3.333 \text{ fills}$$

There will be at total of 2 refills after the initial fill by the pharmacy.

Now, calculate the quantity of the short-fill:

$$\frac{100 \text{ capsules}}{3 \text{ fills} \times (30 \text{ caps/fill})} = 10 \text{ capsules}$$

There will be a short-fill of 10 capsules.

Example: A prescription is written for Lexapro® 20mg #50 Ť PO cap daily with 3 refills. The patient's insurance plan has a 32-day supply limitation. Calculate the number of refills and short-fills (if any) for the adjusted quantity.

First, calculate the total number of capsules over the life of the prescription:

$$50 \text{ capsules} \times 4 \text{ total fills} = 200 \text{ capsules}$$

Next, calculate how many capsules needed per fill:

$$Capsules \text{ per fill} = \frac{1 \text{ cap}}{dose} \times \frac{1 \text{ dose}}{day} \times \frac{32 \text{ days}}{fill} = 32 \text{ caps/fill}$$

Next, calculate how many fills are needed to dispense the quantity as specified by the prescriber:

$$\frac{200 \text{ caps}}{1} \times \frac{1 \text{ fill}}{32 \text{ caps}} = 6.25 \text{ fills}$$

$$Fills = \frac{200 \text{ caps}}{(32 \text{ caps/fill})} = 6.25 \text{ fills}$$

There will be a total of *5 refills* after the initial fill by the pharmacy.

Now, calculate the quantity of the short-fill:

$$\frac{200 \text{ capsules}}{6 \text{ fills} \times (32 \text{ caps/fill})} = 8 \text{ capsules}$$

There will be a short-fill of 8 capsules.

Caveat: Although pharmacy technicians are allowed to reduce the quantity dispensed in a fill, they cannot surpass the total prescribed quantity.

Medical Terminology and Abbreviations

A pharmacy technician should be able to communicate with other pharmacy staff so work can be completed efficiently and safely. To that end, a pharmacy technician must have knowledge of common medical terminology and abbreviations.

Medical terminology is made up of *word parts*: roots, prefixes, and suffixes. These are combined to form medical words.

The following is a list of common word roots, prefixes, and suffixes (and their meanings) used in medical terminology:

Root	Meaning
cardi	heart
gastr	stomach
derm	skin
arthr	joint
pulmon	lung
hem	blood
gynec	woman, female
ped	child
ren	kidney
ophthalm	eye
rhin	nose
crani	skull
cyst	urinary bladder
encephal	brain
cephal	head
aden	gland
col	colon, large intestine
chondr	cartilage
cyt	cell
erythr	red
leuk	white
electr	electricity
onc	tumor
oste	bone
psych	mind

Prefix	Meaning
tachy-	fast
brady-	slow
uni-	one
bi-	two, both
tri-	three
hyper-	increased, above
hypo-	decreased, below
inter-	between
intra-	within
retro-	behind
dys-	bad, painful, difficult, abnormal
aut-	self
sub-	below, under
trans-	across, through

Suffix	Meaning
-logy	study of
-logist	specialist in the study of
-algia	pain
-it is	inflammation
-pathy	disease
-stomy	opening
-tomy	cutting into, incision
-ectomy	cutting out, removal, excision
-phasia	speech
-emia	blood condition
-phagia	eat
-uria	urine
-centesis	surgical puncture to remove fluid
-scope	instrument to visually examine
-scopy	visual examination
-megaly	enlargement
-oma	tumor, mass
-gram	record
-therapy	treatment

Pharmacy technicians may come across medical abbreviations and acronyms in prescriptions, medical charts, and varied forms of drug information. The following is a list of common medical abbreviations and acronyms, and their meanings:

Medical Abbreviation	Meaning
HIV	human immunodeficiency virus
AIDS	acquired immunodeficiency syndrome
BP	blood pressure
HTN	hypertension, high blood pressure
BM	bowel movement
DM	diabetes mellitus
FBS	fasting blood sugar
OA	Osteoarthritis
CAD	coronary artery disease
RA	rheumatoid arthritis
BPH	benign prostatic hyperplasia
CVA	cerebrovascular accident, stroke
DJD	degenerative joint disease
GI	Gastrointestinal
COPD	chronic obstructive pulmonary disease
CHF	congestive heart failure
GERD	gastroesophageal reflux disease
HR	heart rate
P	Pulse
NKDA	no known drug allergies
RBC	red blood cell
WBC	white blood cell
URI	upper respiratory infection
UTI	urinary tract infection
SOB	shortness of breath
ECG	Electrocardiogram
EEG	Electroencephalogram
IBS	irritable bowel syndrome
NPO	nothing by mouth
STI	sexually transmitted infection
PSA	prostate specific antigen
ANA	antinuclear antibody
NSAID	nonsteroidal anti-inflammatory drug
CNS	central nervous system
MS	multiple sclerosis
CXR	chest X-ray

Many of these abbreviations are derived from Latin and may be for routes of drug administration, dosage forms, weights, frequency of drug administration, volumes, names of drugs, and directions for compounding. Pharmacy abbreviations may be written in lower case or capital letters. They should be used with caution as misinterpretation can lead to medication error.

The following is a list of common pharmacy abbreviations and their meanings:

Pharmacy Abbreviation	Meaning
tab	tablet
cap	capsule
oint	ointment
g	gram
mg	milligram
mL	milliliter
mcg	microgram
U	units
NS	normal saline
PO	by mouth
IV	intravenous
BSA	body surface area
mEq	milliequivalent
IM	intramuscular
SQ, SC	subcutaneous
PRN	as needed
q	every, each
cc	cubic centimeter
gr	grain
ac	before meals
hs	bedtime
bid	twice a day
tid	three times a day
qid	four times a day
QS	quantity sufficient
QD	daily
QOD	every other day
°	hour
SL	sublingual (under the tongue)
au	both ears
ad	right ear
as	left ear
gtt	drops
ou	both eyes

120

Pharmacy Abbreviation	Meaning
tab	tablet
cap	capsule
os	left eye
od	right eye
amp	ampule
atc	around the clock
biw	twice a week
tiw	three times a week
wa	while awake
stat	immediately

Equipment/Supplies for Drug Administration

Packaging Requirements

All medication leaving a pharmacy—whether inpatient or outpatient—must be packaged.

Ideally, medication packaging should be sufficient enough to:

- Protect against all adverse external environmental factors that could alter characteristics of a medication (e.g., light, moisture, temperature, and oxygen variables)

- Protect against physical/mechanical damage

- Protect against biological damage

- Provide identification and correct information for drugs

Types of raw materials used in medication packaging include cardboard, paper, glass, plastic, rubber, and metal (e.g., aluminum and stainless steel). The use of these raw materials generates a significant amount of waste. Methods of disposal of uncontaminated medication packaging include recycling, incineration (burning), and landfill. Cardboard, paper, glass, and metal are best disposed via recycling. Plastics and rubber are best disposed via incineration.

In general, packaging should maintain the stability of the medication while furnishing needed safety to patients and others who have to access the medication (e.g., caregivers and nurses).

Light Resistance

Medication packaging must have adequate light resistance. Currently, there are more than 200 medications that are sensitive to light. For example, when nitroprusside is exposed to direct sunlight, it changes into cyanide (a poison). The chemical composition of other medications may be altered by exposure to direct sunlight. As a result, many medications are dispensed in amber-colored containers. Common light-sensitive medications include doxycycline (Vibramycin®), linezolid (Zyvox®), acetazolamide (Diamox®), and zolmitriptan (Zomig®).

Child Resistance

In clinical trials, the addition of child-resistant packaging has greatly reduced child mortality from oral prescription-drug intoxication. The three most common child-resistant closures are the "squeeze-turn," "push-turn," and a combination lock. Most medication containers considered child-resistant require two hands to open. This requirement may cause difficulty for elderly individuals.

The **Poison Prevention Packaging Act (PPPA) of 1970** requires all prescription medications and controlled substances to be dispensed in vials with child-resistant caps. The purpose of the Act was to combat and decrease these poisonings. The **Consumer Products Safety Commission** was empowered by the Act to develop rules about packaging for products that would be applied in households with young children. As a result of the Act, the development and mandatory use of child-resistant caps was instituted, as well as regular safety tests for caps, to ensure standards are met to keep children safe.

Exceptions to the legislation are few and may include a request by patient or physician not to receive the safety caps for oral contraceptives and select emergency sublingual (under the tongue) cardiovascular medications (e.g., nitroglycerin sublingually to treat angina associated with heart disease). If a patient or physician requests not to receive child-resistant caps, make sure that the back of the prescription is signed indicating the request for a non-child resistant container. The request should also be noted in the pharmacy management software system.

Medications dispensed or administered in inpatient environments (e.g., hospitals, long-term care facilities, and nursing homes) are also exempt from the child-resistant packaging legislation. A pharmacist's failure to abide by the PPPA could result in prosecution and imprisonment for no longer than one year, or payment of a fine of no more than $1,000, or both.

Containers and Container Materials

Medication packaging requires many different types of containers.

The following is a list of containers used in medication packaging:

- Round vials for capsules or tablets

- Wide-mouth bottles—for bulk powders or large quantities of capsules, tablets, and high-viscosity (thick) liquids

- Prescription bottles for low-viscosity (thin) liquids

- Applicator bottles to apply liquid medications to the skin

- Dropper bottles for otic, ophthalmic, nasal, or oral liquids requiring administration by dropper

- Hinged-lid or slide boxes for dispensing powders or suppositories

- Ointment jars and collapsible tubes to dispense semi-solid medications

For most medications, the original manufacturer's packaging suffices. In repackaging medications, pharmacy technicians should always be sure to consult the manufacturer's guidelines to determine if light-resistant packaging is required.

122

The following is a list of container classification:

- Tamper-evident packaging refers to a sealed container with medication intended for ophthalmic or otic use—a broken seal is evidence of tampering.

- A well-closed container protects the medication from loss under normal conditions.

- A light-resistant container protects the medication from direct sunlight.

- A tight container prevents contamination by solids, liquids, or vapors.

- A hermetic container is unable to be penetrated by gas or air.

- A single-dose container refers to a single-unit container intended for parenteral (non-oral) administration.

- A single-unit container holds one dose of medication.

- A unit-of-use container holds a specific quantity of medication that's ready to be dispensed but not yet labeled.

- A unit-dose container is a single-dose container for which the intended use is other than parenteral.

- A multiple-unit container allows for multiple withdrawals of a medication without affecting the quality, strength, or purity of the remainder.

- A multiple-dose container is a multiple-unit container intended for parenteral administration.

Other vehicles for the packaging of pharmaceuticals may include:

- **Ampules**: Single-dose containers sealed by fusion that can only be opened by breaking

- **Bags**: Containers composed of flexible surfaces with closed bottoms and sides that can be sealed

- **Blisters**: Multi-dose containers composed of two layers, with one layer constructed to hold single doses

- **Bottles**: Container with a neck and a flat bottom

- **Cartridges**: Containers to hold solid or liquid dosage forms (e.g., prefilled syringes)

- **Gas cylinders**: Containers capable of holding compressed, dissolved, or liquefied gas, and outfitted to regulate the flow of gas

- **Injection needles**: Hollow needles with locking hubs intended to administer liquid dosage forms

- **Injection syringes**: Syringes with or without fixed needles and freely movable pistons

- **Pressurized containers**: Containers capable of holding compressed, dissolved, or liquefied gas, and outfitted to produce the spontaneous, controlled release of a gas

- **Strips**: Multi-dose containers composed of two layers with perforations that holds single doses of solid or semi-solid dosage forms

- **Tubes**: Multi-dose containers made of collapsible material for release of semi-solid dosage forms released through a nozzle when package is squeezed

- **Vials**: Single- and multi-dose containers for parenteral medications containing an overseal and stopper

In May 1992, the United States Food and Drug Administration specified 11 technologies capable of fulfilling the definition of tamper-evident packaging. The list encompasses: blister and bubble packs; film wrappers; heat-shrunk wrappers or bands; bottles equipped with inner-mouth seals; plastic packs or paper foil; breakable cap-ring systems; sealed tubes; tape seals; plastic blind-end heat-sealed tubes; sealed cartons; all metal and composite cans; and aerosol containers.

A variety of plastics, including *polyvinyl chloride* (PVC), have been used in the last 50 years as materials for medication packaging. Plastics are an affordable option, keeping the majority of medications intact and uncontaminated. Plastics are unbreakable, light, and collapsible, which are significant advantages over glass. The main use of plastics is as material for bags for *parenteral solutions* (e.g., IV solutions).

Some medications may be able to bond with the PVC in containers, which may alter the structure and eventually harm the efficacy of a medication. In these scenarios, glass is a great alternative because it's *inert* (nonreactive). For example, sublingual nitroglycerin shouldn't be exposed at length to traditional PVC medication containers. Many pharmacists will dispense this medication in glass vials.

Metal is also used as a raw material in medication packaging. Metal is strong, impervious to gases, and shatterproof. Metal may be included in the structure of tubes, cans, blister packs, and pressurized containers (e.g., gas and aerosol cylinders). Aluminum and stainless steel are the predominant metals used in medication packaging.

Syringes
Pharmacies dispense two general types of syringes: oral/topical syringes and injectable syringes. **Oral/topical syringes** are perfect for precise dosing of oral or topical medications and have a safety feature that doesn't allow the attachment of needles. **Injectable syringes** are available in a wide assortment of sizes with numerous needle options. Historically, prescribers have been responsible for writing prescriptions for syringes and needles needed by patients. However, pharmacy staff may still have to determine the appropriate number of syringes and needles to dispense. In many states, patients are permitted to request syringes without prescriptions, although most insurance carriers don't cover syringes.

Unit Dose Systems
Modern technology has allowed drugs or medications to be packaged in convenient and safe ways involving unit dose systems, which is when a medication is prepared in a labeled individual packet for

124

convenience, safety, or monitoring. Unit dose packaging devices may be manual, semi-automatic, or automatic. The intent of a unit dose is to decrease administration error.

A Unit Dose System:
A syringe as a final unit dose

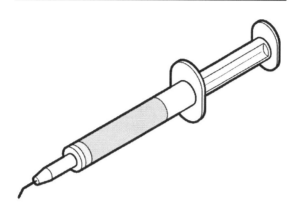

A **modified unit dose system** is a drug delivery system that merges blister packaged, unit dose medications into a multi-dose card rather than placing them in a loose box.

Pills in a Blister Pack

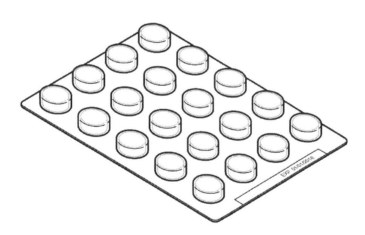

A **blended unit dose system** is a combination of the unit dose system and non-unit dose system. It may contain multiple medications packed in a cassette. An example is a compliance (or bubble or blister) pack, in which multiple medications are arranged in each bubble (or compartment) according to the time of administration in a day or week.

Spacers

Administering certain medications may require specific medical equipment or supplies. **Albuterol inhalation aerosol**, a medication often prescribed for asthma, is dispensed in a canister that requires an inhaler or puffer to administer. The medication is best administered by modifying the inhaler with a device called a spacer. A **spacer** is an elongated closed tube that attaches to the inhaler on one end and has a mouthpiece on the other. Pediatric patients may require a breathing mask, which can be attached to the spacer. The medication is sprayed into the spacer, keeping the aerosol contained, while the patient breathes it in. Spacers are an easier and more effective way to ensure the medication is being inhaled into the lungs rather than being deposited in the mouth or on the tongue, which increases the likelihood of patient adherence.

Diabetic Supplies

Diabetic patients who are dependent on insulin require specialized medical supplies to safely administer medications. Insulin syringes are used to draw insulin from medication vials for administration. The most common insulin syringes are U-100 syringes, meaning a 1-milliliter insulin syringe will deliver up to one hundred units of insulin (the most common concentration of insulin). The **gauge of an insulin syringe** refers to the diameter or thickness of the needle and ranges from a twenty-eight gauge to a thirty-one gauge. The larger the gauge, the smaller the diameter of the needle. Prefilled insulin pens are disposable pens containing up to 300 units of insulin. An insulin pen requires pen needles, which are attached to the end of the insulin pen. The pen is then dialed to the desired dose, and the insulin is injected. Patients should use alcohol swabs to wipe the rubber seal or stopper on vials and insulin pens as well as the site of injection to prevent contamination. Lastly, it is important for diabetic patients to have a sharps container to safely dispose of insulin syringes after each use.

Lot Numbers, Expiration Dates, and the National Drug Code (NDC) Numbers

NDC Number

The **Drug Listing Act of 1972** implemented the **National Drug Code or NDC** as a 10-digit number, which distinguishes each and every medication used by humans. When one breaks down the 10-digit NDC number, each segment correlates specifically to the drug as follows:

- Labeler code is the first segment and refers to the manufacturer who produced the drug.
- Product code is the second segment and refers to the drug's strength and dosage form.
- Packaging code is the third segment and refers to the package size and type.

It is important to note that reassignment of an NDC number to a drug is prohibited, to avoid possible mix-up and to prevent health hazard to patients.

Sample NDC Number

NDC 0049 - 4900 - 66

Labeler

Roerig

Product code

Zoloft
50mg

Package code

100 tablets

Lot Numbers

To identify a product that has been manufactured, a lot number is assigned. A **lot number** helps track the product in the event of a recall. Lot numbers are usually assigned to a large batch of a product and placed on the retail packaging. This makes the product easier to track and trace back to its origin, even as it gets distributed nationwide.

Expiration Dates

For many pharmaceutical drugs, stability studies are performed to validate the potency, efficacy, and safety of a drug. Stability studies involve products placed in controlled experimental conditions and followed by analytical laboratory testing to determine the expiration date of a drug. Some drugs are assigned a month or year expiration date, but drugs typically have a 12- to 60-month expiration date provided by the manufacturer.

Identifying and Returning Medications and Supplies

Dispensing Process

Proper product validation uses National Drug Codes (NDCs), barcode scanning, and visual inspection/verification. The pharmacy technician should make a habit of checking the NDC in the pharmacy management software system against the product being dispensed. The practice not only decreases pharmacy error but may also help avoid billing fraud. Many pharmacies use barcode scanning systems to provide another opportunity to reconcile the NDC in the computer with the one on the stock medication bottle containing the drug to be dispensed. Lastly, visual inspection is the oldest and most common form of verification. A registered pharmacist (RPh) traditionally carries out the validation, but some states allow pharmacy technicians to perform the task.

Visual inspection should verify the following:

- Accurate interpretation of the original prescription to the prescription label
- Accurate patient information on the product
- Appropriate packaging has been used
- Correct drug is being dispensed

After the medication has been filled and checked, it's ready for the patient to pick up. All new patients at a pharmacy should be given a copy of the **Health Insurance Portability and Accountability Act of 1996 (HIPAA)** notice of privacy practices. Pharmacy technicians must be sure to document the receipt of the notice by the patient. Per the **Omnibus Budget Reconciliation Act of 1990 (OBRA-90)**, the pharmacist is required to offer medication counseling. The pharmacy technician may also feel compelled to offer medication counseling. If a patient would like to see the pharmacist for medication counseling, the request should be noted in the pharmacy management software system. The pharmacy should make a valid attempt at privacy for patient counseling sessions and may be achieved through a simple privacy screen or a dedicated room.

Pharmacies are increasingly using drug distribution systems that rely on automated dispensing systems. These systems serve as storage, dispensing, and charging (as in retail) hubs in a pharmacy. Automated dispensing systems simplify inventory control tracking, save time, and reduce medication errors. These automated systems are commonly implemented in hospital pharmacies and may be either decentralized or centralized.

A **decentralized distribution system** is housed in patient care areas, which is supposed to reduce or eliminate system management issues, such as poor recordkeeping and diversion of narcotics. This is done by use of automated dispensing cabinets, ADCs, located in care units. Advantages of a decentralized system include the ability to document medication waste, dispense and return medications, and generate reports. Decentralized systems can also reduce the time to receive ordered medications.

A **centralized distribution system** is used to improve the manual unit-dose cart filling process. With this system, medications are distributed from a central location, instead of from several dispensing systems. The pharmacy technician usually hand-delivers medications to the patient care units in a centralized system. The automated centralized systems help reduce errors in filling medication carts and may require less equipment and fewer staff to maintain it, due to having a single location. One disadvantage of centralized automated dispensing systems is the inability to stock all dosage forms of a medication.

Automated dispensing systems used in decentralized medication management include:

- **Pyxis MedStation™ system**: Barcode scanning ensures accurate dispensing of medications. Active alerts are also included to provide added safety precautions. It is considered one of the industry standards.

- **Cubie™ system**: Allows a nurse to access and remove only one medication at a time. The system reduces the risk of a nurse selecting a medication from the wrong pocket.

- **Pyxis™ anesthesia system**: Provides ease of access to medications needed by anesthesia practitioners by providing visibility to medication inventory. The system has biometric access and an array of drawer types.

- **Pyxis™ CII Safe**: Monitors and tracks the refilling of controlled substance inventory within a hospital.

Inventory control may be utilized to provide pharmacy QA in a variety of fashions, including: ensuring that needed medications are available to provide treatment, establishing parameters for the proper dispensing of medications, removing expired and short-dated medications from inventory, regularly checking for drug recalls and performing all pertinent follow-ups, and separating inventory to diminish the potential for picking the wrong drug. Properly trained pharmacy staff, meticulous attention to detail, and automation are crucial for successful and dependable inventory control. Most pharmacies have established minimum and maximum inventory levels for the medications they stock. This practice ensures that an adequate, but not excessive, amount of a particular medication is stocked on the shelves.

Many pharmacies use computerized systems to monitor inventory levels. When a maximum level of a medication is reached, the pharmacy knows not to exceed that quantity and will hold off on reorders. When a minimum level of a medication is reached, the pharmacy will reorder. Controlling inventory levels helps with order fulfillment and minimizes the potential for drugs expiring while in inventory. Computer systems capable of tracking National Drug Codes (NDCs), expiration dates, and lot numbers have added value and can help monitor for expired drugs, drug recalls, and can even interface with pharmacy management software.

Pharmacy personnel often are required to remove drugs from stock for reasons such as being expired, nearing their expiration date (short-dated), or being recalled. Proper inventory control and periodic manual checking of expiration dates helps to minimize the potential for dispensing expired medications. It also maximizes the usage of available stock before drugs become outdated. If an expiration date on a medication mentions only the month and year, the medication should be treated as expiring on the last day of the month. For example, a drug with an expiration date of 03/2019 should be treated as expiring on March 31, 2019.

Medication Disposition

A drug recall can be opened by either the drug manufacturer or the Food and Drug Administration (FDA). The common causes for drug recall are serious adverse effects during post-marketing surveillance, formulation defects, formulation instability, lack of potency, packaging issues, delivery device (e.g., sprays or puffers) malfunctioning, and lack of good manufacturing practices. Poorly performed manufacturing practices involve a host of problems, such as unsanitary conditions for manufacturing a drug, which may constitute a recall.

Recalled Medication Processes

Six important steps are critical to the drug recall process.

- The manufacturer or wholesaler alerts the pharmacy/facility/institution via e-mail, mail, or fax about the reason for the recall. A recall notice contains the drug manufacturer's name, drug name, strength, package size, lot number or batch number, and expiration date.

- The pharmacy determines if the recalled medication is in stock. Physicians/clinics/institutions check if there are samples with that particular batch number in stock, and then contact the respective company representative for return of the samples.

- The pharmacy contacts patients who have taken the drug. Should the customer have the recalled drug, it must be returned to the pharmacy for a refund or substitute.

- The drug manufacturer directs the pharmacy to follow disposition directions.

- Drugs that have been recalled are returned to the manufacturer and returned for credit.

- The physician is notified of the recall and asked for a new order, especially if the drug will not be available for an extended period of time.

Expired Medications

- Each pharmacy establishes policies regarding the process of pulling drugs that will expire.

- Expired drugs must be kept separate from in-date drugs.

- Both pharmacists and pharmacy technicians must be familiar with the institution's policies regarding out-of-date drugs.

- Should a drug pass its expiration date before or during the course of treatment, it should never be dispensed to a patient. Depending on the contract with pharmacies and hospitals, wholesalers and manufacturers will determine if a drug will be returned for partial or full credit. Properly rotating drugs and employing sound inventory management skills can reduce the incidence of expired drugs.

- Cytotoxic drugs must be destroyed in accordance with the biohazardous waste management protocol.

- Reconstituted or compounded medication cannot be returned to the manufacturer. Partially used bottles of medication are often (but not always) non-returnable.

- Controlled substances with DEA numbers can only be returned by institutions. Long-term facilities cannot return controlled substances to pharmacies because they do not have DEA numbers.

- Destruction of controlled substances involves notifying the DEA at least two weeks before destruction. Form 41 is used for expired controlled substances and must be on file at the pharmacy for at least 2 years after destruction.

Pharmacy Waste

Pharmacy waste can be any chemically-manufactured good, vaccine, or allergenic used in the diagnosis, cure, mitigation, treatment, or prevention of disease or injury in humans or animals.

The following nine recommendations will minimize pharmacy waste:

- Make the best use of opened chemotherapy vials.
- Label medication for home use.
- Prime and flush intravenous lines with a saline (salt) solution.
- Check container sizes in relation to use.
- Substitute prepackaged unit dose liquids with specific oral syringes to patients.

130

- Get rid of stored controlled substances that are also hazardous waste.
- Use hard plastic buckets for delivering chemotherapeutic medication to hospitals.
- Monitor dates on emergency syringes.
- Review inventory control to minimize expired medications.

Pharmacy Waste Disposition

The following strategies pertain to waste disposal:

- Use hazardous waste labels to identify hazardous pharmacy waste.
- When not in use, keep containers covered.
- Limit quantity by allowing 3 days to dispose waste, once maximum capacity occurs.

Hazardous Waste

Characteristics of Hazardous Waste	
Ignitability	Flashpoint of less than 60°C.
Corrosivity	pH of less than 2 or greater than 12.5.
Reactivity	When in contact with water, this substance is liable to explode, react violently, or release toxic gases.
Toxicity	Toxic at a concentration above the limit of a regulated substance.
K-list waste	Contains one or more as corrosive, ignitable, reactive, or toxic substances.
P and U-list waste	Chemical matter that is commercially pure grade or technical grade, or a chemical formulation in which the chemical is the sole active ingredient.
Other	These substances are considered hazardous waste: • Medications with more than one active ingredient • All chemotherapy agents • Medications with low LD50s* • Endocrine disruptors • All drugs on the P and U lists

*LD50 (lethal dose) is the quantity of a consumed substance that kills 50 percent of a test sample. Its unit is expressed in mg/kg or milligrams of substance per kilogram of body weight.

Return to Stock

Most pharmacies have an inventory system that allows them to generate a daily report of prescriptions that have been filled but not picked up by a patient after a specific time frame. Prescriptions that were billed to insurance providers must be returned to stock and claims reversed. In addition, unclaimed medications tie up inventory of dispensable drugs that could be dispensed to other patients. It is recommended to pull unclaimed medications after fourteen days, reverse the insurance claim if applicable, and remove all protected health information such as patient name and address. Most computer systems will generate a return to stock label that includes the name of the drug, the **NDC**, or **national drug code**, and the product's expiration date.

Reverse Distribution

Reverse distribution of dispensable medications usually involves the return of unopened overstock products. A **reverse distributor** is a company that facilitates the movement of saleable and nonsaleable pharmaceutical goods. Reverse distributers operate in a regulated environment and are required to register with the DEA, which allows them to handle controlled substances as well. Dispensable medications processed by reverse distributers often are overstocked medications or medications sent to the pharmacy in error. These dispensable medications are deemed safe for redistribution within the pharmaceutical supply. **Nondispensable medications** include expired medications, medications that have been recalled, or medications that were delivered damaged. These medications are deemed pharmaceutical waste and are processed accordingly.

Glossary

Albuterol Inhalation Aerosol	This is a medication often prescribed for asthma, is dispensed in a canister that requires an inhaler or puffer to administer.
Alligation (Tic-Tac-Toe) Method	It uses a grid that looks similar to a tic-tac-toe grid. The problem is set up by placing the desired concentration in the middle box, the higher concentration in the upper left-hand corner, and lower concentration in the lower left-hand corner.
Ampules	These are single-dose containers sealed by fusion that can only be opened by breaking.
Bags	These are containers composed of flexible surfaces with closed bottoms and sides that can be sealed.
Blended Unit Dose System	This is a combination of the unit dose system and non-unit dose system. It may contain multiple medications packed in a cassette.
Blending	This is the act of mixing two substances together.
Blisters	These are multi-dose containers composed of two layers, with one layer constructed to hold single doses.
Body Surface Area (BSA)	Body surface area (BSA) can be calculated using Mosteller's equation as follows. $$BSA\ (\text{m}^2) = \sqrt{\frac{\left(Height\ (\text{cm})\ \times\ Weight\ (\text{kg})\right)}{3,600}}$$
Bottles	This is a container with a neck and a flat bottom.
Cartridges	These are containers to hold solid or liquid dosage forms (e.g., prefilled syringes).
Centralized Distribution System	This is used to improve the manual unit-dose cart filling process.
Communition	This is making a substance into small, fine particles.
Consumer Products Safety Commission	This was empowered by the Act to develop rules about packaging for products that would be applied in households with young children. The development and mandatory use of child-resistant caps was instituted, as well as regular safety tests for caps, to ensure standards are met to keep children safe.
Corrosivity	This describes a pH of less than 2 or greater than 12.5.
Cubie™ System	This allows a nurse to access and remove only one medication at a time. The system reduces the risk of a nurse selecting a medication from the wrong pocket.
Decentralized Distribution System	This is housed in patient care areas, which is supposed to reduce or eliminate system management issues, such as poor recordkeeping and diversion of narcotics.
Drug Listing Act of 1972	This implemented the National Drug Code (NDC) as a 10-digit number, which distinguishes each and every medication used by humans.
Emulsifying Agents	These have chemical properties that make them both water and oil soluble, or amphiphilic, are used to stabilize the emulsion.
External Phase	This is the second phase of emulsion consists of the medium in which it is dispersed.
Gas Cylinders	These are containers capable of holding compressed, dissolved, or liquefied gas, and outfitted to regulate the flow of gas.
Gauge of an Insulin Syringe	This refers to the diameter or thickness of the needle and ranges from a twenty-eight gauge to a thirty-one gauge.
Geometric Dilution	This is mixing two different ingredients together of unequal quantities, starting with the ingredient of smallest quantity and adding the same quantity of the other ingredient (of larger amount), continuing to repeat until all the ingredients are used.
Ignitability	This is a flashpoint of less than 60°C.
Injection Needles	These are hollow needles with locking hubs intended to administer liquid dosage forms.

133

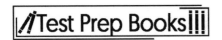

Injection Syringes	These are syringes with or without fixed needles and freely movable pistons; they are available in a wide assortment of sizes and needle options.
Internal Phase	The first phase of emulsion consists of the dispersed liquid.
Inventory Control	This may be utilized to provide pharmacy QA in a variety of fashions.
K-List Waste	This contains one or more as corrosive, ignitable, reactive, or toxic substances.
Levigation	This is the use of water or another solvent to carry an insoluble drug powder through the process.
Lot Number	This helps track the product in the event of a recall. Lot numbers are usually assigned to a large batch of a product and placed on the retail packaging.
Medical Terminology	This is made up of word parts: roots, prefixes, and suffixes. These are combined to form medical words.
Modified Unit Dose System	This is a drug delivery system that combines unit dose medications, which are blister packaged, into a multi-dose card instead of being placed loose in a box.
Nondispensable Medications	These include expired medications, medications that have been recalled, or medications that were delivered damaged. These medications are deemed pharmaceutical waste and are processed accordingly.
Nonsterile Emulsions	These are thermodynamically unstable mixtures composed of at least two liquids that are immiscible—liquids that are insoluble in one another and do not mix easily.
Omnibus Budget Reconciliation Act of 1990 (OBRA-90)	The pharmacist is required by OBRA-90 to offer medication counseling.
Oral/Topical Syringes	These are perfect for precise dosing of oral or topical medications and have a safety feature that doesn't allow the attachment of needles.
P and U-List Waste	Chemical matter that is commercially pure grade or technical grade, or a chemical formulation in which the chemical is the sole active ingredient.
Pharmaceutical Compounding	This refers to the formulation of a product in a pharmacy, distinct from one supplied by a commercial manufacturer, in order to meet the unique needs of a patient as specified by the physician.
Pharmacy Waste	This can be any chemically-manufactured good, vaccine, or allergenic used in the diagnosis, cure, mitigation, treatment, or prevention of disease or injury in humans or animals.
Poison Prevention Packaging Act (PPPA) of 1970	This requires all prescription medications and controlled substances to be dispensed in vials with child-resistant caps. The purpose of the Act was to combat and decrease these poisonings.
Pressurized containers	These containers are capable of holding compressed, dissolved, or liquefied gas, and outfitted to produce the spontaneous, controlled release of a gas.
Proportional Calculations	These are often used in the pharmacy to determine how much of a medication should be dispensed, to calculate a dose, or to measure the amount in compounding.
Pulverization By Intervention	For powders that do not crush easily, a solvent (usually an alcohol) dissolves the powder can be used to intervene.
Pyxis MedStation™ System	Barcode scanning ensures accurate dispensing of medications. Active alerts are also included to provide added safety precautions. It is considered one of the industry standards.
Pyxis™ Anesthesia System	This provides ease of access to medications needed by anesthesia practitioners by providing visibility to medication inventory. The system has biometric access and an array of drawer types.
Pyxis™ CII Safe	This monitors and tracks the refilling of controlled substance inventory within a hospital.
Reactivity	When in contact with water, this substance is liable to explode, react violently, or release toxic gases.
Reverse Distribution	This usually involves the return of unopened overstock products.
Reverse Distributor	This is a company that facilitates the movement of saleable and nonsaleable pharmaceutical goods.
Spacer	This is an elongated closed tube that attaches to the inhaler on one end and has a mouthpiece on the other.

Strips	These are multi-dose containers composed of two layers with perforations that holds single doses of solid or semi-solid dosage forms.
Toxicity	This means that a substance is toxic at a concentration above the limit of a regulated substance.
Tubes	These are multi-dose containers made of collapsible material for release of semi-solid dosage forms released through a nozzle when package is squeezed.
Vials	These are single- and multi-dose containers for parenteral medications containing an overseal and stopper.

135

Practice Quiz

1. If the adult dosage for amoxicillin is 500 mg, what would be the appropriate dose for an infant that is 6 months old and what is the name of the formula used for infant dosages?
    a. 20 mg, Fried's Rule
    b. 1.67 mg, Fried's Rule
    c. 500 mg, Young's Rule
    d. 20 mg, Clark's Rule

2. How many 400 mg tablets are needed to make 1 liter of a 1:250 solution?
    a. 30 tablets
    b. 10 tablets
    c. 4 tablets
    d. 400 tablets

3. How many tablespoons are in 4 ounces?
    a. 8
    b. 22
    c. 1
    d. 120

4. A drug needs to be stored at room temperature (68 °F). What is the equivalent temperature in degrees Celsius?
    a. 36 °C
    b. 72 °C
    c. 68 °C
    d. 20 °C

5. Pharmacy technicians have many tasks in the pharmacy. Which of the following is NOT a legal task for them to perform?
    a. Answering phones
    b. Providing medical advice to a patient
    c. Processing orders using pharmacy software
    d. Being on alert for potential errors and notifying the pharmacist

See answers on the next page.

Answer Explanations

1. A: Fried's Rule is the formula that should be used to calculate dosages for infants and toddlers up to two years old. The 20 mg is found by entering the given values into the formula:

$$Child's\ dose = \frac{Child's\ age\ \times\ adult\ dose}{150} = \frac{6 \times 500mg}{150} = \frac{3,000mg}{150} = 20mg$$

The other formulas are not specifically intended for infants and Clark's Rule is based on weight.

2. B: Using proportions, one can calculate how many grams of the medication are needed for the solution. Afterwards, the number of grams can be converted to the number of tablets.

First, set up the proportion and make it equal to variable we're looking for over the total amount of milligrams (mg) being dealt with. Since 1 liter equals 1,000,000 milligrams, our set up looks like this:

$$\frac{1}{250} = \frac{x}{1,000,000\ mg}$$

Essentially, the equation is saying what number of milligrams needed is 1/250th of 1,000,000.

To get x by itself, multiply each side by 1,000,000 mg. You get:

$$\frac{1,000,000\ mg}{250}$$

$$4,000\ mg$$

Then you need to determine how many tablets are needed to get 4,000 mg. This is pretty straightforward since the tablets are 400 mg each. Just divide the total number of milligrams needed (4,000) by the amount per tablet (400) to get 10.

3. A: Recalling conversion factors, $1\ tbsp. = 14.79\ mL$, and $1\ ounce = 29.57\ mL$, so there are:

$$4\ ounces \times \frac{29.57\ mL}{1\ ounce} = 118.28\ mL$$

To find the number of tablespoons use the tablespoon to ounce conversion factor:

$$118.28\ mL \times \frac{1\ tbsp.}{14.79\ mL} = 8.00\ tbsp$$

The other answers are incorrect because they do not apply the conversions correctly.

4. D: The correct answer of 20 °C can be found using the appropriate temperature conversion formula:

$$°C = (°F − 32) × \frac{5}{9}$$

$$(68 − 32) × \frac{5}{9}$$

$$36 × \frac{5}{9} = 20°C$$

5. B: Certified Pharmacy Technicians are not allowed to provide medical advice to patients; this falls outside of their scope of practice. They are asked to do all of the other tasks listed as options in the answer bank.

Practice Test #1

1. After opening, how long is Lantus stable at room temperature?
   a. fourteen days
   b. twenty-one days
   c. twenty-eight days
   d. forty-two days

2. Before initiating therapy with warfarin, patients should be advised that increased bleeding can occur with concurrent use of warfarin and all of the following *except:*
   a. non-steroidal anti-inflammatory drugs (NSAIDs)
   b. spinach
   c. garlic
   d. heparin

3. A patient presents to the pharmacy with a prescription that reads: amoxicillin 250mg/5mL oral suspension – 5 mL PO TID x 7 days. How much amoxicillin is required to complete therapy as directed?
   a. 100 mL
   b. 80 mL
   c. 120mL
   d. 50 mL

4. Storage conditions for medications are determined by whom?
   a. Drug Manufacturers
   b. Occupational Safety and Health Administration (OSHA)
   c. United States Pharmacopeia (USP)
   d. U.S. Food and Drug Administration (FDA)

5. Reconstituting medications with the incorrect diluent may result in which of the following reactions?
   a. Trituration
   b. Precipitation
   c. Liquefaction
   d. Levigation

6. To display therapeutic equivalence, parameters that must be comparable between medications include all of the following *except*:
   a. safety profile
   b. clinical efficacy
   c. active ingredients
   d. cost equivalency

7. To achieve blood pressure lowering effects, medications from the following classes are commonly prescribed. Select all that apply.

       I. Angiotensin-converting enzyme inhibitors (ACE Inhibitors)
       II. Angiotensin receptor blockers (ARBs)
       III. Calcium channel blockers (CCBs)
       IV. Beta Blockers

    a. I and II
    b. I, II, and III
    c. II and III
    d. I, II, III, IV

8. A patient calls the pharmacy days after picking up Prometrium capsules. She explains that she experienced difficulty breathing and chest tightness after ingesting the capsules and later developed a rash. After checking with her physician, she stated her reaction could have resulted from a food allergy. What food allergy is contraindicated with Prometrium oral capsules?
    a. Shellfish Hypersensitivity
    b. Peanut Hypersensitivity
    c. Egg Hypersensitivity
    d. Canola Oil Hypersensitivity

9. You receive a prescription order with the following information: NS 1 Liter w/ 10 mL MVI x 1 dose over 8 hours. Select the order that best correlates to that information.
    a. 1000 mL ½ NS with 10 mL multivitamin added given at 126.25 mL/hour
    b. 1000 mL NS with 10 mL multivitamin added given at 150 mL/hour
    c. 1000 mL NS with 10 mL multivitamin added given at 126.25 mL/hour
    d. 1000 mL ½ NS with 10mL multivitamin added given at 150 mL/hour

10. To reduce the incidence of this common side effect, angiotensin-converting enzyme inhibitors (ACE Inhibitors) are often replaced with a different class of medications.
    a. cough
    b. headache
    c. excessive salivation
    d. hypokalemia

11. The Dietary Health and Supplement Act of 1994 specifies criteria that must be met for dietary supplements, including all of the following *except*:
    a. mandatory marketing as a sole source of nutrition
    b. labeling that explicitly states "dietary supplement"
    c. product availability as a capsule, liquid, powder, or tablet
    d. amino acid, botanical, herbal, mineral, and/or vitamin ingredient composition

12. If no stability information is available, what is the beyond-use date of aqueous oral formulations?
    a. no longer than thirty days from the date compounded at controlled cold temperatures
    b. no longer than seven days from the date compounded at controlled cold temperatures
    c. no longer than fourteen days from the date compounded at controlled cold temperatures
    d. no longer than fifteen days from the date compounded at controlled cold temperatures

13. Select the answer choice that best completes the following statement. When given intramuscularly, ertapenem sodium is routinely reconstituted with _____, decreasing the medication's _____.
 a. sterile water, potency
 b. lidocaine hydrochloride, stability
 c. sodium chloride, tonicity
 d. dextrose, bioavailability

14. Of the following, select the medication-indication combination that is correctly paired.
 a. Microzide – type II diabetes mellitus
 b. Singulair – chronic obstructive pulmonary disease
 c. Digitek – heart failure
 d. Skelaxin – constipation

15. A chemical incompatibility is one in which components in a compounded preparation do what?
 a. lose product uniformity
 b. change in odor
 c. alter in palatability
 d. lose potency and integrity

16. A patient presents to the pharmacy requesting an antihistamine with a decreased potential for drowsiness. What medication should be recommended?
 a. fexofenadine
 b. chlorpheniramine
 c. doxylamine
 d. diphenhydramine

17. Narrow therapeutic index drugs exhibit a small window between _____ and _____.
 a. efficacy and toxicity
 b. ease of administration and tolerability
 c. cost efficiency and inefficiency
 d. uniformity and potency

18. Which of the following medication pairs does not represent pharmaceutical alternatives?
 a. Toprol XL and Lopressor
 b. Atarax and Vistaril
 c. Glucotrol and Diabeta
 d. Epitol and Tegretol XR

19. Per federal law, what is the maximum amount of pseudoephedrine that can be purchased daily?
 a. 3.6 grams
 b. 9 grams
 c. 7.5 grams
 d. 3.9 grams

141

20. Hydrochlorothiazide, a commonly prescribed diuretic, is commercially available in combination with all of the following medications *except*:
    a. valsartan
    b. nebivolol
    c. spironolactone
    d. ramipril

21. Select the route of administration that produces 100% bioavailability for medications when utilized.
    a. rectal
    b. sublingual
    c. intravenous
    d. transdermal

22. Patients receiving therapy with statins (ex. pravastatin, atorvastatin, lovastatin) should avoid which of the following?
    a. ginger root
    b. grapefruit
    c. green tea
    d. lemon juice

23. How many milliliters (mL) of fluid can a IV-ounce amber bottle hold?
    a. 120 mL
    b. 180 mL
    c. 240 mL
    d. 150 mL

24. Common side effects of which of the following class of medications include insulin resistance, depression, edema, osteoporosis, and glaucoma?
    a. antibiotics
    b. antitussives
    c. antihypertensives
    d. steroids

25. The following information is required on medication labels. Select all that apply.

    I. Prescription number
    II. Name of prescriber's office
    III. Date prescription is filled
    IV. Pharmacy address

    a. I and II
    b. I, II, and III
    c. I, III, and IV
    d. I, II, III, and IV.

26. Intravenous Vancomycin is a narrow therapeutic index antibiotic eliminated by what process?
    a. Hepatic excretion
    b. Renal excretion
    c. Fecal excretion
    d. Respiratory excretion

27. Of the following classes of medications, which are *not* commonly prescribed to treat depression?
    a. selective serotonin reuptake inhibitors (SSRIs)
    b. serotonin and norepinephrine reuptake inhibitors (SNRIs)
    c. tricyclic antidepressants (TCAs)
    d. monoamine oxidase inhibitors (MAOIs)

28. With what medical condition should sympathomimetic agent containing medications like pseudoephedrine and phenylephrine be avoided?
    a. cancer
    b. diabetes mellitus
    c. hypertension
    d. lung disease

29. How many milligrams are in one gram?
    a. 1000
    b. 100
    c. 10
    d. 0.001

30. Of the following medications, which is available as an ophthalmic solution, topical ointment, injection solution, and intravenous solution?
    a. gentamicin sulfate
    b. ciprofloxacin hydrochloride
    c. vancomycin hydrochloride
    d. levofloxacin

31. Select the medication that works by decreasing calcium entry into the cells of the heart and blood vessel walls.
    a. ramipril
    b. valsartan
    c. metoprolol
    d. amlodipine

32. Two or more pharmaceutically comparable products that demonstrate equivalent bioavailability when tested are referred to as what?
    a. pharmaceutical equivalents
    b. pharmaceutical alternatives
    c. bioequivalents
    d. biosimilars

33. JP, a 43-year-old male, presents to the pharmacy requesting a cold and sinus medication that will not interfere with his blood pressure. What medication should be recommended?
    a. pseudoephedrine
    b. chlorpheniramine
    c. phenylephrine
    d. ephedrine

34. Select the statement that is *in*correct.
    a. Medication guides are provided to patients to mitigate the occurrence of adverse events.
    b. Patient package inserts are submitted voluntarily to the FDA and do not require approval.
    c. Over-the-counter medications are regulated by the FDA.
    d. Instructions for use are produced by drug manufacturers and approved by the FDA.

35. Which of the following factors should be considered when assigning beyond-use dates?

Select the best answer.

    I. The medication's chemical nature
    II. Information obtained from published literature regarding the medication
    III. Storage conditions
    IV. Potential microbial growth

    a. I, II, and III only
    b. I and II only
    c. I, III, and IV only
    d. I, II, III, and IV

36. What is the brand name and medication classification for ezetimibe?
    a. Zetia, cholesterol absorption inhibitor
    b. Zestril, angiotensin-converting enzyme inhibitor
    c. Zoloft, selective serotonin reuptake inhibitor
    d. Zocor, statin (HMG-CoA Reductase Inhibitor)

37. While working in a compounding pharmacy, you notice that a bottle of disinfectant is leaking and spreading all over the floor. When you report to the pharmacist, he asks you to take care of it. What would be the appropriate spill-handling procedure?
    a. Wear gloves and wipe it
    b. Pour some rubbing alcohol on it and wipe it off
    c. Spread paper towels on the spill
    d. Consult MSDS for handling the chemical

38. How long after a Schedule II medication is dispensed must a prescription be kept?
    a. At least one year
    b. At least two years
    c. At least five years
    d. At least seven years

39. Hazardous wastes produced in a pharmacy include which of the following?

> I. Antibiotics
> II. Chemotherapy drugs
> III. Hormonal contraceptives

  a. I
  b. II
  c. III
  d. I, II, and III

40. Choose the answer that includes only examples of Schedule IV substances
  a. Carisoprodol, lorazepam, and temazepam
  b. Heroin, LSD, and peyote
  c. Methylphenidate, oxycodone, and codeine
  d. Phendimetrazine, clonazepam, and triazolam

41. You have retrieved a DEA form 222 from a file and noted an error relative to the requirements for that form. Identify which of this information would indicate an error.
  a. A note was made that a copy sent to the DEA office.
  b. A spelling error was crossed out and written above.
  c. The copy of the form has been on file for over one year.
  d. The form was completed on paper, not electronically.

42. Select the choice that identifies appropriate disposal for the substance named.
  a. Biohazards should be disposed of in a labeled receptacle that is usually dark blue.
  b. Expired OTC medications should be disposed of in a labeled receptacle that is usually red.
  c. Hazardous drugs should be disposed of in white "Hazardous Drug Waste" bags.
  d. Infectious sharps should be disposed of in a container labeled bio-hazard.

43. Select the option which includes safe, environmentally sound disposal method(s) for pharmaceutical waste.

> I. Rinse down sink
> II. Incineration
> III. Waste collection company

  a. I only
  b. II only
  c. III only
  d. I, II, and II

44. Which choice accurately describes information that must be maintained in a log of dispensed prescriptions?
  a. Date the medication was prescribed and dispensed
  b. Medication strength and dosage form
  c. Patient's name and known allergies
  d. Prescribing physician's name and address

145

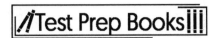

45. What action should you prioritize upon discovering the theft of a controlled substance from the pharmacy?
    a. Alert local law enforcement authorities to the theft.
    b. Engage the pharmacy's lawyers to communicate with the DEA.
    c. File a Form 222 electronically or in hard copy within one day.
    d. Notify the local DEA Diversion Field Office immediately by phone.

46. What do you know about the registrant based on the following DEA number: PR312511?
    a. A registered nurse with a last name starting with P
    b. A physician with a last name starting with P
    c. A nurse practitioner with a last name starting with R
    d. A manufacturer with a last name starting with R

47. Which is true about the following DEA number: ML6298548?
    a. The check digit is invalid.
    b. The number of digits is incorrect.
    c. SUM1 is equal to 20.
    d. SUM2 is equal to 28.

48. Identify the error-prone abbreviation that is matched with the correct substitution suggested to avoid misinterpretation.
    a. The abbreviation cc should be substituted with "units."
    b. The abbreviation IU should be substituted with "intravenous."
    c. The abbreviation qhs should be substituted with "nightly."
    d. The abbreviation UD should be substituted with "unit dose."

49. To prevent dispensing errors, verify the patient's

    I. Address
    II. Birthdate
    III. Therapeutic use of the drug

    a. I and II only
    b. I and III only
    c. II and III only
    d. I, II, and III

50. Identify the correct use of tall man lettering for the following LASA medication names.
    a. acetazolAMIDE, acetohexAMIDE
    b. chlorPROMazine, chlorPROPamide
    c. DAUNORUBICIN, DOXORUBICIN
    d. DOBUTamine, DOPamine

51. What is one disadvantage of using barcodes for the automation of prescription filling?
    a. Barcodes increase risk of dispensing errors.
    b. Barcodes cannot be used at patients' bedsides.
    c. Barcodes are not available for all dosage forms.
    d. Barcodes compare dosage with doctor's orders.

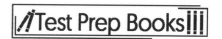

52. The pharmacist asks you to review a filled prescription, written as sertraline, 25.0 mg tablet, 1 tablet BT, disp#30. The pharmacist has dispensed 90 tablets of 25 mg sertraline with instructions for the patient to take twice daily. What is the error in this scenario?
    a. The prescription was written for less than a month's supply.
    b. The pharmacist dispensed the incorrect dose of tablets.
    c. The medication should be taken once daily at bedtime.
    d. There is no error in this scenario.

53. The system has flagged a prescription for a 25 mg dose of hydrochlorothiazide. The patient is an adult male, 62 years of age with a medical history including hypertension and type 2 diabetes, which is managed with metformin. How should the technician proceed?
    a. Consult with the pharmacist.
    b. Consult with the prescribing physician.
    c. Fill the prescription.
    d. Reject to fill the prescription.

54. A pharmacy customer asks for advice on OTC pain medication. The young woman complains of a terrible headache that came on about 12 hours prior. The pharmacist confirms that the patient is also suffering extreme neck stiffness and a high fever. Review of the patient's information reveals no medical history; her only prescription medication is for oral contraceptives, which she has been taking for several years. How is the pharmacist likely to respond?
    a. Ask questions to determine if this is an adverse drug event.
    b. Direct the patient to appropriate OTC pain and fever medications.
    c. Encourage the patient to seek further medical intervention.
    d. Point out OTC drugs that may interact with her prescription medications.

55. An elderly pharmacy patient is picking up his prescription for 200 mg theophylline when he remarks that he's been suffering nausea and abdominal pain. A review of his patient information indicates that he is also taking 5 mg donepezil and 50 mg atenolol. What indication do you have that this may be an adverse drug event?
    a. The prescribed dosage for at least one of the medications
    b. The interaction between a drug and the patient's disease
    c. The interaction between two or more of the medications
    d. The therapeutic index of at least one of the medications

56. A patient on limited income has admitted to taking half the dose of her medication to make it last longer. What is this best described as?
    a. Drug-patient interaction
    b. Medication abuse
    c. Non-compliance
    d. Overprescribing

57. A patient brings in a paper prescription from Dr. Valdez, a psychiatrist. It is written as methylphenidate 20 mg, 1 tablet tid, Disp #90, Refills 3. What aspect of the prescription indicates it may be a forgery?
    a. Dosing instructions
    b. Number of refills
    c. Prescriber information
    d. Quantity prescribed

58. Infection control guidelines include which of the following?
    a. Dispense antibiotics responsibly
    b. Ensure proper immunization of staff
    c. Provide hand sanitizer for customers
    d. Use disposable tools

59. A patient is seeking to refill a prescription for clonazepam before it is due. He claims to have accidentally spilled much of the bottle in the toilet, rendering it useless. His file indicates that he previously asked for an early refill, as well. How should the pharmacy technician proceed?
    a. Consult with the pharmacist
    b. Counsel the patient on the missed dose
    c. Refill the prescription
    d. Seek a formulary substitution

60. Identify the words that appropriately fill the blanks in the following description of the standard procedure for washing hands to prevent the spread of infection:

    1. Remove _____
    2. Wet hands with _____
    3. Apply _____
    4. Vigorously rub all parts of the hands and wrists for _____
    5. Rinse and dry with a paper towel
    6. Turn off tap with _____

    a. Gloves, water, disinfectant, at least 20 seconds, hands
    b. Jewelry, warm water, soap, 10-20 seconds, paper towel
    c. Rings, water, disinfectant, 10 seconds, elbow
    d. Watches and rings, warm water, soap, up to 10 seconds, towel

61. Personal protective equipment (PPE) use
    a. Completely prevents the spread of infection
    b. Eliminates the need for hand washing
    c. Typically utilizes reusable materials
    d. Varies depending on contaminant type

62. Which describes a proper practice in mask use?
    a. Carefully pull mask away from the face without dragging it.
    b. Remove mask with gloved hands before removing gloves.
    c. Wash hands after removing first gloves and then mask.
    d. Wear an N95 mask when exposed to hazardous vapors.

63. Which disinfectant is accurately identified and labeled with the correct level?
    a. 3% hydrogen peroxide, intermediate level disinfectant
    b. Boiling item for 10 minutes, intermediate level disinfectant
    c. Household bleach, high level disinfectant
    d. Sterilization, high level disinfectant

64. The guidelines set forth in *USP 797* describe
    a. Appropriate PPE for various substances and situations
    b. Equipment disinfection and sterilization products
    c. Infection control of environment and equipment
    d. Guidelines governing hygiene for sterile preparations

65. Which is true about the pharmacy's laminar flow hood?
    a. It must be properly cleaned before each use.
    b. It serves as a storage area for items with hazardous fumes.
    c. It should run for at least 30 minutes before cleaning.
    d. Its HEPA filter should be cleaned with 70% ethanol.

66. A newly hired pharmacy technician has created a schedule for cleaning items and equipment. He cleans counting trays and spatulas daily in 70% ethanol, wipes down counting trays with cleaning wipes throughout the day, marks tools for use with substances known to cause allergies, and immediately cleans tools used to dispense liquid and cream medications. Has he made any errors?
    a. No, he did not make any errors according to cleaning protocol.
    b. Yes, counting trays and spatulas should be cleaned with hot, soapy water.
    c. Yes, counting trays should be cleaned after each use.
    d. Yes, both options b.   and c. describe errors in cleaning protocol.

67. At the completion of her shift, before leaving for the day, a pharmacy technician completes the following tasks: washes counters and surfaces, rinses dispensing tools, washes keyboards and phones, takes out pharmacy trash, vacuums pharmacy floor, disinfects pharmacy waiting area. What did she miss?
    a. Clean dispensing tools with disinfectant.
    b. Ensure medication bottle tops are tightened.
    c. Put on PPE before cleaning the pharmacy.
    d. Wet mop the pharmacy floor with disinfectant.

68. What is the proper sequence for applying PPE for sterile preparations?

      1. Put on facial, shoe, and hair covers
      2. Put on gown with sleeves fitted around wrists
      3. Put on sterile gloves
      4. Remove debris from under fingernails
      5. Scrub hands with alcohol-based scrub
      6. Wash hands and arms up to the elbow

    a.   1, 4, 6, 2,5, 3
    b.   1, 6, 4, 2, 5, 3
    c.   6, 4, 5, 3, 2, 1
    d.   4, 6, 3, 5, 1, 2

69. A pharmacy technician observes an error in the dosage for a medication. She informs her supervisor who completes the incident report and submits it through MedWatch. The report includes the specifics of the affected patient, date, time, and location of incident, description, name, and signature, and date filed. What part of this scenario was conducted incorrectly?

    a.   Important information is missing from the report.
    b.   MedWatch is not an appropriate tool for this scenario.
    c.   The wrong person made the report.
    d.   There were no incorrect actions in this scenario.

70. A new pharmacist is unsure if a do not crush warning should be added when dispensing a medication. To what should she refer?

    a.   ISMP
    b.   MERP
    c.   SERP
    d.   VERP

71. Which is true about adverse reactions to medication?

    a.   Consumers must report adverse reactions to manufacturers.
    b.   ISMP includes all MedWatch-reported adverse effects.
    c.   Reviews of FAERS can highlight trends in product safety.
    d.   Only clinicians can report adverse effects to the FDA.

72. A pharmacy receives a prescription for a compounded ointment. The pharmacist on duty has extensive knowledge of the chemical properties of the ingredients and their compatibilities with other ingredients. However, the pharmacy does not have equipment or an area designated for this purpose. How should the pharmacy proceed?

    a.   Order the equipment needed.
    b.   Refer the patient to another pharmacy.
    c.   Substitute with a similar ointment.
    d.   Use other equipment found in the pharmacy.

73. Which is a true statement about documentation for a compounding pharmacy?
    a. Equipment maintenance must be tracked and kept in records.
    b. Ingredient records must be kept but not the quantity and dose calculations
    c. Master formulation records describe the process used in compounding.
    d. Records should be kept for at least two years at an offsite location.

74. Equipment important for formulating a pharmaceutical compound includes:
    a. Beakers
    b. Counting trays
    c. Ointment
    d. Weighing papers

75. The materials used in compounding should be:

    I. Chemically inert
    II. Non-hazardous
    III. Produced by the FDA

    a. One of the above
    b. Two of the above
    c. All of the above
    d. None of the above

76. Which of the following is an improper practice in chemical compounding?
    a. Analyze whether the admixture will be absorbed properly.
    b. Assess the effect of pH on bioavailability of oral admixtures.
    c. Compound more than one mixture at the same time.
    d. Have a dedicated area for the compounding process.

77. When are nonsterile emulsions used?
    a. When liquid materials do not dissolve in or mix with each other easily
    b. When materials used in compounding do not need to be sterile
    c. When solid materials used in compounding require an emulsifying agent
    d. When the amount of internal phase exceeds the amount of external phase

78. Which suffix is correctly matched with its meaning?
    a. -algia, blood condition
    b. -itis, visual examination
    c. -phagia, eat
    d. -stomy, cutting into

79. Which medical abbreviation is accurately listed with its meaning?
    a. EEG, electrocardiogram
    b. HTN, hypotension
    c. NPO, nothing by mouth
    d. RA, reactive allergy

151

80. Interpret the following: 1 mg/kg SQ BID.
    a. 1 microgram per kilogram skin cream applied on body part designated
    b. 1 microgram-kilogram injected into the muscle each day
    c. 1 milligram per kilogram administered beneath the skin twice daily
    d. 1 milligram- kilogram soft capsule taken every other day

81. A medication is directed to be administered "au." In what type of container is it likely to be packaged?
    a. Collapsible tube
    b. Dropper bottle
    c. Prescription bottle
    d. Round vial

82. Which choice accurately matches the non-sterile compounding technique with its description?
    a. Communition – mixing two ingredients of varying quantities
    b. Geometric dilution – mixing two substances together with water
    c. Levigation – use of a solvent to carry an insoluble drug powder
    d. Pulverization by intervention – making a substance into small particles

83. Identify the true statement.
    a. Cardi is a prefix meaning heart
    b. Hem is a root word meaning blood
    c. Hypo is a prefix meaning increased
    d. Tachy is a root word meaning fast

84. What is the purpose of the amber color of many prescription medication containers?
    a. Prevent physical damage to the medication
    b. Protect the medication from light exposure
    c. Provide accurate identification of medication
    d. Reduce counterfeit medication distribution

85. According to the PPPA, which of the statements are correct?

    I. All medications must have childproof caps
    II. Medications in inpatient environments are exempt
    III. Patients may ask for any medication to be an exception

    a. I and II
    b. I and III
    c. II and III
    d. I, II, and III

86. According to the FDA, which of these is approved as temper-evident packaging?
    a. All metal tubes
    b. Bottles with childproof caps
    c. Bubble packs
    d. Injection needles

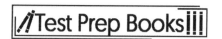

87. Select the option that lists the correct conversion factor.
    a. 1 liquid ounce = 14.79 mL
    b. 1 pint = 8 ounces
    c. 1 tablespoon = 29.57 mL
    d. 1 teaspoon = 4.929 mL

88. You are asked to use Clark's rule to calculate the child dose of a medication. The child weighs 13,000 grams. What number would you use for body weight in the calculation?
    a. 0.013 kilograms
    b. 5.900 pounds
    c. 13 kilograms
    d. 28.665 pounds

89. You receive a prescription written as 5 gtt ad qd x 14. What size bottle of the medication should be dispensed?
    a. One 5 mL bottle
    b. One 10 mL bottle
    c. One 15 mL bottle
    d. Two 10 mL bottles

90. What condition is a prescription written as 5 gtt ad qd x 14 most likely written for?
    a. Ear infection
    b. Eye inflammation
    c. Nasal congestion
    d. Opioid addiction

Answer Explanations #1

1. C: twenty-eight days. Once opened, Lantus (insulin glargine) is stable for twenty-eight days at room temperature. Answer choices A, C, and D – fourteen days, twenty-one days, and forty-two days, respectively, are incorrect.

2. B: spinach. Considered a leafy green, answer choice B, spinach, is rich in Vitamin K and can work in the body to produce a blood-clotting factor. Answer choice A, non-steroidal anti-inflammatory drugs, can increase bleeding risk. Choice C, garlic, has also been shown to increase the chance of bleeding when taken with warfarin. Finally, answer choice D, heparin, is an anticoagulant used to prevent blood clot formation in the body, thus creating an increased bleed risk.

3. C: 120 mL. The directions for the patient's prescription call for 5 milliliters (mL) of amoxicillin by mouth (PO) three times daily (TID) or 15 milliliters orally daily for seven days. A total of 105 milliliters of amoxicillin are needed to complete the course as directed. Answer choice A, 100 mL, would be an insufficient quantity. Answer choices B, 80 mL, and D, 50 mL, would also be insufficient quantities. Only choice C, 120 mL, provides the amount of medication necessary to complete the course of therapy.

4. A: Drug Manufacturers. Storage conditions for medications are determined by the manufacturers that produce them. Answer choice D, U.S. Food and Drug Administration, is incorrect as FDA regulations defer to drug manufacturing requirements to determine storage conditions. Answer choice B, OSHA, is incorrect as the agency regulates safety conditions for workers. Answer choice C, USP, develops quality standards for medications but also defers to drug manufacturers for medication storage conditions.

5. B: Precipitation. Answer choice B, precipitation, is correct. Reconstitution with an improper diluent can cause active medications to precipitate, forming crystals within the solution. Answer choice A, trituration, is the process of grinding medicines into fine powders. Answer choice C, liquefaction, occurs when solid ingredients are combined and produce a liquid or fluid resulting compound. Answer choice D, levigation, refers to a process of trituration with wetting agents.

6. D: cost equivalency. For medications to be deemed therapeutic equivalents, they must display the same safety profiles – choice A, clinical efficacy – choice B, and active ingredients – choice C per U.S. Food and Drug Administration guidelines. Answer choice D, cost equivalency, is not a parameter that must be comparable between therapeutically equivalent medications.

7. D: I, II, III, and IV. In the treatment of hypertension, angiotensin-converting enzyme inhibitors (ACE Inhibitors), angiotensin II receptor blockers (ARBs), calcium channel blockers (CCBs), and beta-blockers are commonly prescribed. Answer choice D is correct. Answer choices A, B, and C do not include all classes listed and are therefore incorrect.

8. B: Peanut Hypersensitivity. Prometrium oral capsules contain peanut oil and should not be taken by patients with peanut allergies. Therefore, the correct answer choice is B, peanut hypersensitivity. Answer choices A – shellfish hypersensitivity, C – egg hypersensitivity, and D – canola oil hypersensitivity are not documented contraindications to Prometrium and are thus incorrect.

9. C: 1000 mL NS with 10 mL multivitamin added given at 126.25 mL/hour. The abbreviation NS represents Normal Saline, not ½ NS as listed in answer choices A and D, which are incorrect. 1 Liter of fluid is equivalent to 1000 milliliters (mL). 1000 mL of normal saline plus 10 mL of multivitamin (MVI)

154

equals 1,010 milliliters of fluid. This volume over 8 hours would produce a rate of 126.25 mL per hour, not 150 mL per hour as stated in answer choice B. The correct answer is choice C, 1000 mL NS with 10 mL multivitamin added at 126.25 mL/hour.

10. A: Cough. Though answer choice B, headache, is a side effect commonly attributed to angiotensin-converting enzyme inhibitors (ACE inhibitors), there is insufficient literature to suggest that this side effect warrants switching to another class of medication. Answer choice C, excessive salivation, is not a common side effect of ACE Inhibitors. Likewise, answer choice D, hypokalemia is not a common side effect of ACE Inhibitors; instead, it is hyperkalemia.

11. A: mandatory marketing as a sole source of nutrition. Answer choice A is prohibited, not mandatory, as The Dietary Health and Supplement Act of 1994 states dietary supplements may not be purposefully marketed as sole nutrition items. Answer choices B, C, and D are all criteria that dietary supplements must meet as set forth by the Dietary Health and Supplement Act of 1994.

12. C: no longer than 14 days from the date compounded at controlled cold temperatures. In the absence of stability data for water containing oral formulations, beyond use date guidelines advise that these preparations expire no later than 14 days from the date of compounding when stored at controlled cold temperatures. Therefore, answer choice C is correct. Choice A, thirty days, and choice D, fifteen days, are beyond the length of drug stability time specified by guidelines and therefore incorrect. Choice B, seven days is before the length of drug stability time specified by guidelines and, therefore, incorrect.

13. B: lidocaine hydrochloride, stability. Invanz (ertapenem sodium) should be reconstituted with 1% lidocaine hydrochloride injection when administered intramuscularly. After reconstitution, the medication's stability is decreased. The correct answer is B. Intravenous –

not intramuscular – ertapenem is reconstituted with sterile water or sodium chloride as stated in answer choices A and C. Invanz should not be diluted with dextrose as suggested in choice D.

14. C: Digitek – heart failure. Answer choice A, Microzide – type II diabetes mellitus, is incorrect, as Microzide is indicated to treat hypertension and edema adjunctively. Choice B is also incorrect, as Singulair (montelukast sodium) is indicated to treat asthma and rhinitis. Answer choice D is also inappropriately paired, as Skelaxin is indicated to relieve musculoskeletal pain, not constipation. The correct choice is C, Digitek – heart failure.

15. D: lose potency and integrity. In a physical incompatibility, compounds may lose product uniformity, change in odor, or alter in palatability, as indicated by answer choices A, B, and C, respectively. However, the question seeks to define what occurs in a chemical incompatibility rendering choices A, B, and C incorrect. A chemical incompatibility is when compounds in preparation react chemically and result in a loss of potency and integrity. Choice D is correct.

16. A: fexofenadine. Answer choices B, chlorpheniramine, C, doxylamine, and D, diphenhydramine, are first-generation antihistamines that can cause sedation and drowsiness. Answer choice A, fexofenadine has not been shown to have sedating effects.

17. A: efficacy and toxicity. Medications with a narrow therapeutic index have a small window between being effective and toxic. The correct choice is A. Answer choice B, ease of administration and tolerability, are unrelated parameters to therapeutic index. Choice C, cost efficiency and inefficiency,

155

also have no bearing on therapeutic index. Finally, answer choice D includes medication properties uniformity and potency, which are also not related to therapeutic index.

18. C: Glucotrol and Diabeta. Medications with the same therapeutic structure formulated as different salts are referred to as pharmaceutical alternatives. Thus, answer choice A, Toprol XL (metoprolol succinate) and Lopressor (metoprolol tartrate), exemplifies pharmaceutical alternatives. Choice *B*, Atarax (hydroxyzine hydrochloride) and Vistaril (hydroxyzine pamoate), represents pharmaceutical alternatives. Choice *D*, Epitol (carbamazepine) and Tegretol XR (carbamazepine extended – release), also illustrates pharmaceutical alternatives. Answer choice C, Glucotrol (glipizide) and Diabeta (glyburide), represents two structurally different medications, not pharmaceutical alternatives.

19. A: 3.6 grams. The Combat Methamphetamine Epidemic Act of 2005 established limits for purchasing products containing ephedrine, pseudoephedrine, and phenylpropanolamine. The daily limit is 3.6 grams, as reflected in answer choice A. Choice *B*, 9 grams, represents the 30-day purchase limit and is incorrect. Choice *C*, 7.5 grams, denotes the mail-order monthly limit and is incorrect. Choice *D*, 3.9 grams, also does not reflect the accurate daily limit for the purchase of ephedrine, pseudoephedrine, and phenylpropanolamine-containing products.

20. B: Nebivolol. Hydrochlorothiazide (HCTZ) is commercially available in combination with choice A, valsartan, as Diovan HCT. Choice *C*, spironolactone, is available in combination with HCTZ as Aldactazide. Answer choice D, ramipril, is available with HCTZ as Altace HCT. However, answer choice B, nebivolol, is not commercially available in combination with HCTZ, making it the correct selection.

21. C: intravenous. Medications administered intravenously display 100% bioavailability. Answer choices A, B, and D – rectal, sublingual, and transdermal, respectively, undergo metabolism and absorption changes, thus decreasing bioavailability.

22. B: grapefruit. Because grapefruit juice can inhibit statin metabolism, patients taking statins should be advised to avoid consuming large amounts of grapefruit and/or grapefruit juice. Answer choice A, ginger root, has not been shown to interact with statin therapy. Answer choice C, green tea, has also not been proven to interact with statin therapy, and neither has choice D, lemon juice. The best answer is choice B.

23. A: 120 milliliters (mL). There are approximately 29.57 mL in one fluid ounce. This number is commonly rounded to 30 mL for simplicity's sake. The roman numeral IV represents four. Therefore, a four-ounce amber bottle can be filled with 118.28 mL of fluid or 120 milliliters. The correct selection is choice A. Choice *B*, 180 mL, would require a six-ounce bottle. Choice *C*, 240 mL, would require an eight-ounce bottle; and choice D, 150 mL, would require a five-ounce container at minimum.

24. D: steroids. Common side effects of answer choice A, antibiotics, include anaphylaxis, stomach upset, and diarrhea; therefore, it is not the correct selection. Antitussives – answer choice B – have been associated with drowsiness, headache, blurred vision, and constipation. Choice *C*, antihypertensives, common side effects include dizziness, lightheadedness, erection problems, and nervousness. Choices *B* and *C* are incorrect. The best selection is choice D, steroids.

25. C: I, III, and IV. Medication labels should include the following: name and address of dispensing pharmacy, prescription number, date filled, name of prescriber (not the name of prescriber's office), name of patient, name and strength of medication, directions for use, cautionary statements, name of pharmacist, date of expiration, and any other information as required by state law (such as refill

156

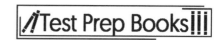

information). Roman numeral II should not be included in required criteria; therefore, answer choices A, B, and D are incorrect.

26. B: Renal excretion. When administered intravenously, vancomycin is cleared from the body by glomerular filtration in the kidneys. Answer choice A, hepatic excretion is incorrect as this would indicate vancomycin is cleared from the body by the liver. Answer choice C, fecal excretion is also incorrect as glomerular filtration is associated with urine production, not fecal production. Choice D, respiratory excretions, suggests vancomycin is cleared from the body through the lungs and is incorrect.

27. D: monoamine oxidase inhibitors (MAOIs). Though each of the classes listed in answer choices A, B, C, and D can be prescribed for the treatment of depression, the question seeks to define which class is *not* commonly prescribed for the treatment of depression. The correct choice is D, monoamine oxidase inhibitors (MAOIs). Due to severe interactions with food and serious side effects, MAOIs are not commonly prescribed.

28. C: hypertension. Medications containing sympathomimetics can cause blood pressure increases and should be avoided in patients with hypertension. There is no literature to support the avoidance of sympathomimetic-containing agents in patients with choice A, cancer, choice B, diabetes mellitus, or choice D, lung disease. The correct answer choice is C.

29. A: 1000. One gram contains one thousand milligrams. The correct choice is A. Answer choice B, one hundred, reflects the number of centigrams in one gram. Choice C, ten, represents the number of decigrams in a gram. Answer choice D, 0.001 represents the number of grams in a milligram – not milligrams in a gram. Answer choices B, C, and D are incorrect.

30. A: gentamicin sulfate. Neither answer choice B, ciprofloxacin hydrochloride, nor D, levofloxacin, are available as topical ointments. Choices *B* and *D* are incorrect. Choice *C*, vancomycin hydrochloride, is not available as an ophthalmic solution or topical ointment and is also incorrect. The correct choice is A, gentamicin sulfate.

31. D: amlodipine. Calcium channel blockers work by slowing calcium entry to heart cells and blood vessel walls. The correct answer choice is D, amlodipine, the only calcium channel blocker listed. Answer choice A, ramipril, is an angiotensin-converting enzyme inhibitor and works via a different mechanism; it is not the correct choice. Answer choice B, valsartan, is an angiotensin receptor blocker that works via a different mechanism; it is not the correct choice. Answer choice C, metoprolol, is also incorrect as it is a beta-blocker that does not work via calcium channels.

32. C: bioequivalents. Choice *A*, pharmaceutical equivalents, refers to two or more medications with equal quantities of active ingredients, the same dosage form, and the same route of administration. Choice *B*, pharmaceutical alternatives, describes medications with the same therapeutic structure and different salt formulations. Choice *D*, biosimilars, defines a biological copy of an already approved biological product manufactured by another company. The correct answer is choice C, bioequivalents.

33. B: chlorpheniramine. Answer choices A, C, and D – pseudoephedrine, phenylephrine, and ephedrine, respectively – are all decongestants with the potential to increase blood pressure. Choice *B*, chlorpheniramine, is an antihistamine that has not been shown to affect blood pressure. The correct answer choice is B.

34. B: Patient package inserts are submitted voluntarily to the FDA and do not require approval. Drug manufacturers develop and submit patient package inserts voluntarily to the FDA; however, FDA approval is required. Answer choices A, C, and D are factual statements, but not correct answers as the question seeks to define which of the statements is incorrect.

35. D: I, II, III, and IV. All of the factors listed must be considered when specifying beyond-use dates for medications. Answer choices A, B, and C, do not include all factors and are thus not the best answer. Answer choice D is the best selection.

36. A: Zetia, cholesterol absorption inhibitor. Answer choice A is correct; ezetimibe is the generic name for Zetia, a cholesterol absorption inhibitor. Answer choices B, C, and D are incorrect.

37. D: The MSDS (Material Safety Data Sheet) is a document that carries information about potentially hazardous chemicals and how to handle them safely. Consult the MSDS for cleaning the spill.

38. B: The log or file of dispensed prescriptions must be kept and available for review and/or inspection by the authorities or Board of Pharmacy for at least two years. Therefore. Choices *A, C,* and *D* are incorrect.

39. B: Hazardous wastes include chemotherapy drugs, as well as expired medications, incorrectly compounded medications, items contaminated by bodily fluids, and disposable equipment used to dispense or make hazardous items. Choices *A, C,* and *D* are incorrect because antibiotics and hormonal contraceptives are nonhazardous.

40. A: Schedule IV substances have low potential for abuse compared with Schedule III substances; they include carisoprodol (Soma®), lorazepam (Ativan®), and temazepam (Restoril®). Choice *B* is incorrect because heroin, LSD, and peyote are Schedule I substances. Choice *C* is incorrect because oxycodone and codeine are Schedule II substances, while methylphenidate is a Schedule IIN substance. Choice *D* is incorrect because while clonazepam (Klonopin®) and triazolam (Halcion®) are Schedule IV substances, phendimetrazine is a Schedule IIIN substance.

41. B: If an error is made on a form 222, a new copy should be completed. Choice *A* is incorrect because when a hard copy is completed, the pharmacy and supplier should each keep a copy on file for two years while also sending a copy to the DEA office. Choice *C* is incorrect because the copy should remain on file for two years, so it should still be there after over a year. Choice *D* is incorrect because form 222 may be completed on paper or electronically.

42. D: Infectious sharps and biohazards should be disposed of in containers labeled "bio-hazard," which are often red or dark orange in color. Choice *A* is incorrect because biohazards should be disposed of in containers labeled "bio-hazard," which are often red or dark orange in color. Choice *B* is incorrect because expired or unused non-hazardous drugs should be disposed of in containers which are often dark blue in color. Choice *C* is incorrect because while hazardous drugs should be disposed of in labeled "Hazardous Drug Waste" bags, and the bags can be different colors, they are never white.

43. C: Disposing of waste through a third-party company with expertise in appropriate waste collection, handling, and disposal techniques is the safest, most environmentally sound option. Choice *A* is incorrect because flushing pharmaceutical waste down a toilet or sink can introduce hydrophilic, biologically-active chemicals into the environment and drinking water supplies. Choice *B* is incorrect

because incineration pollutes the air. Therefore, choice *D* is also incorrect because it includes options I and II.

44. B: The log or records of dispensed medication should include the patient's name and address as well as the date the medication was dispensed, drug name, strength, dosage form, and quantity dispensed. Choice *A* is incorrect because the log should include the date the medication was dispensed but not the date it was prescribed. Choice *C* is incorrect because the log should include the patient's information but not their known allergies. Choice *D* is incorrect because the log need not include the physician's information.

45. A: Though not required by Federal law or policies, it is important to notify local law enforcement and state regulatory agencies of the theft, because it is a crime. Choice *B* is incorrect because the notice to the DEA should come directly from the registrant or authorized individual of the registrant; intermediaries should not be engaged. Choice *C* is incorrect because the correct form in this instance is a DEA Form 106 (Report of Theft or Loss of Controlled Substances); Form 222 documents the transfer, order, or return of Schedule II substances. Choice *D* is incorrect because the DEA Diversion Field Office must be notified in writing.

46. D: The first letter in the DEA number represents the type of registrant; the letter P indicates a manufacturer or researcher. The second letter in the DEA number represents the first letter of the registrant's last name. Choice *A* is incorrect because registered nurses cannot write prescriptions. Choice *B* is incorrect because the last name of the registrant in this example is R, represented by the second letter in the DEA number. Further, a first letter of P does not indicate a physician as the type of registrant; practitioners are designated by the letters A, B or F. Choice *C* is incorrect because nurse practitioner is a mid-level practitioner, which is designated by an M as the first letter in a DEA number.

47. C: SUM1 is equal to the sum of digits 1, 3, and 5: $6 + 9 + 5 = 20$. Choice *A* is incorrect because the check digit, the last digit in the number is correct. The check digit is found by adding $SUM1 + PROD2$. $SUM1 \ (above) = 20$. $PROD2 = SUM2 \times 2$. SUM2 equals the sum of digits 2, 4, and 6: $2 + 8 + 4 = 14$. So $PROD2 = 14 \times 2 = 28$. The check digit is the last digit of $SUM1 + PROD2 = 20 + 28 = 48$, so the check digit is 8. Choice *B* is incorrect because DEA numbers have six digits plus a single check digit. Choice *D* is incorrect because SUM2=14 as shown above. $PROD2 = SUM2 \times 2 = 28$.

48. C: The abbreviation qhs means nightly at bedtime, but is easily confused with qhr (every hour); therefore, the substitution "nightly" should be used. Choice *A* is incorrect because the abbreviation cc means cubic centimeters" it is often confused with "units" and should be substituted with mL. Choice *B* is incorrect because IU (international unit) is easily confused with IV and should be substituted with unit. Choice *D* is incorrect because the abbreviation UD (ut dictum, meaning as directed) is easily confused with unit dose and should be substituted with "as directed."

49. D: Asking the patient to verify two unique identifiers (often address and birthdate), as well as the use of the drug helps to prevent errors in dispensing the wrong medication. Choices *A, B,* and *C* are incorrect because they exclude at least one of the correct options.

50. D: The goal of tall man (mixed case) lettering is to highlight the differences in two LASA (look-alike, sound-alike) medications. The capital letters in this example highlight the different prefixes in these LASA medication names. Choice *A* is incorrect because the capital letters in this choice highlight the portions of the LASA medication names, which are the same. Tall man lettering should be used to

159

highlight their differences (i.e., acetaZOLAMIDE, acetoHEXAMIDE). Choice *B* is incorrect because the capital letters do not highlight the entire difference between the two medication names (i.e., chlorproMAZINE, chlorproPAMIDE). Choice *C* is incorrect because correct tall man lettering only uses capital letters for the portions of the medication names that differ (i.e., DAUNOrubicin, DOXOrubicin).

51. C: Barcodes may not be included on all medications or unique dosage forms. Choice *A* is incorrect because barcodes generally reduce the risk of dispensing errors. Choice *B* is incorrect because barcodes can be used at patients' bedsides. Choice *D* is incorrect because barcodes can compare dispensed dosages with the doctor's orders, which is an advantage in their use.

52. C: The abbreviation BT in the prescription indicates the medication should be taken at bedtime. The pharmacist dispensed the prescription for instructions to take the medication twice daily, which is abbreviated BID. Choice *A* is incorrect because 30 tablets are a one-month supply if taken once daily at bedtime, as prescribed. Choice *B* is incorrect because the pharmacist correctly dispensed 25 mg tablets, despite the prescriber's erroneous use of a trailing zero (25.0 mg) in the prescription. Choice *D* is incorrect because there is an error in how the pharmacist interpreted the prescription.

53. A: The flag resulted because of a drug-disease (hydrochlorothiazide-type 2 diabetes) interaction. Diuretics like hydrochlorothiazide can make it very difficult to control blood sugar in patients with type 2 diabetes. The drug utilization review (DUR) and consult with prescribing physician should be conducted by the pharmacist, not a pharmacy technician. Choice *B* is incorrect because the pharmacist, not the pharmacy technician, should follow-up with the prescribing physician if necessary. Choices *C* and *D* are incorrect because the pharmacist, not the technician, should apply the override code necessary to fill or reject to fill the prescription.

54. C: A headache that comes on quickly and is accompanied by extreme neck stiffness or pain and a fever could indicate incidence of meningitis. Based on these red flags, the pharmacist would likely recommend emergency medical attention. Choice *A* is incorrect because the patient has been on the same medication for several years, and her symptoms are not known to be side effects of oral contraceptives. Choices *B* and *D* are incorrect because the totality of the patient's symptoms indicates the need for more serious intervention than OTC medication.

55. D: Theophylline has a narrow therapeutic index and toxicity symptoms that include nausea and abdominal pain. Choice *A* is incorrect because the dosages listed for the three medications are reasonable and acceptable. Choice *B* is incorrect because the listed medications do not interact with the patient's implied conditions, asthma/COPD, Alzheimer's, and high blood pressure. Choice *C* is incorrect because none of these medications is known to interact with any of the others.

56. C: Noncompliance occurs when the patient fails to take their medication as prescribed. In addition to taking a smaller dose than prescribed, noncompliance may include discontinuing medication before the full course is taken, taking it at the wrong time of day, stopping medication use, and taking expired medications. Choice *A* is incorrect because drug-patient interaction is not a term; drug-patient precaution describes the possibility that medication is inappropriate for a patient based on their age, gender, allergies, pregnancy, or other factors. Choice *B* is incorrect because medication abuse involves using or overusing medication for an unintended purpose. Choice *D* is incorrect because the prescription was verified to be correct based on the patient's needs, but the patient is choosing to under-dose herself to make the medication last longer.

57. B: Refills on Schedule II substances like methylphenidate (Ritalin®) are prohibited. Choice *A* is incorrect because methylphenidate is prescribed to adults in 20-30 mg doses taken 2-3 times per day, usually not exceeding 60 mg per day. Choice *C* is incorrect because a psychiatrist is a medical specialist known to prescribe this medication. Choice *D* is incorrect because a one-month prescription of 3 tablets per day would require that 90 tablets be dispensed.

58. B: Immunization of staff is a component of personal care for disease prevention, which helps to control the spread of infection. Choice *A* is incorrect because infection control guidelines are intended to prevent the spread of disease within the staff and materials used in the pharmacy; they do not address medications dispensed to patients. Choice *C* is incorrect because infection control guidelines focus on pharmacy staff, not patients or customers. Choice *D* is incorrect because tools need not be disposable but should be cleaned regularly according to appropriate protocols.

59. A: The repeated requests of this patient for early refills indicate possible misuse of a commonly abused medication, clonazepam. This situation should be brought to the attention of the pharmacist whose responsibility is to conduct a Drug Utilization Review (DUR) and/or determine the appropriate next steps for managing the patient's case. Choice *B* is incorrect because it is the pharmacist's, not the pharmacy technician's, job to counsel patients on missed doses. Choice *C* is incorrect because the situation raises red flags that should be addressed with the pharmacist before proceeding. Choice *D* is incorrect because were formulary substitution be deemed appropriate, that would be a decision made by the pharmacist and possibly prescriber.

60. B: This choice describes the standard procedure for washing hands. Choice *A* is incorrect because handwashing procedure does not assume a person is wearing gloves; further, soap, not disinfectant should be used in step 3, and one should us a paper towel to turn off the tap. Choice *C* is incorrect because all jewelry should be removed, soap, not disinfectant should be used in step 3, and one should us a paper towel to turn off the tap. Choice *D* is incorrect because scrubbing should occur for 10-20 seconds, and a paper, not cloth towel should be used to turn off the tap.

61. D: The amount and type of PPE required depends on the materials being handled. Choice *A* is incorrect because the use of PPE significantly reduces but does not completely prevent the spread of infection. Choice *B* is incorrect because PPE does not eliminate the need for proper handwashing; hands should still be washed thoroughly and according to established guidelines before putting on PPE. Choice *C* is incorrect because PPE is generally disposable and should not be reused or shared.

62. A: A mask should be removed carefully to avoid contaminating the skin of the face or the airway. Choices *B* and *C* are incorrect because gloves should be removed and hands washed before removing a mask to avoid contaminating the face. Choice *D* is incorrect because N95 masks are certified to provide adequate protection against airborne particles but not against gas or vapor.

63. D: Sterilization is a high-level disinfectant. Choice *A* is incorrect because 3% hydrogen peroxide is a low-level disinfectant; a 6% hydrogen peroxide soak for 5 minutes is an intermediate-level disinfectant. Choice *B* is incorrect because an item must be boiled for at least 20 minutes to provide intermediate-level disinfection. Choice *C* is incorrect because household bleach is a low-level disinfectant.

64. D: Chapter *USP 797* in the USP National Formulary describes appropriate hygiene for pharmaceutical sterile preparations. Choice *A* is incorrect because *USP 797* only describes PPE necessary for sterile preparations. Choice *B* is incorrect because *USP 797* describes personnel hygiene, not cleaning of

161

equipment or products used in sterilization. Choice *C* is incorrect because *USP 797* does not describe infection control.

65. A: The laminar flow hood must be appropriately cleaned before each use. Choice *B* is incorrect because the hood should not be used to store items. Choice *C* is incorrect because the hood should run for 5-20 minutes before cleaning and at least 30 minutes before use. Choice *D* is incorrect because disinfectant should not be applied to the HEPA filter, as it can damage the filter.

66. B: Counting trays and spatulas should be cleaned at least once per day in hot, soapy water. Choice *A* is incorrect because the technician need not clean counting trays and spatulas in 70% ethanol. Choice *C* is incorrect because counting trays should be cleaned regularly, at least once per day, but they needn't be cleaned after each use. Choice *D* is incorrect because option c. is incorrect.

67. D: In addition to being swept with a broom or vacuum, the pharmacy floor should also be wet mopped daily with disinfectant. Choice *A* is incorrect because dispensing tools need only be rinsed. Choice *B* is incorrect because tightening medication caps is not a part of daily clean-up. Choice *C* is incorrect PPE is not explicitly required for cleaning the pharmacy.

68. A: Choice *A* describes the correct order staff should follow before creating sterile preparations. Choices *B, C,* and *D* are incorrect.

69. C: The incident report should be completed by the staff member who noticed the error. Choice *A* is incorrect because the report included all necessary information. Choice *B* is incorrect because MedWatch provides a voluntary online reporting form for medication errors. Choice *D* is incorrect because the wrong person made the report in this scenario.

70. A: Institute of Safe Medication Practices (ISMP) provides impartial, timely, and accurate drug safety information including "do not crush" lists, black box warnings, error-prone abbreviations lists, confused drug names lists, high alert medications, and tall man letters. Choice *B* is incorrect because MERP is the National Medication Errors Reporting Program, which provides information on errors, not specific information for dispensing. Choice *C* is incorrect because SERP is not an acronym affiliated with pharmacy practice. Choice *D* is incorrect because VERP is the Vaccine Errors Reporting Program, which is not related to prescription drugs.

71. C: The Food and Drug Administration's Adverse Event Reporting System (FAERS) includes all MedWatch-reported adverse effects and product integrity concerns; the data may be reviewed to detect trends in safety concerns. Choice *A* is incorrect because consumers are not required to report adverse effects but may report them to the prescriber and/or manufacturer. Choice *B* is incorrect because the Institute of Safe Medication Practices (ISMP) provides impartial, timely, and accurate drug safety information including "do not crush" lists, black box warnings, error-prone abbreviations lists, confused drug names lists, high alert medications, and tall man letters. Choice *D* is incorrect because the FDA requires manufacturers to forward to them any adverse drug effects reported by prescribers or consumers.

72. B: It is critical for the pharmacist to have relevant knowledge of materials, calculations, and methods as well as an appropriate environment and equipment. If these criteria cannot be met, the patient should be referred to a pharmacy capable of meeting them. Choice *A* is incorrect because aside from the fact that the equipment may take time to arrive, the pharmacy also lacks a designated space and proper resources for safe compounding. Choice *C* is incorrect because the prescriber ordered a compounded

product to meet the specific needs of the patient. Choice *D* is incorrect because equipment used in compounding must have specific characteristics to promote proper technique and avoid contamination.

73. A: Standard operating procedures (SOPs) including equipment maintenance are required documentation for a compounding pharmacy. Choice *B* is incorrect because ingredient records AND quantity/dose calculations used must be kept in records. Choice *C* is incorrect because compound records describe the process of compounding; master formulation records include the details of ingredients and preparation for the compounding procedure. Choice *D* is incorrect because records must be kept for a time specified by state law; they should be kept available at the pharmacy.

74. D: Weighing papers, wax papers, or measuring boats are important for weighing ingredients necessary for pharmaceutical compounding. Choice *A* is incorrect because graduated cylinders, not beakers are used to precisely measure liquids used in compounding. Choice *B* is incorrect because counting trays are used for dispensing, not compounding. Choice *C* is incorrect because ointment is a substance that might be compounded; ointment slabs and cream/ointment bases are equipment used in that process.

75. D: Materials used in compounding may be chemically reactive and hazardous, though special care should be taken to avoid contamination when handling such materials. Compounding materials are not produced by the FDA but are preferably produced in an FDA-registered manufacturing facility. Therefore, choices *A, B,* and *C* are incorrect.

76. C: Only one compound should be performed at a time to avoid errors and cross-contamination. Choice *A* is incorrect because admixtures should be analyzed to ensure that they will be absorbed properly, whether topically or systemically. Choice *B* is incorrect because orally-administered admixtures should be assessed to determine the effect of gastro-intestinal pH and hepatic (liver) metabolism on the bioavailability of the active ingredients. Choice *D* is incorrect because it is important to perform compounding in a designated, clean and sanitized area.

77. A: Nonsterile emulsions are thermodynamically unstable mixtures composed of at least two liquids that are immiscible—liquids that are insoluble in one another and do not mix easily. Choice *B* is incorrect because not all nonsterile compounded preparations are emulsions. Choice *C* is incorrect because nonsterile emulsions involve only liquids. Choice *D* is incorrect because the internal phase of an emulsion is the dispersed liquid, and the external phase is the medium which it is dispersed; these do not relate to the amounts of the two substances.

78. C: The suffix -phagia means eat. Choice *A* is incorrect because the suffix -algia means pain; the suffix -emia means blood condition. Choice *B* is incorrect because the suffix -itis means inflammation; the suffix -scopy means visual examination. Choice *D* is incorrect because the suffix -stomy means opening; the suffix -tomy means incision or cutting into.

79. C: NPO means nothing by mouth because PO (per os) means by way of mouth. Choice *A* is incorrect because EEG means electroencephalogram. Choice *B* is incorrect because HTN means hypertension or high blood pressure. Choice *D* is incorrect because RA means rheumatoid arthritis.

80. C: The abbreviations are interpreted as follows: mg – milligram, / – per, kg – kilogram, SQ (or SC) = subcutaneously, or under the skin; BID = twice daily. Therefore, choices *A, B,* and *D* are incorrect.

163

81. B: The abbreviation au means the medication should be administered in both ears; therefore, it is likely to be contained in a dropper bottle. Choices *A, C,* and *D* are incorrect because these containers don't facilitate delivery of medication into the ears.

82. C: Levigation is the use of water or another solvent to carry an insoluble drug powder through the compounding process. Choice *A* is incorrect because communition is the process of making a substance into small, fine particles. Choice *B* is incorrect because geometric dilution involves the mixing of two substances in uneven quantitates by starting with the smaller quantity. Choice *D* is incorrect because pulverization by intervention is used for powders that do not crush easily and is a process by which a solvent (usually an alcohol) is used to intervene in dissolving the powder.

83. B: Hem is a root word meaning blood. Choice *A* is incorrect because cardi is a root word meaning heart. Choice *C* is incorrect because hypo is a prefix meaning decreased. Choice *D* is incorrect because tachy is a prefix meaning fast.

84. B: The amber color provides light resistance that is particularly important for the more than 200 medications that are sensitive to light. Choice *A* is incorrect because the package may protect from physical damage, but the color is irrelevant to that purpose. Choice *C* is incorrect because the identifying information must be labeled on the container. Choice *D* is incorrect because counterfeit medication is a result of issues in the supply chain and is not impacted by the container in which medication is dispensed.

85. A: The Poison Prevention Packaging Act (PPPA) of 1970 requires all prescription medications and controlled substances to be dispensed in vials with child-resistant caps; however, medications dispensed and administered in inpatient environments are exempt to this legislation. Choices *B, C,* and *D* are incorrect because only select medications may be exceptions to this rule at the request of patients or physicians.

86. C: The FDA specifies 11 technologies capable of fulfilling the definition of tamper-evident packaging including blister and bubble packs; film wrappers; heat-shrunk wrappers or bands; bottles equipped with inner-mouth seals; plastic packs or paper foil; breakable cap-ring systems; sealed tubes; tape seals; plastic blind-end heat-sealed tubes; sealed cartons; all metal and composite cans; and aerosol containers. This list excludes the packaging listed in Choices *A, B,* and *D.*

87. D: One teaspoon is equal to 4.929 mL. Choice *A* is incorrect because one liquid ounce is equal to 29.57 mL. Choice *B* is incorrect because one pint is equal to 16 ounces. Choice *C* is incorrect because one tablespoon is equal to 14.79 mL.

88. D: Clark's Rule uses the body weight in pounds, which would be calculated as follows:

$$13,000 \text{ grams} \frac{1 \text{ kilogram}}{1,000 \text{ grams}} \times \frac{2.205 \text{ pounds}}{1 \text{ kilogram}} = 28.665 \text{ pounds}$$

Therefore, Choices *A, B,* and *C* are incorrect.

89. A: The prescription reads that 5 drops (gtt) should be delivered per day (qd) for 14 days. There are 20 drops in one mL of liquid, so:

$$\frac{5 \text{ drops}}{1 \text{ day}} \times \frac{1 \text{ mL}}{20 \text{ drops}} \times 14 \text{ days} = 3.5 \text{ mL}$$

Therefore, one 5 mL bottle would be needed to provide enough medicine for the full course. Choices *B*, *C*, and *D* are incorrect because they provide excess medication, which would result in waste.

90. A: The abbreviation ad means the medication is to be placed in the right ear. Choice *B* is incorrect because a medication to treat a condition of the eye would include either ou (both eyes), os (left eye), or od (right eye). Choice *C* is incorrect because drops for nasal congestion are most likely to be delivered nasally. Choice *D* is incorrect because drops administered for opioid addiction would likely be administered sublingually (sl).

Practice Test #2

1. Examples of stimulant medications include all of the following, *except*:
   a. methylphenidate
   b. venlafaxine
   c. dextroamphetamine
   d. lisdexamfetamine

2. _____, a common side effect of antipsychotic medication treatment, is characterized by rapid and involuntary movement of the face, lips, and tongue.
   a. paranoia
   b. akathisia
   c. tardive dyskinesia
   d. dystonia

3. Select the sequence that accurately reflects topical steroids listed in order from **least** to **most** potent.
   a. hydrocortisone → betamethasone → triamcinolone → fluticasone
   b. triamcinolone → fluticasone → betamethasone → hydrocortisone
   c. hydrocortisone → fluticasone → triamcinolone → betamethasone
   d. betamethasone → triamcinolone → fluticasone → hydrocortisone

4. A patient presents to the pharmacy with a prescription for Vistaril 25mg. The pharmacy has hydroxyzine hydrochloride tablets available. Can the prescription be filled as written with the available tablets?
   a. Yes. Vistaril is the brand name for hydroxyzine hydrochloride.
   b. Yes. A prescription for Vistaril can be filled with hydroxyzine hydrochloride tablets.
   c. No. A prescription for Vistaril must be filled with Vistaril only.
   d. No. A prescription for Vistaril should be filled with generic hydroxyzine pamoate if available.

5. Patients taking angiotensin-converting enzyme inhibitors should use caution with which of the following supplements? Select the best answer.
   a. sodium
   b. potassium
   c. magnesium
   d. calcium

6. Select the medication and indication combination that is *in*correct.
   a. Actos: acne
   b. Symbicort: Chronic Obstructive Pulmonary Disease
   c. Lasix: edema
   d. Propecia: male pattern baldness (alopecia)

7. The FDA has issued a black box warning to draw attention to the severe risks of oral contraceptive use in women ages 35 and up, and what?
    a. alcohol
    b. obesity
    c. cigarette smoking
    d. opioids

8. Foscarnet sodium, lamivudine, and maraviroc belong to what medication class?
    a. antipsychotics
    b. antivirals
    c. antimetabolites
    d. antibiotics

9. _____ is a chronic, progressive, obstructive airway disease characterized by coughing, wheezing, shortness of breath, *and* sputum production.
    a. Asthma
    b. Bronchitis
    c. Emphysema
    d. Chronic obstructive pulmonary disease (COPD)

10. Patients taking methotrexate (MTX) should be counseled to avoid what during MTX therapy and for six months after?
    a. folic acid
    b. acetaminophen
    c. calcium
    d. pregnancy

11. Each of the following clinical conditions requires the initiation of total parenteral nutrition therapy *except*:
    a. short bowel syndrome
    b. severe burns
    c. short-term colonic ileus
    d. severe malnutrition

12. What resource lists all FDA-approved drug products with therapeutic equivalence evaluations?
    a. The Purple Book
    b. The Orange Book
    c. The Blue Book
    d. The Pink Book

13. Patients with peptic ulcers or gastroesophageal reflux disease (GERD) should avoid _____ therapy.
    a. proton pump inhibitor (PPI)
    b. prokinetic agent
    c. non-steroidal anti-inflammatory drug (NSAID)
    d. histamine blocker

14. A patient calls the pharmacy to ask if it is appropriate to treat her young child's diarrhea with Pepto-Bismol. Which of the following statements is accurate regarding her concern?
   a. Bismuth subsalicylate is appropriate for use in children ages 6-12.
   b. Bismuth subsalicylate is appropriate for use in ages 2 - 12.
   c. Bismuth subsalicylate is appropriate for use in children ages 12+.
   d. Bismuth subsalicylate is appropriate for use in children of all ages.

15. A patient presents to the pharmacy with a prescription that reads: Ciprodex 7.5mL, IV GTT AD BID x 7d. Select the order string that accurately reflects the directions of the prescription.
   a. Ciprodex 7.5 mL bottle, instill 4 drops in right ear twice daily for seven days
   b. Ciprodex 7.5 mL bottle, instill 4 drops in right eye twice daily for one week
   c. Ciprodex 7.5 mL bottle, instill 4 drops in left ear twice daily for seven days
   d. Ciprofloxacin 7.5mL intravenously twice daily for seven days

16. Legend medications are drugs that require what?
   a. a written indication
   b. a prior authorization
   c. a generic substitution
   d. a prescription

17. Patients who take multiple medications are engaging in _____, a practice that occurs commonly in the _____ population and increases the risk of adverse events, drug-drug interactions, and drug-disease interactions.
   a. polypharmacology; pediatric
   b. polypharmacy; geriatric
   c. polypharmaceutics; pediatric
   d. polymedicine; geriatric

18. JP, a 43-year-old male, takes Ibuprofen 800mg orally at 4p.m. The half-life of his dose is estimated to be 2 hours. How many minutes must pass before 75% of the medication is eliminated?
   a. 60 minutes
   b. 180 minutes
   c. 240 minutes
   d. 120 minutes

19. Patients taking theophylline should use caution with which of the following antibiotics?
   a. ciprofloxacin
   b. doxycycline
   c. vancomycin
   d. clindamycin

20. What abbreviation would a doctor use to prescribe a medication to be administered under the tongue?
   a. ou
   b. po
   c. sl
   d. top

21. Select the choice that correctly lists an example drug from the hormone class with the condition it treats.
    a. Estradiol treats postmenopausal symptoms.
    b. Levothyroxine treats hyperthyroidism.
    c. Ondansetron treats menstrual disorders.
    d. Raloxifene treats osteoporosis.

22. Patients on which of the following medications should avoid drinking grapefruit juice?
    a. Pramipexole
    b. Pravastatin
    c. Pregabalin
    d. Propranolol

23. What is the active ingredient in Xarelto®?
    a. Cetirizine
    b. Latanoprost
    c. Lisinopril
    d. Rivaroxaban

24. Medications with the suffix -lol belong to which drug class?
    a. Antibiotic
    b. Beta-blocker
    c. Protein pump inhibitor
    d. Vasodilator

25. Medication directions that include the abbreviation qd indicate that the medication should be taken:
    a. As needed
    b. Daily
    c. Every other day
    d. Twice a day

26. What are angiotensin receptor blockers used to treat?
    a. Asthma
    b. A blood clot
    c. Hyperlipidemia
    d. Hypertension

27. What is common side effect of ACE inhibitors?
    a. Bradycardia
    b. Chronic dry cough
    c. Edema
    d. Hypertension

28. Which of the following options accurately describes a known drug-drug interaction?
    a. Naproxen can decrease the effects of warfarin.
    b. Tetracycline can increase the effect of Yasmin.
    c. Vardenafil can increase the effect of nitroglycerin.
    d. Warfarin can decrease the effect of ampicillin.

29. Which nervous system medication class is likely to be prescribed as a short-term treatment for someone experiencing alcohol withdrawal?
    a. Antidepressant
    b. Antipsychotic
    c. Benzodiazepine
    d. Stimulant

30. Medications with the same moiety that are formulated as different complexes and thus may have different strengths are described as what?
    a. Bioalternatives
    b. Bioequivalents
    c. Pharmaceutical alternatives
    d. Pharmaceutical equivalents

31. Which pharmaceutical dosage form is necessary for IM administration?
    a. Capsule
    b. Liquid
    c. Suppository
    d. Tablet

32. An individual's nasal culture has resulted as positive for influenza. Which class of medication is the doctor likely to prescribe?
    a. Antibiotic
    b. Antimetabolite
    c. Antiviral
    d. Steroid

33. A patient's medical history should include which information?

    I. Prescription medications taken
    II. OTC drugs and dietary supplements taken
    III. Allergies to foods

    a. I only
    b. I and II only
    c. I and III only
    d. I, II, and III

34. What part of a prescription is called the inscription?
    a. Instructions to the pharmacist filling the prescription
    b. Name, strength, dosage form, and quantity of medication
    c. Patient's name, contact information, and medical history
    d. Prescriber's name, title, and contact information.

35. A prescription for amitriptyline contains the following details. Identify the information which would indicate an error on the prescription.

      I. Intramuscular injections
      II. 400 mg per day
      III. Administered twice daily

    a. I only
    b. II only
    c. III only
    d. I, II, and III

36. Standard parameters for medication storage include a range of temperatures. Select the choice that correctly pairs a temperature with the corresponding standard parameter for medication storage.
    a. Cold, 40°F
    b. Cool, 45°F
    c. Freezer, 13°F
    d. Warm, 78°F

37. Your pharmacy plans to advertise a drug take-back event. What should patrons be encouraged to do before surrendering their medications?
    a. Destroy identifying information on the container.
    b. Flush all liquid medications down the toilet.
    c. Mix medications with coffee grounds or cat litter.
    d. Register their contact information with the DEA.

38. What does the term reverse distributor refer to?
    a. A company who collects and appropriately disposes of hazardous waste.
    b. A pharmacy or pharmacist that sells unused drugs to the manufacturer.
    c. A private firm that dispenses unexpired medications from a pharmacy at a discount.
    d. A third-party that facilitates the granting of credits for controlled substances.

39. Proper risk management involves which of the following inventory storage practices?
    a. Storage of all insulin brands together in a single location
    b. Storage of internal and external medications in separate locations
    c. Storage of similar-looking drugs in areas near each other
    d. Storage of volatile substances in a sealed, protective outer bag

40. A prescription is written as "Lorazepam, 2.0mg tablet, 1 tablet TID, disp#90." What error did the prescriber make in writing this prescription?
    a. Lorazepam does not exist in tablet form.
    b. The prescriber wrote the strength incorrectly.
    c. The dose exceeds the daily maximum for lorazepam.
    d. There are no errors in this prescription.

41. What additional oversight is required of patients taking thalidomide?
    a. Pregnancy testing
    b. Tracking neutrophil counts
    c. Two types of birth control
    d. Use of the iPledge system

42. According to the Combat Methamphetamine Epidemic Act, what restrictions are placed on drug purchases?
    a. The date and time of sale must be recorded when purchasing sertraline.
    b. No more than 9 grams of phenylephrine may be purchased in a thirty-day period.
    c. Phenylpropanolamine must be kept behind the pharmacy counter or in a locked cabinet.
    d. State or federal identification is necessary to purchase cetirizine or loratadine.

43. Which of the following is true about **Risk Evaluation and Mitigation Strategy (REMS)**?
    a. REMS include requirements for prescriber, patient, and pharmacy for safe use.
    b. REMS may be necessary for drugs for which adverse effects are unknown.
    c. The FDA is responsible for developing and implementing REMS for relevant drugs.
    d. The iPledge program is an example of a REMS for medications that contain thalidomide.

44. Fifteen people taking the same dietary supplement have recently suffered heart attacks with no other apparent risk factors. Which Class of recall would this qualify for under MedWatch?
    a. Class I
    b. Class II
    c. Class III
    d. Class IV

45. What is the pharmacy's responsibility upon being notified of an FDA market recall?
    a. Instruct affected patients to destroy the recalled product.
    b. Notify prescribers that the product has been recalled.
    c. Record the names and addresses of patients affected.
    d. Return remaining stock of the recalled product to the FDA.

46. What government agency was formed to oversee the safety of prescription and OTC medications?
    a. CSA
    b. DEA
    c. EPA
    d. FDA

47. What accurately describes risk management?

    I. Occurs only after a mistake has been made
    II. Involves quality control, assurance, and improvement
    III. Is an ongoing process requiring updates

    a. I and II
    b. I and III
    c. II and III
    d. I, II, and III

48. Which legislation was enacted to protect supply chains and minimize the distribution of counterfeit medications?
    a. CMEA
    b. CSA
    c. DSCSA
    d. FD & C

49. Which action is included in a root cause analysis?
    a. Identify causal pathways for medication errors.
    b. Penalize the individual(s) responsible for the error.
    c. Select an individual to conduct the investigation.
    d. Submit the corrective action plan to MedWatch.

50. A patient calls the pharmacy after picking up a new prescription. Based on the bottle directions, she is unable to determine how many tablets she should take each day. What type of error is this?
    a. A medication dispensing error
    b. A near miss error
    c. A noncompliance error
    d. An adverse effect error

51. Which situations are likely to increase medication dispensing errors in a pharmacy?

    I. Frequent phone calls to the pharmacy
    II. High turnover in staffing
    III. Staff frequently working overtime

    a. I and II
    b. II and III
    c. I and III
    d. I, II, and III

52. Identify the situation which would prevent you from refilling a prescription.
    a. Refill a medication for which a practitioner changed dosage
    b. Refill a prescription that is greater than one month old
    c. Refill a Schedule II substance for second time in two months
    d. Refill a Schedule IV substance for the fifth time in six months

53. What strategy is effective in identifying the majority of dispensing errors?
    a. Pharmacist to patient counseling sessions
    b. Prescription confirmation with practitioner
    c. Proper storage of sound-alike medications
    d. Providing sufficient work breaks for staff

54. A prescriber sends the following electronic prescription to the pharmacy: Neurontin, 300 mg, Sig: 1 cap po, #90. What information is missing?
    a. Dosage form
    b. Frequency of administration
    c. Route of administration
    d. Strength

173

55. A physician sends a prescription without indicating the number of refills required. How should you proceed?
    a. Ask the pharmacist to clarify.
    b. Assume no refills are permitted.
    c. Contact the prescriber.
    d. Refer to the ISMP guidelines.

56. The pharmacist asks you to compare a medication label he dispensed with the original prescription. The prescription reads Latanoprost .005%, 2.5 mL bottle, Sig: 1 drop ou qd hs. The pharmacist dispenses a 2.5 mL bottle of 0.005% Latanoprost with directions to place one drop in each ear every day at bedtime. In what portion of the prescription did the pharmacist make an error?
    a. Frequency of administration
    b. Dosage form
    c. Route of administration
    d. Strength of medication

57. A prescription medication order list labeled ASAP, which means it must be filled
    a. At regularly scheduled intervals
    b. Quickly, but not necessarily within 15 minutes
    c. When the patient requests the medication
    d. Within 15 minutes of receipt

58. What is an example of off label use?
    a. Formulary substitution to a less expensive, generic equivalent form
    b. Prescription of medication for a condition other than what it was approved for
    c. Misuse or overuse of narcotics beyond therapeutic levels with a goal to get high
    d. Noncompliance by a patient who chooses to discontinue use due to side effects

59. What is an identified best practice for the use of gloves to prevent contamination and infection?
    a. Gloves should be changed after contact with contaminated items.
    b. Gloves should be rated N-95 or higher by regulatory board standards.
    c. Gloves should be removed quickly to prevent skin contamination.
    d. Gloves should be washed before being removed from hands.

60. A patient calls the pharmacy after missing a dose of her oral contraceptives. How should you proceed?
    a. Consult with the pharmacist.
    b. Counsel her on the recommendations.
    c. Instruct her to call her physician.
    d. Refer her to the manufacturer.

61. A pharmacist licensed and trained to administer vaccines would also be able to

      I. Counsel patients on vaccination schedules
      II. Educate patients on potential vaccine side effects
      III. Treat patients' adverse reactions to vaccinations

    a. I and II
    b. I and III
    c. II and III
    d. I, II, and III

62. Which of the following is a common dispensing error?
    a. Adding zeroes before decimal points
    b. Confusing the abbreviation od for qd
    c. Including commas in large dose values
    d. Mistaking "u" (units) for zero in a number

63. What is one indication that a prescription may be forged?
    a. Abbreviations or codes used in place of longhand
    b. Handwritten prescriptions written in ink
    c. Incorrect dosing for a particular medication
    d. Refills requested on Schedule III medications

64. Adulterated products, counterfeit products, and misbranded products should all be reported to MedWatch as:
    a. Adverse effects
    b. Drug-drug interactions
    c. Medication errors
    d. Product integrity concerns

65. A prescription labeled PRN indicates
    a. Patient must take medication orally.
    b. Patient must take medication at set intervals.
    c. Patient may request medication at any time.
    d. Patient may request medication within set parameters.

66. Which of these is a high-alert medication?
    a. Ephedrine
    b. Lansoprazole
    c. Midazolam
    d. Propranolol

67. Common antimicrobial agents used in hand washing include
    a. Alcohol (60%)
    b. Chlorhexidine (10%)
    c. Hydrogen peroxide
    d. Iodine compounds

68. Biaxin-XL is the brand-name of a slow-release tablet with the active ingredient clarithromycin. Which special considerations should be made for dispensing this medication?
    a. Do not crush warning
    b. High-alert medication
    c. Both a. and b.
    d. Neither a. nor b.

69. What type of information is reported using VAERS?
    a. Certification to administer vaccines
    b. Failure to follow vaccine schedules
    c. Inappropriate use of vaccines
    d. Patients' reactions to vaccines

70. Which of the following is true about a DUR?
    a. A DUR is typically performed by a pharmacy technician.
    b. A formulary substitution is an example of a DUR conflict.
    c. The need for a DUR is usually not detected by pharmacy software.
    d. The patient's address is a critical piece of data for a DUR.

71. What is the proper sequence for cleaning the laminar flow hood?

    1. Remove items that don't belong in the hood
    2. Spray internal surfaces with disinfectant
    3. Turn the hood on and allow it to run
    4. Allow the hood to dry
    5. Clean with sterile wipes
    6. Dress in personal protective equipment

    a. 1, 3, 6, 2, 4, 5
    b. 3, 6, 1, 5, 2, 4
    c. 5, 1, 6, 2, 4, 3
    d. 6, 3, 1, 2, 5, 4

72. Insulin should be stored at a temperature between 36°F and 46°F. Which of the following readings on a Celsius thermometer would be a proper temperature for storing insulin?
    a. -8 °C
    b. -2 °C
    c. +6 °C
    d. +10 °C

73. Which age-based dose calculation rule is best used to calculate the dose of a medication for an 8-month-old child?
    a. Clark's Rule
    b. Dilling 's Rule
    c. Fried's Rule
    d. Young's Rule

74. Which option below lists the correct child dose for a 7-year-old using Young's Rule and an adult dose of 300 mg?
- a. 6.73 mg
- b. 105 mg
- c. 110.5 mg
- d. 168 mg

75. The adult dose of diazepam is 10 mg. What is the correct dose for a 9-month-old child?
- a. 0.050 mg
- b. 0.375 mg
- c. 0.588 mg
- d. 0.600 mg

76. Based on an adult dose of 200 mg, what is the correct dose of docusate for a 12-year-old child with height of 150 cm and weight of 40 kg and what formula was used to calculate it?
- a. 1.29 mg, as calculated by body surface area
- b. 117.6 mg, as calculated by body weight
- c. 53.3 mg, as calculated by Clark's Rule
- d. 73.7 mg, as calculated by Dilling 's Rule

77. A vancomycin prescription is written as 10mg/kg/dose slowly IV for a pediatric patient weighing 18.6 kg. What quantity of vancomycin should the patient receive in each dose?
- a. 1.86 mg
- b. 1.86 mL
- c. 186 mg
- d. 186 mL

78. An adult cardiac patient is prescribed a liquid suspension of furosemide in a dose of 60 mg. The pharmacy is supplied an oral solution in the concentration of 40mg/5mL. What volume should the patient be prescribed for each dose?
- a. 3.33 mL
- b. 7.5 mL
- c. 10 mL
- d. 480 mL

79. A 100 milliliter bag of normal saline solution includes 0.9 grams of sodium chloride. What are the type of ratio, proper units, and percentage for this solution?
- a. V/V, mL/g, 111%
- b. V/W, mL/g 0.111%
- c. W/W, g/mL, 0.009%
- d. W/V, g/mL 0.9%

80. Calculate the days supply for a prescription written as sumatriptan 50 mg #16 i tab PO PRN at first sign of migraine aura; may repeat i tab once, not to exceed ii tab in 24 hours.
- a. 4 days
- b. 8 days
- c. 16 days
- d. 30 days

81. The pharmacy has a policy to pull unclaimed medications after 14 days and reverse the insurance claim on the medication. What term describes this process?
   a. Nondispensable medication
   b. Patient non-compliance
   c. Return to stock
   d. Reverse distribution

82. The pharmacy receives a prescription for Basaglar® (insulin glargine) written as 20 mL 60 units SC daily at bedtime. Calculate the days supply.
   a. 3 days
   b. 12 days
   c. 33 days
   d. 100 days

83. Ciprodex® is dispensed in a 7.5 mL bottle. Is one bottle enough for a 7-day prescription written as 4 gtt au bid?
   a. Yes, with 2 days supply remaining in the bottle
   b. Yes, with 9 days supply remaining in the bottle
   c. Yes, with 18 days supply remaining in the bottle
   d. No; two bottles should be dispensed

84. A patient is prescribed atorvastatin 10 mg tabs #60 ii tab daily PO with 3 refills. The patient's insurance plan has a 32-day supply limitation. Calculate the number of fills and short fills.
   a. 2 fills and a short fill of 45 tablets
   b. 2 fills and a short fill of 48 tablets
   c. 3 fills and a short fill of 45 tablets
   d. 3 fills and a short fill of 48 tablets

85. Because of their insurance's supply limitations, a patient's third prescription refill has a short-fill of 15 tablets. As the pharmacy technician, how should you proceed?
   a. Dispense the full amount and bill the insurance for the 15 tablets.
   b. Consult with the insurance company for guidance.
   c. Reduce the quantity dispensed by 15 tablets.
   d. Refuse to refill the prescription.

86. A nurse is given a bubble pack with multiple medications for a single patient in each compartment, arranged by day of the week. What type of unit dose system is this?
   a. Ampule unit dose
   b. Blended unit dose
   c. Daily unit dose
   d. Modified unit dose

87. The NDC for amitriptyline hydrochloride is 0832-1222-11. What do you know about this medication?
   a. The number 1222 refers to the drug's dosage form.
   b. The number 11 refers to the drug manufacturer.
   c. The number 0832 refers to the number of pills in the container.
   d. The number 0832-1222-11 refers to the lot number.

88. Choose the option that correctly pairs the type of automated dispensing system with one of its advantages or disadvantages.
    a. Centralized distribution systems cannot stock all dosage forms.
    b. Centralized distribution systems require no hand delivery.
    c. Decentralized distribution systems create longer wait times for medications.
    d. Decentralized distribution systems increase risk of narcotics diversion.

89. A drug recall

    I. May only be initiated by the FDA.
    II. Affects all pharmacies that have the medication in stock.
    III. Notice is first sent to prescribing physicians.

    a. One of these is true.
    b. Two of these are true.
    c. All of these are true.
    d. None of these is true.

90. Which is a characteristic of a medication that qualifies as hazardous waste?
    a. A pH between 2 and 12.5
    b. Active ingredient is pure grade
    c. High LD50 (lethal dose)
    d. Only one active ingredient

Answer Explanations #2

1. B: venlafaxine. Venlafaxine is a serotonin and norepinephrine reuptake inhibitor used to treat depression, not a stimulant. The correct answer choice is B. Answer choices A - methylphenidate, C – dextroamphetamine, and D – lisdexamfetamine are stimulants.

2. C: tardive dyskinesia. Answer choice A, paranoia, describes feelings of suspicion or mistrust of others and anxiety. Choice B, akathisia, is characterized by restlessness and an inability to remain still. Dystonia – answer choice D – is a movement disorder that causes uncontrollable muscle contraction; however, these movements are usually slower and present as unnatural postural changes. The correct answer is C, tardive dyskinesia.

3. C: hydrocortisone → fluticasone → triamcinolone → betamethasone. Hydrocortisone is the lowest potency of the topical steroids listed, a class 7 topical steroid. Fluticasone is mid potency, class 5. Triamcinolone is mid-potency, class 4. Finally, betamethasone is the highest potency, class 1. Answer choice C accurately reflects topical steroids listed in order of potency from least to most potent. Answer choices A, B, and D are incorrect.

4. D: A prescription for Vistaril should be filled with generic hydroxyzine pamoate if available. Answer choice A is incorrect because Vistaril is the brand name for hydroxyzine pamoate, not hydroxyzine hydrochloride. Choice B is incorrect because Vistaril should not be filled with hydroxyzine hydrochloride, as they are not the same medications. Choice C is also incorrect as a prescription with Vistaril is not required to be filled with Vistaril only. The correct answer is D. Vistaril is the brand name for hydroxyzine pamoate and can be filled generically with hydroxyzine pamoate as such.

5. B: potassium. Hyperkalemia is a common side effect of angiotensin-converting enzyme (ACE) inhibitors and caution should be used with potassium supplement and ACE inhibitor therapy. Answer choice A, sodium, is affected by ACE Inhibitor therapy but to a lesser degree than potassium. Therefore, it is not the best answer. Choices C and D, magnesium, and calcium, respectively, have not been shown to interact with ACE Inhibitor therapy. The best answer is choice B.

6. A: Actos: acne. Answer choice A, Actos, is indicated to treat type II diabetes mellitus not, acne, and is thus incorrectly paired. Choice B, Symbicort, is indicated to treat asthma and chronic obstructive pulmonary disease (COPD); it is correctly paired. Choice C, Lasix, is indicated to treat edema, hypertension, and pulmonary edema and is correctly paired. Choice D, Propecia, is indicated to treat benign prostatic hyperplasia and male pattern alopecia and is correctly paired.

7. C: cigarette smoking. Oral contraceptive use with cigarette smoking increases the risk of cardiovascular disease in women ages 35 and up who smoke. Women over the age of 35 who smoke should not use oral contraceptives. There is no FDA black box warning with oral contraceptive use and alcohol, obesity, or opioids. Answer choices A, B, and D are incorrect.

8. B: Antivirals. Foscarnet sodium is an antiviral indicated to treat AIDS-induced cytomegaloviral retinitis and herpes simplex. Lamivudine is an antiretroviral indicated to HIV infection and chronic type B hepatitis. Maraviroc is an antiretroviral indicated to treat HIV infection. Each medication listed belongs to the antiviral class. Answer choices A, C, and D are incorrect.

9. D: Chronic Obstructive Pulmonary Disease (COPD). Answer choice A, asthma, is a chronic lung disease in which airways narrow, causing difficulty breathing; however, it differs from COPD markedly in nature as COPD progressively worsens over time. Choice B, bronchitis, describes inflammation of the smooth lining of the bronchial tubes. Choice C, emphysema, is a lung condition in which air sacs in the lungs are damaged. Choices *B* and *C* can cause breathing difficulties in patients with COPD; however, COPD is defined as a chronic, progressive, obstructive airway disease characterized by coughing, wheezing, shortness of breath, *and* sputum production. The correct answer is choice D.

10. D: pregnancy. Patients taking methotrexate (MTX) should avoid pregnancy during MTX therapy and for six months after, as it is an abortifacient and has teratogenic effects. The correct answer choice is D. Answer choice A, folic acid, is incorrect, as folic acid should be taken with methotrexate to replenish the folic acid loss that occurs with methotrexate. Choice B, acetaminophen, has no interaction with methotrexate and is therefore incorrect. Choice C, calcium, also has no interaction with MTX and is incorrect.

11. C: short-term colonic ileus. Parenteral nutrition therapy should not be initiated when it is not anticipated to be used for longer than three days. Short-term colonic ileus is a condition usually resolved within 1-3 days; therefore, short-term colonic ileus does not require parenteral nutrition therapy. The correct answer choice is C. Answer choices A, B, and D, short bowel syndrome, severe burns, and severe malnutrition, respectively, all require total parenteral nutrition therapy.

12. B: The Orange Book. The Orange Book, officially named *Approved Drug Products with Therapeutic Equivalence Evaluation*, identifies FDA-approved drug products with patent and therapeutic equivalence evaluation information. The correct answer is B. Answer choice A, The Purple Book, provides information about FDA-approved biologic products. Choice C, the Blue Book, provides medication price information. Choice D, The Pink Book, provides information on vaccine-preventable diseases.

13. C: non-steroidal anti-inflammatory drug (NSAID) therapy. NSAID therapy can exacerbate gastroesophageal reflux disease (GERD) and peptic ulcer symptoms and should be avoided in patients with either condition. Answer choice C is correct. Proton pump inhibitors, prokinetic agents, and histamine blockers – answer choices A, B, and D, respectively – are treatment options for GERD and are thus incorrect.

14. C: Bismuth subsalicylate is appropriate for use in children ages 12+. Patients younger than 12 should not take bismuth subsalicylate, the active ingredient in Pepto Bismol, as its use is associated with Reye's Syndrome, a rare but fatal disease if not treated. Answer choices A, B, and D indicate that it is safe for patients younger than 12 to ingest bismuth subsalicylate and are therefore incorrect.

15. A: Ciprodex 7.5 mL bottle, instill 4 drops in right ear twice daily for seven days. The abbreviations in the prescription are translated as follows: IV – four, GTT – drops, AD – right ear, BID – twice daily, 7d = 7 days. Answer choice A correctly reflects the prescription as written. Choice B is incorrect as AD is translated to right eye; the abbreviation for right eye is OD. Choice C is incorrect as AD is translated to left ear; the abbreviation for left ear is AS. Choice D is incorrect as IV is incorrectly translated as intravenously, and the abbreviations AD and GTT are not represented in the directions.

16. D: a prescription. Legend drugs require a prescription. The correct answer choice is D. Answer choice A, written indication, is incorrect. Choices *B* and *C*, prior authorization, and generic substitution, respectively, are also incorrect.

181

17. B: polypharmacy; geriatric. Polypharmacy occurs when patients take multiple medications, generally more than five. Polypharmacy commonly occurs in the elderly population. The correct answer choice is B. Answer choice A, polypharmagoloy; pediatric, is incorrect. Answer choice C, polypharmaceutics; pediatric, is incorrect. Choice D, polymedicine; geriatric, is also incorrect.

18. C: 240 minutes. A medication's half-life represents the amount of time it takes the body to eliminate 50% of the medication. In this instance, approximately 50% of the ibuprofen circulating in JP's body is eliminated after 2 hours (120 minutes). This means after 120 minutes, the amount of ibuprofen circulating in JP's body is halved to 400mg. After 4 hours, the amount of medication circulating in JP's body is halved again to 200mg, meaning approximately 75% (600mg) of the medication has been cleared. Answer C is the correct answer. Answers A, B, and D are incorrect.

19. A: ciprofloxacin. Concurrent administration of ciprofloxacin and theophylline may lead to toxic plasma elevations of theophylline. The correct answer choice is A. Choice B, doxycycline, has not been shown to interact with theophylline. Choice C, vancomycin, has no documented interaction with theophylline. Choice D, clindamycin, has also not been proven to interact with theophylline. Choices B, C, and D are incorrect.

20. C: The abbreviation sl means that a medication is to be administered sublingually, or under the tongue. Choice A is incorrect because the abbreviation ou means the medication is administered in both eyes. Choice B is incorrect because the abbreviation po means the medication is administered orally or by mouth. Choice D is incorrect because the abbreviation top means the medication is administered topically, or applied to the skin.

21. A: Estradiol is a hormone that is used to treat postmenopausal symptoms. Choice B is incorrect because levothyroxine is a hormone used to treat hypothyroidism. Choice C is incorrect because ondansetron is an antiemetic used to treat nausea and vomiting. Choice D is incorrect because raloxifene is an estrogen modulator used to treat osteoporosis.

22. B: Pravastatin is a statin used to treat hyperlipidemia, and statins can negatively interact with grapefruit juice. Grapefruits and their juice decrease statin metabolism, causing them to accumulate in the body, which can result in muscle or liver damage. Choice A is incorrect because pramipexole is a dopamine agonist; it does not interact with grapefruit juice. Choice C is incorrect because pregabalin is an anticonvulsant; it does not interact with grapefruit juice. Choice D is incorrect because propranolol is a beta-blocker; it does not interact with grapefruit juice.

23. D: Rivaroxaban is the active ingredient in the brand-name blood thinner Xarelto®. Choice A is incorrect because cetirizine is the active ingredient the antihistamine Zyrtec®. Choice B is incorrect because latanoprost is the active ingredient in the anti-glaucoma medication Xalatan®. Choice C is incorrect because lisinopril is the active ingredient in the ACE inhibitor Zestril®.

24. B: Beta blockers including atenolol, propranolol, metoprolol, carvedilol, and nebivolol. Choices A, C, and D are incorrect because medications in those categories do not end in -lol. Antibiotics (Choice A) have a variety of suffixes. Protein pump inhibitors (Choice C) commonly end in the suffix -ole. Vasodilators (Choice D) end in the suffix -fil.

25. B: The abbreviation qd means every day, or daily. Choice A is incorrect because prn is the abbreviation for as needed. Choice C is incorrect because qod is the abbreviation for every other day. Choice D is incorrect because bid is the abbreviation for twice a day.

26. D: Angiotensin receptor blockers (ARB) are used to treat hypertension by relaxing the veins and arteries to facilitate blood flow. Choice *A* is incorrect because asthma is treated with anti-inflammatories, steroids, and bronchodilators. Choice *B* is incorrect because blood clots are treated with blood thinners. Choice *C* is incorrect because hyperlipidemia is treated with statins.

27. B: ACE Inhibitors (ACEIs), or angiotensin-converting enzyme inhibitors are a class of drugs used to treat hypertension (high blood pressure) and cardiovascular disease. Their most common side effect is a chronic dry cough; other side effects include low blood pressure (hypotension), dizziness, fatigue, headache, and elevated blood potassium levels (hyperkalemia). Bradycardia (choice *A*), edema, or swelling (choice *C*), and hypertension (choice *D*) are not frequent side effects of ACEIs.

28. C: Vardenafil, an erectile dysfunction drug, can enhance the vasodilator effect of nitroglycerin, which can cause an irreversible drop in blood pressure and possible fatality. Choice *A* is incorrect because the NSAID naproxen can increase the blood-thinning effects of warfarin. Choice *B* is incorrect because antibiotics like tetracycline can decrease the efficacy of oral contraceptives like Yasmin. Choice *D* is incorrect because there is no known effect of the blood thinner warfarin on antibiotics like ampicillin.

29. C: Benzodiazepines are used to treat alcohol withdrawal, as well as a short-term treatment of anxiety; they have significant risk for physical dependence. Choice *A* is incorrect because antidepressants are used to treat mood disorders; while they may be paired with benzodiazepines, they are not directly used for people experiencing alcohol withdrawal. Choice *B* is incorrect because antipsychotics are used to treat psychoses, like schizophrenia and bipolar disorder. Choice *D* is incorrect because stimulants are used to treat attention-deficit hyperactivity disorder (ADHD) as well as cardiac arrest and shock emergencies.

30. C: Pharmaceutical alternatives have the same therapeutic structure (moiety) but are formulated as different salts, esters, or complexes. These include different dosage forms and strengths of a single medication (e.g., standard vs. extended release). Choice *A* is incorrect because bioalternatives are not a type of therapeutic equivalence. Choice *B* is incorrect because bioequivalents are pharmaceutically-comparable products with identical rates of and extent of absorption. Choice *D* is incorrect because pharmaceutical equivalents have the same active ingredients in the same dosage form and same route of administration; they have equal strength.

31. B: IM stands for intramuscular administration; to be administered into a muscle, the dosage form must be a liquid. Choices *A* and *D* are incorrect because capsules and tablets are solid dosage forms; they cannot be injected into muscle. Choice *C* is incorrect because suppositories are also solid dosage forms, which are inserted into body cavities.

32. C: Influenza is caused by a virus; antivirals either halt replication of or block the function of viruses. Choice *A* is incorrect because antibiotics are used to treat bacterial infections; they are not effective against viruses. Choice *B* is incorrect because antimetabolites are used to suppress abnormal cell growth and immune system function. Choice *D* is incorrect because steroids are used to treat issues related to inflammation and swelling.

33. D: All of this information is helpful in determining risks that certain medications may pose for the patient. Additionally, the patient's medical history should include medical conditions, patient's prescription compliance, allergies to substances and medications, as well as previously noted drug interactions.

34. B: This information is called the inscription of the prescription. Choice *A* is incorrect; it describes the subscription. Choice *C* is incorrect; it describes the patient information. Choice *D* is incorrect; it describes the prescriber information.

35. B: Amitriptyline dose should not exceed 300 mg per day. Choice *A* is incorrect because amitriptyline may be administered as oral tablets or intramuscular injections. Choice *C* is incorrect because amitriptyline may be taken once, twice, or three times daily. Choice *D* is incorrect because options I and III would not be apparent errors on a prescription for amitriptyline.

36. A: Cold temperatures are those that do not exceed 46 °F; 40°F is less than that. Choice *B* is incorrect because 45°F is below the standard for cool temperature, which is between 46° and 59 °F. Choice *C* is incorrect because 13°F is greater than the freezer standard, which is between -13° and -14° F. Choice *D* is incorrect because 78°F is below the standard warm temperature range, which is between 86° and 104 °F.

37. A: Labels on medications should be removed or made illegible before disposal; no personal information is necessary for the process. Choice *B* is incorrect because no medications should be flushed down the toilet, unless specified on the label. Choice *C* is incorrect because medications need only be mixed with coffee grounds or cat litter if being disposed of in the trash; this step is unnecessary when the drugs will be handled by a pharmaceutical waste management organization. Choice *D* is incorrect because personal information is not required to return substances in a take-back program.

38. D: A reverse distributor registered with the DEA evaluates unused or expired controlled substances transferred from a pharmacy to determine if credit may be granted. Choice *A* is incorrect because reverse distributors may dispose of controlled substances if necessary, but not other forms of hazardous wastes. Choice *B* is incorrect because reverse distributors act as a go-between between pharmacies and manufacturers. Choice *C* is incorrect because reverse distributors do not dispense medications.

39. B: Internal and external medications should be stored separately. Choice *A* is incorrect because all insulin brands should be stored separately. Choice *C* is incorrect because look-alike and sound-alike drugs should be stored in different areas. Choice *D* is incorrect because volatile substances should be stored in cool, well-ventilated areas; oncology medications should be stored in sealed, protective outer bags to prevent leakage.

40. B: Prescribers must not use trailing zeros after decimal points (e.g., 2.0mg) or leading zeros before decimal points, as this increases the potential for dosage errors. Choice *A* is incorrect because lorazepam exists both as a table and an injection. Choice *C* is incorrect because the daily dose prescribed is 6mg per day, which is the maximum for lorazepam. Choice *D* is incorrect because there is an error in the way the strength is written.

41. A: The S.T.E.P.S (System for Thalidomide Education and Prescribing Safety) program requires mandatory counseling, pregnancy testing, and registration. Choice *B* is incorrect because patients' white blood cell counts and absolute neutrophil counts must be tracked when taking clozapine. Choices *C and D* are incorrect because the iPledge system, as well as pregnancy testing and two forms of birth control are required in patients taking isotretinoin.

42. C: The Federal Combat Methamphetamine Epidemic Act regulates the sale of products containing ephedrine, pseudoephedrine, and phenylpropanolamine; they must be kept behind the pharmacy counter or in a locked cabinet. Choice *A* is incorrect because that information is not required for the sale

of sertraline; however, the pharmacy must record the customer's name, address, date and time of sale, product name, quantity sold, and signature when selling products containing ephedrine, pseudoephedrine, and phenylpropanolamine. Choice *B* is incorrect because the sale of phenylephrine is not limited; however, the purchase of products containing ephedrine, pseudoephedrine, and phenylpropanolamine is limited to 3.6 grams per day and no more than 9 grams in a thirty-day period. Choice *D* is incorrect because identification is not necessary to buy cetirizine or loratadine; however, it is necessary to purchase products containing ephedrine, pseudoephedrine, and phenylpropanolamine.

43. A: REMS may be required by the FDA for medications with serious risks that may outweigh benefits and include requirements for prescriber, patient, and pharmacy to support safe and effective use. Choice *B* is incorrect because a REMS is used for medications with known, serious risks. Choice *C* is incorrect because the drug manufacturer is responsible for developing and implementing REMS for drugs, as required by the FDA. Choice *D* is incorrect because the iPledge program is an example of a REMS for medications that contain isotretinoin.

44. A: Class I recalls are the most serious and involve substances or devices that cause serious adverse health conditions or death. Choice *B* is incorrect because Class II recalls involve substances or devices that cause temporary health problems but are unlikely to be linked to a serious health condition, such as a heart attack. Choice *C* is incorrect because Class III recalls involve substances or devices that violated an FDA regulation but are unlikely to cause adverse health conditions. Choice *D* is incorrect because there is no Class IV category of recalls under MedWatch.

45. B: Someone from the pharmacy should notify prescribing physicians of the recall. Choice *A* is incorrect because patients should be notified and instructed to return the recalled product to the pharmacy for a refund or substitution. Choice *C* is incorrect because pharmacies do not need to record personal information of patients. They must, however, record the number of customers affected, the dates the customers were notified, the number of customers that responded to the notification, and the amount of medication that was returned as a result of the recall. Choice *D* is incorrect because remaining stock should be returned to the manufacturer per the instructions included in the recall notification.

46. D: The Food and Drug Administration (FDA) is the government agency that oversees the production and safety of food and drugs. Choice *A* is incorrect because the Comprehensive Drug Abuse Prevention and Control Act (CSA) is what guides Federal law on the manufacture, regulation, and sale of certain controlled substances. Choice *B* is incorrect because the Drug Enforcement Agency (DEA) implements laws related to controlled substance use and drug trafficking. Choice *C* is incorrect because the Environmental Protection Agency (EPA) regulates the proper disposal of pharmaceutical waste.

47. C: Risk management is an ongoing and fluid process that involves quality assurance (QA – prevention to keep problems from happening), quality control (QC – identifying and fixing flaws with existing practices), and quality improvement (using knowledge and experiences to improve practices). Choices *A*, *B*, and *D* are incorrect because the all include option I; risk management is a continuous process meant to both prevent and address issues.

48. C: The Drug Supply Chain Security Act (DSCSA) established guidelines for tracing medications in the supply chain and requires distributors and logistics providers to obtain licensure with the FDA. Choice *A* is incorrect because the Combat Methamphetamine Epidemic Act (CMEA) limits the sale of products containing ephedrine, pseudoephedrine, and phenylpropanolamine. Choice *B* is incorrect because

Controlled Substances Act (CSA) provides guidance for the development of laws related to the manufacture, regulation, and sale of certain controlled substances. Choice *D* is incorrect because the Federal Food, Drug, and Cosmetic Act (FD&C) gives the FDA supervision of the safety of the food, drug, and cosmetic industries.

49. A: The root cause analysis is a team effort to collect data, analyze medication error incidents, and identify contributing factors to such incidents. Choice *B* is incorrect because the goal of the root cause analysis is to identify the factors that contribute to medication errors, not to blame anyone involved. Choice *C* is incorrect because the investigation is conducted by a team, not an individual. Choice *D* is incorrect because the corrective action plan is an internal document meant to help the team avoid future errors; it is not submitted to MedWatch.

50. A: Inadequate labeling is an example of a medication dispensing error. Choice *B* is incorrect because a near miss is a type of medication error that has the potential to do harm but does not because it does not reach the patient. Choice *C* is incorrect because a noncompliance error occurs when the patient does not take the medication as directed. Choice *D* is incorrect because the patient has not experienced an adverse effect from the medication.

51. D: These situations increase workload and stress, create work interruptions, and/or contribute to staff fatigue – all factors which increase the chance of medication dispensing errors. Choices *A, B,* and *C* are incorrect because they each exclude one correct option.

52. C: Schedule II controlled substances cannot be refilled. Choice *A* is incorrect because a patient may need an early refill if the prescriber updated the medication dosage. Choice *B* is incorrect because prescriptions do not become invalid until they are on year old. Choice *D* is incorrect because Schedule III and IV controlled substances may be filled five times within a six-month period.

53. A: The majority of dispensing errors (83%) are identified during medication counseling sessions between the patient and pharmacist. Choices *B, C, and D* are incorrect because while these practices are all important, they do not individually prevent as many errors as counseling patients at pick-up.

54. B: The prescription does not indicate how often the patient should take the medication. Choice *A* is incorrect because "cap" indicates that the dosage form is caplets. Choice *C* is incorrect because "po" indicates the tablets should be taken by mouth. Choice *D* is incorrect because the strength is indicated at 300 mg.

55. B: When the prescriber doesn't indicate the number of refills, it is assumed that no refills are permitted. Choices *A* and *C* are incorrect because convention dictates that no refills are permitted. Choice *D* is incorrect because the Institute of Safe Medication Practices (ISMP) provides impartial, timely, and accurate drug safety information but does not dictate the number of refills on a prescription.

56. C: Ou indicates the medication should be placed in each eye; the pharmacist mistakenly wrote the label indicating the medication should be placed in each ear. Choice *A* is incorrect because qd hs indicates the medicine should be used every day at bedtime, which the pharmacist relayed accurately. Choice *B* is incorrect because the dosage form dispensed matches the prescription. Choice *D* is incorrect because the strength of the medication dispensed matches that in the prescription; the pharmacist simply added a zero before the decimal point, which is convention for avoiding dispensing errors.

57. B: ASAP indicates a prescription has priority but not the priority of a STAT order, which should be processed within 15 minutes. Choice *A* is incorrect because standing orders refer to medications administered at regularly scheduled intervals. Choice *C* is incorrect because PRN orders refer to medications filled or administered at the patients request within parameters set by the prescriber. Choice *D* is incorrect because STAT orders are of the highest priority and must be filled within 15 minutes of receipt.

58. B: An off-label use is when a medication is prescribed to treat a health issue it was not originally approved for. Choice *A* is incorrect because generic equivalents and other formulary substitutions are not off label uses. Choice *C* is incorrect because misuse is a decision made by a patient to use the medication for an alternative purpose; off label uses are directed by a prescriber. Choice *D* is incorrect because noncompliance is a patient incorrectly following a prescription; it is not an alternate use directed by a prescriber.

59. A: Gloves should be changed after contact with contaminated items. Choice *B* is incorrect because masks, not gloves, have N-95 ratings. Choice *C* is incorrect because gloves should be removed carefully, not necessarily quickly. Choice *D* is incorrect because hands should be washed after removing gloves.

60. A: Technicians should consult with the pharmacist on missed doses of medication, as well as formulary substitutions and patient misuse/overuse of medication. Choice *B* is incorrect because pharmacists, not technicians, should offer counsel on missed doses. Choices *C* and *D* are incorrect because the pharmacist is able to counsel the patient on a missed dose.

61. A: Pharmacists trained to administer vaccinations are also trained to counsel patients on side effects and vaccination schedules. Choices *B, C,* and *D* are incorrect because they all include option III; although pharmacists are trained to recognize adverse reactions, they are not necessarily able to treat them.

62. D: Using the abbreviation "u" for units can result in the u being mistaken for a zero, which can lead to overdosing (e.g., 5u mistaken as 50). Choice *A* is incorrect because leading zeroes should be added before decimal points to avoid overdosing. Choice *B* is incorrect because the abbreviation for od (right eye) is often confused for the abbreviation ad (right ear). Choice *C* is incorrect because large dose values in the tens of thousands or more should have commas to avoid errors in transcription and dispensing.

63. C: Mistakes in dosing or unusual dosages for a particular medication both indicate a prescription may be forged. Choice *A* is incorrect because prescribers typically use abbreviations; only if they're used incorrectly should they raise concern. Choice *B* is incorrect because handwritten prescriptions are typically written in ink. Choice *D* is incorrect because refills are permitted on Schedule III medications; they are prohibited on Schedule II medications.

64. D: Product integrity concerns might include an adulterated product, misbranded drugs, counterfeit products, or an improperly labeled product. Choice *A* is incorrect because adverse effects describe drugs' effects on consumers, not supply chain issues that create the problems listed in the question. Choice *B* is incorrect because drug-drug interactions occur when a patient takes two contradictory drugs. Choice *C* is incorrect because medication errors relate to dispensing medication.

65. D: PRN is a medication order that may be filled at the patient's request within parameters set by the prescriber. Choice *A* is incorrect because po is the abbreviation that indicates a medication should be taken orally. Choice *B* is incorrect because a standing order refers to a medication that the patient takes

at set intervals. Choice *C* is incorrect because PRN orders place prescriber-set parameters on how often patients may request a medication.

66. C: Midazolam is a moderate sedative agent, which is a high-alert medication. Choices *A*, *B*, and *D* are incorrect because ephedrine (decongestant), lansoprazole (protein pump inhibitor), and propranolol (beta blocker) are not in categories included within the list of high-alert medications.

67. D: Iodine compounds are among the most common antimicrobial agents used for hand washing in healthcare settings. Choice *A* is incorrect because alcohol is used as an antimicrobial handwashing agent in concentrations of 70-90%. Choice *C* is incorrect because chlorhexidine is used as an antimicrobial handwashing agent in concentrations of 2% or 4%. Choice *C* is incorrect because hydrogen peroxide is not typically used in handwashing.

68. A: As a slow-release tablet, Biaxin-XL should receive a do not crush warning on its label. Choices *B* and *C* are incorrect because clarithromycin is an antibiotic, which is not labeled as a high-alert medication. Choice *D* is incorrect because Biaxin-XL should have a do not crush warning.

69. D: Pharmacists should report adverse reactions to the Vaccine Adverse Event Reporting System (VAERS). Choices *A*, *B*, and *C* are incorrect because none of this information is reported to VAERS.

70. B: A DUR is an authorized, systematic, and ongoing review about the prescribing, dispensing, and use of a medication in respect to a specific patient's condition(s). DUR conflicts include formulary substitutions, as well as drug-drug interactions, drug-disease interactions, drug-patient precautions, inappropriate treatment duration, medication abuse and misuse, and drug dosage modifications. Choice *A* is incorrect because a DUR is performed by the pharmacist. Choice *C* is incorrect because pharmacy software typically does detect and flag DUR conflicts for pharmacist review. Choice *D* is incorrect because information important to a DUR includes the patient's health history (including age, gender, allergies, and pregnancy) and medication profile; knowing or verifying their address is not necessary.

71. D: When cleaning the laminar flow hood, one should first dress in PPE, then turn on the hood and allow it to run for five to twenty minutes. After removing items that don't belong in the hood, spray internal surfaces with disinfectant and use sterile wipes to clean in a sweeping back and forth motion before letting the hood dry. Choices *A*, *B*, and *C* are incorrect because they list steps in incorrect order for cleaning the laminar flow hood.

72. C: A temperature of +6°C is within the range of acceptable temperatures between +2.22 °C and +7.78 °C, as calculated below.

$$°C = (36°F - 32) \times \frac{5}{9} = +2.22°C$$

$$°C = (46°F - 32) \times \frac{5}{9} = +7.78°C$$

Therefore, Choices *A, B, and D* are incorrect.

73. C: Fried's rule uses the age of the child expressed in months and is best used in infants under 2 years of age. Choice *A* is incorrect because Clark's rule is based on body weight, not age. Choice *B* is incorrect because Dilling 's rule uses the child's age expressed in years, which is better applied for older children. Choice *D* is incorrect because Young's rule also uses age in years and is best used for children aged 1-12.

188

74. C: Using Young's rule, the correct dose for the 7-year-old child would be calculated as follows:

$$Child\ dose = Adult\ dose\ x\ \frac{Age\ in\ years}{(Age + 12)} = 300\ \text{mg}\ x\ \frac{7}{7 + 12} = 110.5\ \text{mg}$$

Choices *A, B,* and *D* are incorrect because they use the wrong formulas or incorrectly calculate using Young's rule.

75. D: Fried's Rule is best used for infants up to 2 years of age. Using this Rule, the dose is calculated as follows:

$$Child\ dose = Adult\ dose\ \times\ \frac{Age\ in\ months}{(150)} = 10\ \text{mg}\ \times\ \frac{9}{(150)} = 0.6\ \text{mg}$$

Choice *A, B,* and *C* are incorrect because they use the wrong formulas or incorrectly calculate using Fried's Rule.

76. B: The calculation by body weight (also known as Clark's Rule) is based on weight in pounds (not kg), so the weight would need to be converted as follows:

$$\frac{40\ \text{kg}}{X\ \text{lb}} = \frac{1\ \text{kg}}{2.205\ \text{lb}}$$

$$X = \frac{40\ \text{kg}\ \times\ 2.205\ \text{lb}}{1\ \text{kg}} = 88.2\ \text{lb}$$

Then the child dose would be calculated with the formula below:

$$Child\ dose = Adult\ dose\ \times\ \frac{Body\ weight\ in\ lb}{(150)} = 200\ \text{mg}\ x\ \frac{88.2\ \text{lb}}{(150)} = 117.6$$

Choice *A* is incorrect because this answer uses Mosteller's equation to calculate the child's body surface area (BSA).

$$BSA\ (\text{m}^2) = \sqrt{\frac{(Height\ (\text{cm})\ \times\ Weight\ (\text{kg}))}{3,600}} = \sqrt{\frac{(150\ \text{cm}\ \times\ 40\ \text{kg})}{3,600}} = \sqrt{1.67} = 1.29\ \text{m}^2$$

But to calculate a child dose, that number must then be multiplied by the adult dose in units of mg/m², which is not provided in this problem.

Choice *C* is incorrect because it applies Clark's Rule but fails to first convert body weight to pounds. When used correctly, Clark's Rule produces the dose listed in Choice *A*. Choice *D* is incorrect because the dose calculated using Dilling 's Rule would be as follows:

$$Child\ dose = Adult\ dose\ \times\ \frac{Age\ in\ years}{(20)}\ 200\ \text{mg}\ \times\ \frac{12}{(20)} = 120\ \text{mg}$$

77. C: Using a proportional calculation, the number of milligrams of vancomycin in each dose can be calculated as follows:

$$\frac{10 \text{ mg}}{1 \text{ kg}} = \frac{X}{18.6 \text{ kg}}$$

$$X = \frac{10 \text{ mg} \times 18.6 \text{ kg}}{1 \text{ kg}} = 186 \text{ mg}$$

Choice *A* is incorrect because it is not calculated correctly. Choice *B* is incorrect because it is not calculated correctly and has incorrect units. Choice *D* is incorrect because although the value is calculated correctly, the units are incorrect.

78. B: Using a proportional calculation, the number of milliliters (ml) of suspension in each dose can be calculated as follows:

$$\frac{40 \text{ mg}}{5 \text{ ml}} = \frac{60 \text{ mg}}{X}$$

$$X = \frac{60 \text{ mg} \times 5 \text{ ml}}{40 \text{ mg}} = 7.5 \text{ ml}$$

Choices *A, C,* and *D* are incorrect because they are not calculated correctly.

79. D: This solution is a weight/volume (W/V) ratio, which equals $\frac{0.9 \text{ grams}}{100 \text{ mL}} = 0.9\%$. Choices *A, B,* and *C* are incorrect because they list incorrect ratio types and incorrectly calculated percentages.

80. B: When calculating for PRN (as needed) tablets, the days supply should be calculated using the highest dose with the shortest interval. In this example, the patient may take up to two tablets in one day (24 hours). The calculation would be completed as follows:

$$Days \; supply = \frac{16 \text{ tabs}}{2 \text{ tab} \times 1 \text{ day}} = 8 \text{ days}$$

Choices *A, C,* and *D* are incorrect because they do not correctly apply the formula.

81. C: The process described is called return to stock. Choice *A* is incorrect because nondispensable medications are pharmaceutical waste and include expired medications, medications that have been recalled, or medications that were delivered damaged. Choice *B* is incorrect because non-compliance occurs when a patient fails to take the prescribed medication as directed by the prescriber. Choice *D* is incorrect because reverse distribution is the return of unopened overstock of products to a reverse distributor company.

82. B: Like most insulins, this brand contains 100 units per mL. Based on the volume and units written in the prescription, the days supply would be calculated as follows:

$$Days \; supply = \frac{20 \text{ mL} \times 100 \text{ units}}{(60 \text{ units per day})} = 33.33 \text{ days} = 33 \text{ days}$$

Choices *A, C,* and *D* are incorrect because they do not correctly apply the formula.

190

83. A: The prescription calls for 4 drops (gtt) in each ear twice daily. Using the conversion factor of 20gtt/mL, the days supply can be calculated as follows:

$$Days\ supply = \frac{7.5\ mL \times \frac{20\ gtt}{mL}}{(8\ gtt\ \times\ 2\ doses\ per\ day)} = \frac{150\ gtt}{(16\ gtt\ per\ day)} = 9.375\ days = 9\ days$$

One bottle contains 9 days supply, which is enough for a a 7-day prescription with 2 days supply remaining in the bottle. Therefore, choices *B*, *C*, and *D* are incorrect.

84. D: The number of fills and quantity in the short-fill can be calculated as follows:

Total number of tablets over the life of the prescription:

$$60\ tablets \times 4\ total\ fills = 240\ tablets$$

Tablets needed per fill:

$$Tablets\ per\ fill = \frac{2\ tab}{dose} \times \frac{1\ dose}{day} \times \frac{32\ days}{fill} = 64\ tabs/fill$$

Number of fills needed to dispense quantity as specified by the prescriber:

$$Fills = \frac{240\ tabs}{(64\ tabs/fill)} = 3.75\ fills$$

There will be 3 total fills or 2 refills after the initial fill by the pharmacy. And the total number of tablets dispensed in the 3 fills is:

$$3\ fills \times 64\ \frac{tabs}{fill} = 192\ tablets$$

The short-fill, or how many of the total number prescribed are left after the 3 complete fills are dispensed:

$$240\ tablets\ prescribed - 192\ tablets\ dispensed = 48\ tablets$$

There will be a short-fill of 48 tablets.

85. C: When a short-fill occurs, pharmacy technicians are allowed to reduce the quantity dispensed. Choice *A* is incorrect because the pharmacy technician cannot surpass the prescribed quantity. Choice *B* is incorrect because the insurance company's policy is clear in their supply limitations. Choice *D* is incorrect because the prescription can be filled with the reduced quantity dispensed.

86. B: A blended unit dose system combines a unit dose system with a non-unit dose system by packaging multiple medications in a single cassette. Choice *A* is incorrect because an ampule is a single dose container that is opened by breaking; it is different from a bubble pack. Choice *C* is incorrect because daily unit dose is not a recognized term. Choice *D* is incorrect because a modified unit dose combines unit dose medications, which are blister packaged, into a multi-dose card instead of being placed loose in a box.

87. A: In an NDC, the second segment (1222 in this example) refers to the drug's strength and dosage form. Choice *B* is incorrect because the third segment in an NDC (11 in this example) refers to the package size and type. Choice *C* is incorrect because the first segment in an NDC (0832 in this example) refers to the drug manufacturer. Choice *D* is incorrect because lot numbers are assigned to batches of product, making them easier to trace in the event of a recall. The NDC is a number is unchanging and is assigned to each specific medication, no matter what lot it is produced in.

88. A: A disadvantage of centralized distribution systems is the inability to stock all dosage forms of a medication. Choice *B* is incorrect because pharmacy technicians usually hand-deliver medications to patient care units in a centralized system. Choice *C* is incorrect because decentralized systems can reduce wait times for ordered medications. Choice *D* is incorrect because the location of the decentralized system within the patient care unit generally decreases the diversion of narcotics.

89. D: None of these statements is true. Drug recalls may be initiated by the FDA or the manufacturer. Recalls only affect pharmacies carrying medication with the batch numbers being recalled. Notice is first sent to pharmacies and other facilities that dispense medications, not to prescribers. Therefore, choices *A, B,* and *C* are incorrect.

90. B: All drugs on the P and U lists are hazardous wastes; they include medications in which a commercially pure grade or technical grade chemical is the sole active ingredient. Choice *A* is incorrect because corrosive hazardous wastes have a pH of less than 2 or greater than 12.5. Choice *C* is incorrect because medications with low LD50 are hazardous, meaning lower concentrations of such drugs are toxic, as measured by killing 50 percent of a test sample. Choice *D* is incorrect because medications with more than one active ingredient are hazardous.

Practice Test #3

1. A patient has brought in a prescription for Diazepam. Which of the following conditions is the most likely reason that the patient needs this prescription?
   a. Hypertension
   b. ADHD
   c. Epilepsy
   d. Depression

2. How is a Schedule V controlled drug class described?
   a. High potential for abuse and severe psychological or physical dependence
   b. Low potential for abuse because they contain limited quantities of narcotics
   c. High potential for abuse and no currently accepted medical use
   d. Relatively low potential for abuse but may cause high psychological dependence

3. To prevent a mix-up between chlorpromazine and chlorpropamide, all EXCEPT which of the following strategies will be applicable?
   a. Tall man lettering
   b. A computer alert for LASA medications
   c. Bar-code scanning of bottles at the filling station
   d. Better lighting on the shelves

4. What is the difference between the Orange Book and the MSDS?
   a. They are the same reference materials, but both should be kept in every pharmacy
   b. Neither should be kept in the pharmacy, but they differ in the information they contain about medications and chemicals
   c. The Orange Book catalogs all products approved by the FDA whereas the MSDS is the safety information from the manufacturer about the chemical
   d. Neither of these documents is important in a pharmacy

5. Which agency is responsible for child-resistant packaging?
   a. DEA
   b. FDA
   c. The Joint Commission
   d. Consumer Products Safety Commission

6. Which of the following is NOT an organization that influences quality assurance (QA) in the pharmacy setting?
   a. United States Pharmacopeia (USP)
   b. Occupational Safety and Health Administration (OSHA)
   c. American Board of Internal Medicine (ABIM)
   d. American Pharmacy Association (APhA)

7. Who is the last person of defense to prevent a medication error?
   a. Physician
   b. Pharmacist
   c. Nurse
   d. Patient

8. Substances or combination of substances that can produce harmful effects on the health and safety of a person are classified as which type of waste?
   a. Solid waste
   b. Biodetrimental waste
   c. Infectious waste
   d. Hazardous waste

9. What does the abbreviation PO mean?
   a. Daily
   b. By mouth
   c. As needed
   d. Bedtime

10. The Class A prescription balance is commonly used in compounding pharmacies. What is the sensitivity of a Class A prescription balance?
    a. 5 mg
    b. 6 mg
    c. 7 mg
    d. 10 mg

11. Who determines specific storage conditions and types of containers for manufactured drugs?
    a. Drug manufacturers
    b. FDA
    c. DEA
    d. Hospitals

12. Which of the following patient education strategies helps prevent medication errors?

    I. Encouraging the patient to review medications before leaving the pharmacy
    II. Educating the patient about medications dispensed
    III. Educating the patient about high-risk medications

    a. I only
    b. III only
    c. I and II
    d. I, II, and III

13. A patient comes in and states that they need to pick up a new prescription, but they cannot remember the exact name. All they remember is that it is for "a cough that will not go away." Out of these medications in the patient's chart—valsartan, tamsulosin, benzonatate, and rosuvastatin—which one are they most likely referring to?
   a. Valsartan
   b. Tamsulosin
   c. Benzonatate
   d. Rosuvastatin

14. A concerned mom asks if her son's flu medication is available in a liquid form because "he refuses to take pills." The medication is oseltamivir. Is this a medication that is available in a non-pill form, and what would be the next best option?
   a. Yes, it is available in a suspension form.
   b. Yes, it is available as a dissolvable lozenge.
   c. Yes, it is available as a topical cream.
   d. No, it is not available in any dosage form besides a pill.

15. A physician called the pharmacy to give a verbal order of ZyPREXA 10 (olanzapine 10 mg). However, the order was misinterpreted, and the prescription was filled for ZyrTEC 10 (cetirizine 10 mg). Which of the following strategies would help to prevent such dispensing errors associated with LASA medications?

   I. The pharmacist reading back the prescription, including spelling the medication name
   II. The physician's office calling the patient and informing him/her that a prescription order has been placed at the pharmacy
   III. Counseling patient about the medication, including the purpose of the treatment

   a. I and II
   b. I and III
   c. II and III
   d. I, II, and III

16. Which statement is true about dry powder inhalers and metered dose inhalers?
   a. A metered dose inhaler uses breath-actuated triggers to deliver the medication.
   b. A dry powder inhaler uses breath-actuated triggers to deliver the medication.
   c. Metered dose inhalers require the patient to load the medication pack every time.
   d. Dry powder inhalers require the patient to push down the loaded canister to deliver a dose of the medication.

17. Which brand name and generic name pair do NOT match?
   a. Diphenhydramine and Benadryl
   b. Naproxen and Aleve
   c. Loperamide and Imodium
   d. Calcium carbonate and Pepto-Bismol

195

18. Which medication class is known to cause sexual dysfunction?
    a. PDE-5 inhibitor (phosphodiesterase-5 enzyme inhibitor)
    b. SSRI (selective serotonin reuptake inhibitor)
    c. NSAID (non-steroidal anti-inflammatory drug)
    d. PPI (protein pump inhibitor)

19. The strength of a medication in a prescription is written as 1%. The pharmacy technician feels that it might be too high of a dose, and it should probably be 0.1%. What should be an appropriate action for the technician to take?
    a. Ask the patient about the strength
    b. Fill the prescription as written
    c. Inform the pharmacist
    d. Call the physician's office to check the strength

20. Which of the following pieces of information are included in the inscription?

    I. Medication name and strength
    II. Instructions for the pharmacist
    III. Quantity to dispense
    IV. Dosage form

    a. I, II, III
    b. I, III, IV
    c. I, II, IV
    d. All of the above

21. Which medication is used for irritable bowel syndrome?
    a. Norepinephrine
    b. Ondansetron
    c. Lubiprostone
    d. Esomeprazole

22. Which one of the following agencies may initiate a drug recall?
    a. United States Food and Drug Administration (FDA)
    b. Drug Enforcement Administration (DEA)
    c. Occupational Safety and Health Administration (OSHA)
    d. The Joint Commission (TJC)

23. Your pharmacy received an institutional order to supply 2 lbs of salicylic acid ointment (17% w/w) for treatment of warts. What is the quantity of salicylic acid required to prepare the ointment?
    a. 70.12 g
    b. 80.32 g
    c. 154.22 g
    d. 170.78 g

24. Which of the following is the accepted convention for leading zeros?
   a. Use a leading zero with numbers greater than one (e.g., 05 mg)
   b. Use a leading zero with numbers in decimal form less than one (e.g., 0.5 mg)
   c. Add a terminal zero (e.g., 5.0 mg)
   d. Increase the use of decimals (e.g., prescribe 0.5 g instead of 500 mg)

25. Which of the following medications is NOT used to treat hyperlipidemia?
   a. Zocor
   b. Norvasc
   c. Vytorin
   d. Simvastatin

26. How many grams of 1% hydrocortisone cream should be mixed with an appropriate quantity of 2.5% hydrocortisone cream to make 250 grams of 1.5% hydrocortisone cream?
   a. 83.33 g
   b. 166.66 g
   c. 133.33 g
   d. 116.66 g

27. What class of medication is used for the treatment of seizures?
   a. Antipsychotics
   b. SSRIs
   c. NSAIDs
   d. Anticonvulsants

28. What is the correct time interval for pharmacy staff to perform mandatory hand hygiene prior to compounding sterile preparations?
   a. At least 10 seconds
   b. At least 30 seconds
   c. At least 60 seconds
   d. At least 90 seconds

29. What is the generic medication that would be dispensed for the NSAID Celebrex if substitution is allowed?
   a. Citalopram
   b. Celecoxib
   c. Meloxicam
   d. Moxifloxacin

30. Which of the following is the preferred method of transmission of prescriptions to a pharmacy?
   a. Writing
   b. Telephoning
   c. Faxing
   d. Electronic prescribing

31. To formulate 200 g of an ointment mix from the ingredients A, B, and C with a ratio of 1:2:1, what quantity of each of those ingredients will be required?
    a. 40 g, 120 g, 40 g, respectively
    b. 45 g, 110 g, 45 g, respectively
    c. 50 g, 100 g, 50 g, respectively
    d. 60 g, 80 g, 60 g, respectively

32. Which of the following statements is NOT TRUE regarding generic substitution?
    a. Generics are more cost effective.
    b. Medication cannot be substituted if the prescriber writes DAW.
    c. Prescriber approval must be obtained for any generic substitution.
    d. Therapeutically equivalent generics have the same efficacy as their branded counterparts.

33. Which of the following government organizations oversees the MedWatch Program?
    a. Drug Enforcement Administration (DEA)
    b. Occupational Safety and Health Administration (OSHA)
    c. United States Food and Drug Administration (FDA)
    d. The Joint Commission (TJC)

34. Which characteristics define Lopressor 100mg tablets and Toprol XL 100mg tablets as pharmaceutical alternatives to one another?
    a. Same active ingredient, same dosage form, same salt
    b. Same active ingredient, same strength, same salt, same dosage form
    c. Same strength, different salt, same dosage form
    d. Same active ingredient, same strength, different dosage form, different salt

35. How should an expiration date of 03/2019 be treated?
    a. Expiring on March 1, 2019
    b. Expiring on March 15, 2019
    c. Expiring on March 31, 2019
    d. Expiring on March 24, 2019

36. In terms of severity and level of danger of a manufactured drug with defects, what is the order of reporting from greatest harm to least harm?
    a. Class II, Class III, and Class I
    b. Class I, Class II, and Class III
    c. Class III, Class II, and Class I
    d. Class IV, Class III, Class II, and Class I

37. Which of the following items is NOT considered personal protective equipment (PPE)?
    a. Underwear
    b. Facemasks
    c. Laboratory coats
    d. Gowns

38. Which of the following medications is indicated for the treatment of an enlarged prostate or BPH?
    a. Singulair
    b. Tamsulosin
    c. Spironolactone
    d. Uloric

39. For how long can insulin vials be kept after they are opened?
    a. One day
    b. Seven days
    c. Thirty days
    d. Six months

40. Which of the following is TRUE regarding dietary supplements?
    a. The Dietary Supplement Health and Education Act of 1994 states dietary supplements must be labeled as such.
    b. Dietary supplements undergo the same rigorous FDA evaluation processes as legend drugs.
    c. Dietary supplements are deemed safe and effective by the FDA.
    d. Any product claims for a dietary supplement made by its manufacturer must be substantiated.

41. Which of the following medications should be stored in glass rather than plastic?
    a. Doxycycline
    b. Sublingual nitroglycerin
    c. Linezolid
    d. Acetazolamide

42. Which of the following agencies oversees the National Medication Errors Reporting Program (MERP)?
    a. Drug Enforcement Administration (DEA)
    b. The Institute of Safe Medication Practices (ISMP)
    c. Occupational Safety and Health Administration (OSHA)
    d. The Joint Commission (TJC)

43. What medication is commonly used in hypothyroidism?
    a. Methimazole
    b. Sumatriptan
    c. Butalbital
    d. Levothyroxine

44. Which dietary supplement is recommended for a woman of childbearing age to help prevent birth defects?
    a. Vitamin D
    b. Calcium
    c. Folic acid
    d. Echinacea

45. There are three segments to the NDC number. Which segment identifies who manufactured a drug?
    a. Packaging code
    b. Product code
    c. Labeler code
    d. NDC

46. Which of the following statements is correct regarding ASAP and STAT prescription medication orders?
    a. ASAP orders, but not STAT orders, are only encountered in a hospital
    b. ASAP orders need to be filled within fifteen minutes of receiving them, whereas there is more leniency with STAT orders
    c. STAT orders need to be filled within fifteen minutes of receiving them, whereas there is more leniency with ASAP orders
    d. STAT orders, but not ASAP orders, are only encountered in a hospital

47. After opening, which of the following brands of insulin would be stable when refrigerated or at room temperature for greater than twenty-eight days?
    a. Lantus vials
    b. Tresiba FlexTouch insulin pen
    c. Humalog vials
    d. Humulin 70/30 insulin pen

48. What method is most effective at reducing medication dispensing errors?
    a. Counseling sessions between the pharmacist and the patient
    b. Checking medication labels with the prescription
    c. Storing drugs properly and with labels facing forward
    d. Reducing distractions in the workplace and overworked staff

49. Which of the following is true regarding lot numbers?
    a. They have the same digits as the expiration date
    b. They have a distinct number for each drug manufactured and supplied by the manufacturer
    c. They contain only numbers and no letters
    d. They can be used interchangeably among different drugs from the same manufacturer

50. Which of the following is TRUE regarding oral antibiotic suspensions reconstituted with water?
    a. All oral antibiotic suspensions must be refrigerated after mixing.
    b. Clarithromycin oral suspension must be refrigerated after mixing with water.
    c. Amoxicillin oral suspension is stable for fourteen days after mixing with water.
    d. Reconstitution of oral antibiotic suspensions reduces the risk of microbial contamination.

51. PPE must be worn by trained personnel when handling hazardous substances. What does PPE stand for?
    a. Personnel provisional equipment
    b. Personal prescription evaluation
    c. Personal protective equipment
    d. Personal provided wear

200

52. Which of the following is NOT a characteristic of a stable suspension?
    a. An internal phase that is uniformly dispersed in the external phase
    b. Small particle size
    c. Insoluble particles that are easily redistributed after settling
    d. Sedimentation or caking of particles

53. For which of the following patients would it be appropriate to give an easier-to-open cap and not a child-safe cap?
    a. A thirty-five-year-old patient that has no other health conditions
    b. A sixty-year-old patient who has a history of asthma
    c. An eighteen-year-old patient who lives alone and has a history of rheumatoid arthritis
    d. A seven-year-old patient with a history of anxiety that lives with his parents

54. A coworker at the pharmacy accidentally grabbed the bottle for hydrochlorothiazide when filling a prescription for hydrocortisone and filled the bottle with the wrong medication. Thankfully, the pharmacist caught the error when verifying the prescription. Which of these following scenarios is most likely to have led to the error?
    a. The bottles were in alphabetical order on the shelf, meaning that these two bottles were next to each other.
    b. The technician was picking up multiple bottles to fill multiple prescriptions at the same time.
    c. A pharmacist should fill all the prescriptions to ensure that they are correct.
    d. The technician was bouncing back and forth between checking customers out at the counter and filling prescriptions.

55. In a horizontal laminar flow hood, how far should one work from the front edge of the work surface?
    a. At least 4 inches
    b. At least 6 inches
    c. Less than 6 inches
    d. At least 2 inches

56. Which of the following is TRUE regarding narrow therapeutic index medications?
    a. Patients taking these medications require minimal monitoring.
    b. Achieving an optimal therapeutic dose can be difficult.
    c. These types of medications must always be administered intravenously.
    d. They are generally considered safer than medications with a higher therapeutic index value.

57. Which of the following are not packaged in blister packs?
    a. Pills
    b. Topicals
    c. Encapsulated liquid pills
    d. Solid dosages

58. How often should a laminar flow hood be certified?
    a. Every 3 months
    b. Every 6 months
    c. Every 9 months
    d. Every 12 months

59. For which of the following types of medication must INR values be closely monitored?
    a. Blood thinners
    b. Statins
    c. Antibiotics
    d. Anticonvulsants

60. Which task would a pharmacy technician be expected to carry out?
    a. Counsel patients on vaccine schedules
    b. Prepare unit dose medications
    c. Provide medical advice to patients
    d. Recommend appropriate OTC medications

61. Which of the following medications is LEAST likely to have an interaction with Coumadin?
    a. Meloxicam
    b. Aleve
    c. Aggrenox
    d. Digoxin

62. What system encompasses a centralized system in using barcode technology with conveyors capable of choosing drugs from a patient's file, as well as putting the medication in the right drawer for the patient?
    a. Automated pump system
    b. Automated dispensing systems
    c. Robotic dispensing
    d. Automated tracking

63. Which of the following might occur in a patient with an INR value lower than two?
    a. Thromboembolism
    b. Uncontrolled bleeding
    c. Excessive bruising
    d. Insufficient clotting of the blood

64. In the MSDS, the toxicological properties section includes which of the following?
    a. Aquatic toxicity
    b. Lethal dose
    c. Protective equipment
    d. Route of entry

65. What is the name given to the process of formulating a pharmacy product to meet a patient's unique needs, as specified by the physician?
    a. Drug dosage modification
    b. Formulary substitution
    c. Off-label use
    d. Pharmaceutical compounding

66. Which compounding technique requires a wetting agent to increase solubility?
    a. Pulverization
    b. Levigation
    c. Geometric dilution
    d. Trituration

67. Which of the following would a pharmacist use to report an adverse vaccine reaction?
    a. CDC
    b. FDA
    c. VAERS
    d. DEA

68. Which of the following is NOT an observable sign of physical incompatibility?
    a. Cracking
    b. Coalescence
    c. pH change
    d. Liquification

69. Which situation may require the pharmacist to formulate a new product to meet a patient's unique needs?
    a. Medication has a do not crush warning
    b. Patient allergic to active ingredient
    c. Product discontinued for adverse reactions
    d. Taste or texture requires alteration

70. Under what conditions can ingredients be withdrawn from their original container for use?
    a. They may be withdrawn for use up to 30 days after the labeled expiration date.
    b. They may be withdrawn from their original container by any pharmacy staff.
    c. They must be placed in an appropriately labeled secondary container.
    d. They should never be used once removed from the original container.

71. Which of the following is NOT a life-threatening consequence of precipitate formation in an IV administered medication?
    a. Embolism
    b. Tissue irritation at IV site
    c. Receipt of toxic substances
    d. Therapeutic failure

72. Which of the following would NOT be reported to MedWatch?
    a. A malfunctioning medical device
    b. Diversion of a controlled substance
    c. The dispensing of an incorrect medication to a patient
    d. Jaundice occurring after taking a new prescription medication

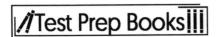
73. Which of the following is NOT a benefit of using an emulsifying agent in a nonsterile compound preparation?
  a. Increased immiscibility
  b. Increased stability
  c. Equal internal phase dispersion
  d. Greater homogeneity

74. Which of the following is an example of a near miss medication error?
  a. A physician prescribes an incorrect dose to a patient, and the patient administers the medication.
  b. A pharmacist dispenses a prescription to an incorrect patient; the wrong patient picks up and administers the medication.
  c. A patient states no known drug allergies when dropping off a prescription but has an adverse allergic reaction to the medication.
  d. A prescription order is keyed for the incorrect medication but is caught by the pharmacist at verification.

75. Which of the following is TRUE regarding the proper storage of a medication that is sensitive to light?
  a. Medication that is sensitive to light should be dispensed in an amber colored bottle or vial.
  b. Only the inactive ingredients or fillers in a drug are affected by light exposure.
  c. Light exposure is not a significant concern during the manufacturing process.
  d. Photodegradation does not have a negative effect on the therapeutic ability of a drug.

76. Lidocaine is considered a high-risk medication because
  a. It is a look-alike medication.
  b. It is a sound-alike medication.
  c. It may cause significant harm.
  d. It should not be crushed.

77. Substances that can harm the health and safety of a person are known as what?
  a. Biological waste
  b. Hazardous waste
  c. Infectious waste
  d. Solid waste

78. Which of the following is NOT accurate regarding the storage and accessibility of controlled medications?
  a. A secure safe or cabinet with locking mechanism is required to protect schedule II medications from diversion.
  b. Controlled medications should be discretely disseminated amongst noncontrolled medications.
  c. Access to controlled drugs should be limited to pharmacy personnel.
  d. Pharmacies should store large quantities of controlled substances in order to better serve their patients.

79. According to federal law, how may a pharmacy receive a new prescription order?
    a. E-mail
    b. Patient request
    c. Verbal order
    d. Via mail

80. Which of the following medications has not been shown to decrease the efficacy of hormonal oral contraceptives when taken simultaneously?
    a. Rifampin
    b. Ritonavir
    c. St. John's Wort
    d. Gabapentin

81. How can pharmacies help to avoid errors in dispensing high-alert medications?

     I. Avoid storing low concentration electrolytes in dispensing areas.
     II. Avoid using tailing zeroes on the dosage (e.g., 2.0 mg).
     III. Avoid using leading zeroes before a decimal (e.g., 0.3 mg).

    a. I only
    b. II only
    c. III only
    d. I, II, and III

82. Select the medication and dosage combination that is *in*correct.
    a. Cephalexin: 500mg orally every 8 hours
    b. Buspirone: 150mg orally daily
    c. Atenolol: 100mg orally daily
    d. Levaquin: 500mg orally daily

83. Which medication should include a do not crush warning on the label?
    a. Ambien because it is slow-release
    b. Aspirin because it is a mucous membrane irritant
    c. Isotretinoin because of risk of rapid absorption
    d. Nexium because it is enteric-coated

84. JP, a 43-year-old male, presents to the pharmacy with a systolic blood pressure of 125 mmHg and diastolic blood pressure of 89 mmHg. What stage of hypertension does JP's blood pressure reading reflect?
    a. Normotensive
    b. Stage II Hypertension
    c. Stage I Hypertension
    d. Prehypertension

85. The potential for errors in dispensing LASA medication can be reduced by
    a. Including only the brand name on pharmacy labels
    b. Printing the medication's use on the prescription
    c. Storing LASA medication on shelves near each other
    d. Using italicized fonts for LASA medication names

205

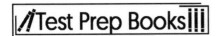
86. Under which guiding document were all Federal laws governing the manufacture, regulation, and sale of controlled substances and narcotics developed?
    a. CSA
    b. DEA
    c. FDA
    d. RCRA

87. Select the Brand – generic medication combination that is correct.
    a. Norvir – nortriptyline
    b. Aldactone – amlodipine
    c. Elavil – enalapril
    d. Abilify – aripiprazole

88. Identify the prescription origin code (POC) that is correctly matched with its descriptor.
    a. 1 = Telephone prescription
    b. 2 = E-prescription
    c. 3 = Written prescription
    d. 4 = Fax prescription

89. The pharmacist asks you to review a lorazepam prescription written for 2.0 mg tablets. How should you respond?
    a. Suggest changing 2.0 mg to 2 mg to avoid overdosing.
    b. Suggest changing 2.0 mg to 2 mg to avoid underdosing.
    c. Suggest changing 2.0 mg to 20 mg to avoid overdosing.
    d. Suggest changing 2.0 mg to 20 mg to avoid underdosing.

90. Vasodilators are associated with all of the following side effects *except*:
    a. hypertension
    b. headache
    c. reflex tachycardia
    d. dizziness

Answer Explanations #3

1. C: Epilepsy is caused by overactive neuronal signaling in the brain, so a central nervous system depressant can calm such activity. Hypertension, ADHD, and depression do not improve with this type of medication and potentially, it can be harmful.

2. B: Schedule V substances like cough preparations containing not more than 200 mg of codeine per 100 mL or per 100 g have small amounts of narcotics and are unlikely to be abused. Choice A is incorrect because Schedule II/IIN substances like meperidine and oxycodone have high potential for abuse and severe psychological or physical dependence. Choice C is incorrect because Schedule I substances like heroin, LSD, and peyote have high potential for abuse and no currently accepted medical use. Choice D is incorrect because Schedule III/IIIN substances like those containing less than 15 mg or hydrocodone or less than 90 mg of codeine per dosage unit have lower potential for abuse the Schedule I or II substances, but their abuse may cause high psychological dependence and moderate or low physical dependence.

3. D: Better lighting will NOT prevent LASA medications mix-up as they are still next to each other on the shelf. Physical separation of LASA medications on the shelves, however, can reduce the possibility of mix-up.

4. C: The *Orange Book* contains all the products the FDA has approved since 1938 and contains the following information about each medication: active ingredient, proprietary name, applicant, and application number. The MSDS is provided by the manufacturer and contains important health and safety information about the referenced chemical. The other answers are incorrect because both the *Orange Book* and MSDS information should be easily accessible in every pharmacy and these reference materials provide different types of information from one another.

5. D: The Consumer Products Safety Commission is an agency that conducts research on products that are worrisome and also on the latest in child-resistant packaging. The DEA is responsible for enforcing laws related to drug use and illegal drug sales. The FDA is responsible for overseeing drug and food production and the safety of these products in the U.S. The Joint Commission is an agency responsible for determining if a hospital has met the standards for healthcare.

6. C: The ABIM is a nonprofit organization that certifies physicians who practice internal medicine and its subspecialties. Only physicians who demonstrate the knowledge, skills, and aptitude to engage in the health care of adults are certified. Choices A, B, and C are all organizations that play a role in molding QA practices in the pharmacy setting.

7. D: Patients are an integral part of the medication safety team. Patients should be educated about their medications and treatment objectives so that they can effectively contribute to preventing medication errors. It is recommended that pharmacists show medications to the patient at the time of dispensing, as this approach significantly decreases dispensing errors.

8. D: Hazardous waste is any substances or mixture of substances that can produce harmful effects on the health and safety of a person. Solid waste, despite its name, refers to all solid, liquid, and gaseous waste. Infectious waste is all waste that contains blood, bodily fluids, blood products, sharps that are infectious, and waste from the laboratory. Biodetrimental waste is fictitious and not an identified type of pharmaceutical waste.

9. B: Pharmacy technicians should be familiar with prescription abbreviations. PO stands for per os, which means by mouth. Daily is QD, PRN is the abbreviation for as needed, and HS is the prescription abbreviation for bedtime.

10. B: The Class A prescription balance can weigh between 120 mg to 120 g. It has a sensitivity of 6 mg, which means just 6 mg of weight will move the balance pointer one division off the equilibrium (or one degree).

11. A: Drug manufacturers determines the storage conditions, such as temperature, and other specifications for a medication.

12. D: As mentioned, patients should be educated about their medications so that they can contribute to preventing medication errors.

13. C: Choice *C* is correct; benzonatate is an antitussive, which is a class of drug commonly used in controlling a cough. Choice *A* is incorrect because valsartan is an ARB, or angiotensin receptor blocker, which is commonly used for lowering blood pressure. Choice *B* is incorrect because tamsulosin is an alpha 1 blocker commonly used in urinary conditions such as BPH, or benign prostatic hyperplasia. Choice *D* is incorrect because rosuvastatin is a statin, which is used to treat high cholesterol. None of those are used for treating a cough, so Choice *C* is correct.

14. A: Choice *A* is correct. Oseltamivir, also known as Tamiflu, is available in both pill and liquid suspension forms. Choices *B* and *C* are not available dosage forms for oseltamivir, and Choice *D* is incorrect because the drug is available in a liquid suspension form.

15. B: Option II is incorrect because the physician's office did not inform the patient about the name of the medication and, thus, the patient cannot help prevent a medication error.

16. B: Choice *B* is correct, as a dry powder inhaler, or DPI, is breath actuated. Choice *A* is incorrect because a metered dose inhaler, or MDI, uses an aerosol propellant and is activated by the patient pressing down on the canister. Choice *C* is incorrect because this is a characteristic of a DPI, not an MDI. Choice *D* is incorrect because that is a characteristic of a MDI, not a DPI.

17. D: Choice *D* is correct because Pepto-Bismol is bismuth subsalicylate, not calcium carbonate. The other answers are correct generic and brand name pairs.

18. B: Choice *B* is correct because SSRIs are well-known for causing sexual dysfunction. Choice *A* is incorrect because PDE-5 inhibitors are medicines such as Viagra/sildenafil that help with sexual dysfunction and do not cause it. Choices *C* and *D* are incorrect because NSAIDs and PPIs are not known to cause sexual dysfunction.

19. C: The correct answer is to *inform the pharmacist.* Choices *A* and *B* are inappropriate. Choice *D* is incorrect because communication with the physician is a pharmacist's responsibility.

20. B: The inscription should include the name of the medication, the strength and dosage form, and the quantity to dispense. The instructions for the pharmacist are part of the subscription. Both the inscription and subscription should be part of the prescription, along with information such as the number of refills, the prescriber's information and signature, and patient information.

21. C: Choice *C* is correct; lubiprostone is Amitiza and is used to treat IBS-C, the constipation form of IBS specifically. Choice *A* is used for sepsis and shock, Choice *B* is used as an antiemetic, and Choice *D* is a PPI used as an antacid.

22. A: The FDA has the authority to initiate a drug recall, whether class I, II, or III. Reasons for drug recalls vary and may include health hazards, mislabeling, contamination, and manufacturing defects. In recent years, there has been a surge in drug recalls initiated by the FDA. The agencies in Choices *B*, *C*, and *D* do not have the authority to initiate a drug recall.

23. C: The correct answer is *154.22 g*. Here's the calculation:

$$Amount\ (in\ g)\ of\ ointment = 2\ \text{lb.} \times 453.6\ \text{g/lb} = 907.2\ \text{g}$$

$$Amount\ of\ salicylic\ acid\ required = amount\ of\ ointment \times concentration\ of\ salicylic\ acid$$

$$(907.2\ \text{g} \times 0.17)$$

$$154.22\ \text{g}$$

24. B: Using leading zeros with numbers in decimal form less than one (e.g., 0.5 mg) helps prevent dispensing larger doses for prescriptions. Choice *A* is incorrect because it does not make sense to include a leading zero with a whole number, and this option could be confusing to the reader. Choice *C* is incorrect because terminal zeros are not typically used as the decimal could be missed, and a ten-fold over-dose could be prescribed. Choice *D* is incorrect because the opposite practice is encouraged; that is, if it is possible to write a prescription without the use of decimal points, it should be done.

25. B: Choice *B* is correct because Norvasc, a calcium channel blocker, is used to control hypertension. *A* and *D* are incorrect because they are not only both statins, but they are the same medication. Simvastatin is the generic equivalent to the brand medication Zocor; both are used to treat hyperlipidemia. Choice *C*, Vytorin, is a combination medication used to treat hyperlipidemia that includes the absorption inhibitor Ezetimibe and the statin Simvastatin.

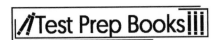
26. B: The correct answer is *166.66 g*. The calculation is below. Review the alligation method of pharmaceutical calculations.

Alligation Method of Pharmaceutical Calculation

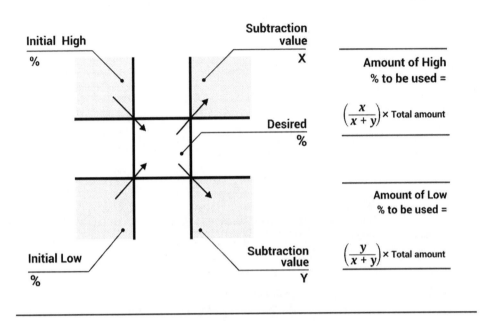

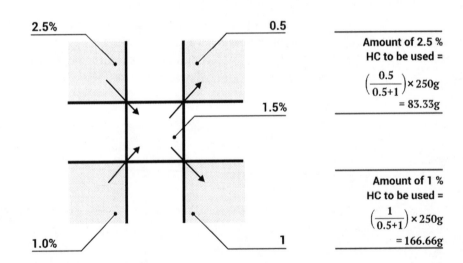

27. D: Choice *D*, anticonvulsant, is the class of medications used to treat seizure disorders such as epilepsy. Some examples of anticonvulsants include Dilantin and Phenobarbital. Antipsychotics, Choice *A*, are used to treat mental health disorders such as schizophrenia or bipolar disorder. Choice *B* is incorrect because SSRIs are used to treat anxiety and depression. Nonsteroidal anti-inflammatory drugs or NSAIDs are used to treat pain and inflammation; therefore, Choice *C* is also incorrect.

28. B: USP 797 mandates that pharmacy staff remove debris from beneath fingernails using warm running water followed by brisk washing from hands to elbows with antibacterial or non-antibacterial

soap for at least 30 seconds prior to compounding sterile preparations. Choices *A*, *C*, and *D* are incorrect as they all present the incorrect duration.

29. B: Celecoxib, Choice *B*, is the generic name for the branded NSAID Celebrex. Choice *A* is incorrect because Citalopram is the generic name for the antidepressant Celexa. Meloxicam, while also an NSAID, is the generic name for Mobic; therefore, Choice *C* is incorrect. Choice *D* is incorrect because Moxifloxacin is the generic for the brand name antibiotic Avelox.

30. D: Electronic prescribing, or e-prescribing, allows physicians and other medical personnel to send prescriptions to a pharmacy electronically. This technology is quickly replacing other modes of prescription transmission such as written, faxed, or called-in prescriptions. E-prescribing has the advantage of providing the ability to transmit accurate, error free, and understandable prescriptions. As a result, it can decrease medication errors.

31. C: The correct answer is *50 g, 100 g, 50 g, respectively*. Here's the calculation:

$$Total\ parts\ of\ the\ ingredients\ (1:2:1) = 4$$

$$Quantity\ of\ A\ in\ 200\ gm\ ointment\ mix = \frac{1}{4} \times 200 = 50\ \text{gm}$$

$$Quantity\ of\ B\ in\ 200\ gm\ ointment\ mix = \frac{2}{4} \times 200 = 100\ \text{gm}$$

$$Quantity\ of\ C\ in\ 200\ gm\ ointment\ mix = \frac{1}{4} \times 200 = 50\ \text{gm}$$

32. C: Choice *C* is the correct choice because prescriber approval is only required when substituting a narrow therapeutic index medication, as NTIs have a variable window between efficacy and toxicity. Generic medications help to keep drug costs down; they can be significantly less expensive than the brand name versions, so Choice *A* is true of generic substitution. Prescribers can avoid generic substitution by writing "Dispense as Written" on a prescription when they feel the brand medication is the best therapeutic option for the patient; therefore, Choice *B* is also true of generic substitution. To be considered the therapeutic equivalent formulation of a brand name drug, the generic formulation must meet the same efficacy and safety parameters as the brand medication; thus, Choice *D* is true of generic substitution as well.

33. C: The FDA oversees the MedWatch Program, which is a safety information and adverse event reporting service (AERS). MedWatch focuses on drugs and medical devices. MedWatch is a voluntary reporting system and allows the information to be shared amongst healthcare professionals and the lay public. Reports are submitted via the Internet.

34. D: Lopressor and Toprol XL have the same active ingredient, Metoprolol, and both are available as 100mg tablets. Lopressor contains the salt form tartrate and is an immediate release formulation, whereas Toprol is the extended release version that contains the salt succinate. Both medications contain the same active ingredient and are the same strength but are of different dosage forms and contain different salts. Therefore, Choice *D* is correct.

35. C: If an expiration date on a medication mentions only the month and year, it should be treated as expiring on the last day of the month. For example, an expiration date of 04/2019 should be treated as

expiring on April 30, 2019. Since 1979, drug manufacturers have been required to print expiration dates on medications. It represents the last day a drug manufacturer can assure 100% efficacy and safety of a drug. The FDA establishes expiration dates for medications.

36. B: Class I pertains to a reasonable probability that product use will cause or lead to serious adverse health events or even death, followed by Class II, which pertains to a likely probability that product use will cause adverse health events, which are temporary or medically reversible. Class III pertains to product use that will probably not cause an adverse health event.

37. A: PPE is worn to decrease the risk of exposure to workplace hazards that may cause injury or illness. Employers are obligated to train and provide appropriate PPE to their employees. OSHA establishes the standards for PPE. Choices *B*, *C*, and *D* are examples of PPE.

38. B: Singulair is used to treat asthma-like symptoms while Spironolactone is a diuretic indicated for patients with CHF; therefore, Choices *A* and *C* are incorrect. Uloric, Choice *D*, is indicated for the treatment of gout. Flomax (Tamsulosin) is an alpha-blocker used to treat BPH in male patients; thus, the correct choice is *B*.

39. C: Opened insulin vials should be kept no longer than thirty days.

40. A: The FDA regulates dietary supplements under the Dietary Supplement Health and Education Act of 1994 guidelines, which means Choice *A* is correct because it states "Dietary Supplements" must be present on the product labeling. Manufacturers and distributers are required to verify that their products are safe and effective, and that their products meet FDA and DSHEA regulations. The FDA does not require manufacturers of dietary supplements to adopt the same practices as drug manufacturers. In addition, manufacturers cannot make claims that dietary supplements be used for the treatment or cure of a condition or ailment; therefore, Choices *B*, *C*, and *D* are incorrect.

41. B: According to the United States Food and Drug Administration's specifications for tamper-evident packaging, sublingual nitroglycerin should not be stored in plastic containers. The medication can bond with the PVC in plastic containers, which can alter the structure and eventually harm the efficacy of the medication. In those scenarios, glass is a great alternative because it is inert (nonreactive). Sublingual nitroglycerin is an example of a medication that should avoid prolonged exposure to traditional PVC medication containers. To combat this problem, many pharmacists will dispense the medication in glass vials because glass is inert. The other medications are light-sensitive, which means they should be dispensed in amber-colored containers, but they can be plastic.

42. B: The Institute of Safe Medication Practices (ISMP) oversees the MERP. The service provides for confidential and voluntary reporting of medication errors. The MERP performs analyses of the errors reported and circulates recommendations for their prevention to drug manufacturers and regulatory organizations. The ISMP also manages the National Vaccine Errors Reporting Program (VERP).

43. D: Choice *D* is correct because levothyroxine, also commonly known as Synthroid, is the first choice used to treat hypothyroidism. Choice *A* is used to treat hyperthyroidism; Choice *B* is commonly used for treating migraines; and Choice *C* is also commonly used for migraines or other pain conditions.

44. C: Choice *C*, folic acid, is a B vitamin that all people need for healthy blood cells, but it is especially important for women of child bearing age because it can help to prevent birth defects that may develop early in a pregnancy, often before a pregnancy is detected. Choices *A* and *B*, Vitamin D and calcium are

212

both supplements that support healthy bone development. Choice *D* is not correct because echinacea is an herbal dietary supplement used as a natural cold remedy.

45. C: Labeler code is the first segment that reveals the manufacturer who produced the drug.

46. C: There are several types of prescription medication orders. Both STAT and ASAP are relatively urgent orders that are received in hospital settings. STAT refers to a medication order that should be filled within fifteen minutes of its receipt. ASAP orders need to be processed as soon as possible but they are of lower priority than STAT orders. In contrast, PRN and standing orders are of much lower priority.

47. B: Tresiba FlexTouch insulin pens can remain stable at room temperature or when refrigerated for up to fifty-six days after opening. Lantus and Humalog vials maintain stability under these same conditions for up to twenty-eight days; therefore, Choices *A* and *C* are incorrect. Humulin 70/30 insulin pens are stable only at room temperature or when refrigerated for up to ten days; therefore, Choice *D* is incorrect.

48. A: While all of the options listed are important methods that should always be employed to reduce dispensing errors, counseling is the most effective method. The pharmacy staff should always provide medication counseling to patients. The vast majority of dispensing errors (approximately 83 percent) are identified in the counseling process. This important discussion between the pharmacist and the patient should be used to verify the medication, dosage and instructions for usage, and pertinent health information. Any errors or misunderstandings can be clarified and remedied prior to the patient leaving the pharmacy. Dispensing errors account for 21 percent of medication errors and can be fatal.

49. B: A lot number has a distinct number for each drug manufactured that is supplied by the manufacturer. It is important to note that drug manufacturers have their own system for numbering. A Lot number could, for example, be expressed as B11907. The B represents the initial of the company's name followed by in house numbering. Unlike an expiration date, it typically has the month and year expressed, for example as 06/2016, 06/16, or June 2016.

50. C: Not all antibiotics require refrigeration after reconstitution. Refrigeration decreases the stability of reconstituted Clarithromycin oral suspension by altering the viscosity or pourability of the suspension as well as affecting the taste; therefore, Choices *A* and *B* are incorrect. Choice *D* is incorrect because reconstitution of any oral antibiotic increases the risk of microbial growth. Therefore, the correct answer is Choice *C*.

51. C: PPE stands for Personal Protective Equipment. Personal protective equipment (PPE) must be worn by trained personnel when handling hazardous substances. PPE is a lab coat, rubber gloves, and safety glasses worn as a unit. PPE may include a breathing apparatus (mask) and/or outer jumpsuit made of protective material, in place of a lab coat, when working in extreme hazard conditions.

52. D: Choices *A, B,* and *C* are incorrect because even distribution of small particles within a suspension vehicle that easily redistributes with moderate shaking are classic characteristics of a stable suspension. The insoluble particles should be able to separate from each other and flow easily in the external phase. Choice *D* is correct because even distribution of the internal phase is lost when the particles adhere to one another, forming large caking clumps within the suspension that can affect accurate dosing of the medication.

53. C: Choice *C* is the correct answer because a patient with rheumatoid arthritis may not be able to open a child-safe cap due to it being harder to open, and no one is living with them to help them open the bottle. The other choices represent patients who do not need special accommodations for their medication bottles because they either have someone live with them that can help, such as Choice *D,* or their condition does not indicate they need help, such as Choices *A* and *B*.

54. D: Choice *D* is correct because the technician should have focused on one task at a time and either waited to count pills until after helping customers, or asked another technician to cover the counter while they counted pills. Choice *A* is common practice and can lead to errors, but since medications are usually placed in alphabetical order on the shelves, this should not cause errors. Choice *B* is also common practice, but even if the technician grabs multiple bottles from the shelves at the same time, they should only count one prescription at a time. Choice *C* is incorrect because technicians are allowed to fill prescriptions, and they often do.

55. B: One should work at least six inches from the front edge of the work surface to ensure adequate sterile compounding and airflow. When the distance is less than 6 inches, the laminar flow air can start mixing with the outside air, which increases the risk of contamination. It is also important to position hands in a way that helps to avoid blocking airflow.

56. B: Choice *B* is the correct choice because narrow therapeutic index medications require close, frequent monitoring and have several risk factors associated with their administration. Choices *A* and *D* are therefore incorrect. Choice *C* is incorrect because narrow therapeutic index medications are available in various dosage forms including intravenously, oral tablets or capsules, injectables, suspensions, etc.

57. B: There are various drugs packaged in blister packs from pills to encapsulated liquid pills (e.g., liquid Nyquil capsules) but topical ointments or medications do not come in blister packs. Only pills or solid dosages are packaged in blister packs.

58. B: The correct answer is 6 months.

59. A: Choice *A* is correct because monitoring INR values is the standard method for determining if blood thinners have reached a therapeutic level. Choice *B* is incorrect because statins are not monitored via INR values but instead require annual bloodwork to screen cholesterol values. Antibiotics do not typically require monitoring, so Choice *C* is incorrect. Anticonvulsants require monitoring of bloodwork, but INR values do not apply here, so Choice *D* is incorrect.

60. B: Pharmacy technicians carry out many tasks including preparation of unit dose medications. Choices *A, C, and D* are incorrect because only pharmacists should perform these tasks.

61. D: NSAIDs, or non-steroidal anti-inflammatory drugs, are known to interact with anticoagulants like Warfarin. NSAIDs can increase excessive bleeding, especially in the gastrointestinal tract. Choices *A* and *B*, Meloxicam and the OTC pain reliever Aleve, are both NSAIDs. Choice *C*, Aggrenox, is an antiplatelet medication that contains the NSAID aspirin; therefore, the correct choice is *D*, Digoxin.

62. C: Robotic dispensing systems use barcode technology to choose drugs from a patient's file and can even put the medicine in the right drawer for the patient. Choice *A* is incorrect because automated pump systems are computerized infusion pumps that provide controlled flow rates. Choices *B* and *D* are

incorrect because automated dispensing systems and automated tracking are tools to save time and reduce human errors by automatically recording inventory data.

63. A: The optimal therapeutic INR value is between two and three. An INR value below two increases the risk of thromboembolism, the formation of blood clots, which can put the patient at risk of heart attack and stroke. Therefore, the correct answer is Choice *A*. Blood that is not clotting effectively, hemorrhaging or uncontrolled bleeding, and excessive bruising are all indicators of an INR that is too high; therefore, Choices *B*, *C*, and *D* are incorrect.

64. D: The toxicological properties section (Section VI) includes route of entry and hazards, as well as first aid statements, carcinogenicity, and effects of chronic exposure. Choice *A* is incorrect because aquatic toxicity is found in the ecological data section of the MSDS. Choice *B* is incorrect because lethal dose is found in the active ingredients section. Choice *C* is incorrect because protective equipment is found in the preventative measures section.

65. D: Pharmaceutical compounding refers to the formulation of a product in a pharmacy, distinct from one supplied by a commercial manufacturer, in order to meet the unique needs of a patient as specified by the physician. Choice *A* is incorrect because a drug dosage modification occurs when the prescriber alters the prescribed dose that the patient should receive. Choice *B* is incorrect because a formulary substitution is a therapeutic or generic substitution of an equivalent substance. Choice *C* is incorrect because off label use occurs when a doctor prescribes a medication for an issue other than what it has been approved to treat.

66. B: Pulverization and trituration are both dry methods used to break down tablets and powders for use in compounded drugs; therefore, Choices *A* and *D* are incorrect. Choice *C*, geometric dilution, is a process of mixing unequal ingredients in a manner that forms a homogenous mixture. It is achieved by diluting the ingredient with a smaller quantity with an ingredient with a larger quantity until it is thoroughly mixed. Choice *B*, levigation, is the correct choice because it involves the grinding of the active ingredient in a wetting agent.

67. C: Choice *C* is correct. The Vaccine Adverse Event Reporting System, or VAERS, is a vaccine safety program that allows pharmacists, patients, physicians, and others to file a report for any adverse reactions to a vaccine. VAERS is a valuable resource used by the Centers for Disease Control (CDC) and the Food and Drug Administration (FDA) to monitor trends in adverse events; therefore, Choices *A* and *B* are incorrect. The Drug Enforcement Agency's (DEA) focus is solely on the regulation of controlled substances, so Choice *D* is incorrect.

68. C: Cracking and coalescence occur in emulsions and are visible signs of instability; therefore, Choices *A* and *B* are incorrect. Choice *D*, liquification, is incorrect because it is a near instantaneous reaction of two solids with low melting points physically changing in structure during the mixing process. Therefore, Choice *C*, the change in pH of a medication, is correct because this sign cannot be visualized and must be determined using litmus paper or a pH meter.

69. D: Pharmaceutical compounding to formulate new products may be used in a variety of instances including to alter the taste or texture of a medication to increase the patient's compliance with the prescription. Choice *A* is incorrect because do not crush warnings simply advise against the crushing of certain medications; they do not require new formulations. Choice *B* is incorrect because compounding may be used if a patient is allergic to an excipient (filler) in a medication; however, if the patient has a

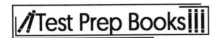

reaction to the active ingredient, another medication should be prescribed. Choice *C* is incorrect because if a product is discontinued because of adverse reactions, it should not be recreated through compounding.

70. C: Ingredients withdrawn from their original container must be kept in an appropriately labeled secondary container. Choice *A* is incorrect because materials may only be reused until they reach the labeled expiration date. Choice *B* is incorrect because ingredients may only be withdrawn by trained staff. Choice *D* is incorrect because ingredients may be removed as long as appropriate protocols are followed.

71. B: Precipitates can enter the blood stream causing blockages in the arteries, which is also known as an embolism and can result in serious complications, including sudden death. Therefore, Choice *A* is incorrect. Precipitate formation is a chemical reaction to medication, which can produce unknown toxic compounds as well as alter the therapeutic capability of the medication; thus, Choices *C* and *D* are also incorrect. The correct choice is *B*, because irritation at the IV site is a rather mild reaction and does not result in serious complications.

72. B: Choice *B* is correct because diversion of controlled substances is regulated by the DEA. A medical device that is a not working as it should is an example of compromised product integrity and would be reported to MedWatch, so Choice *A* is incorrect. Choice *C* is a medication error, and Choice *D* is classified as an adverse reaction and should be reported to MedWatch. Therefore, both Choice *C* and Choice *D* are incorrect.

73. A: An emulsifying agent is necessary to provide an equal distribution of the active ingredient within a preparation which increases the overall stability of the product, so Choices *B* and *C* are incorrect. Immiscibility is defined as two or more products that cannot create a homogenous mixture owing to their inability to dissolve into one another. Choice *D* is incorrect, as adding an emulsifying agent to two immiscible products will benefit the compound because it will decrease the immiscible, or anti-mixable, properties, allowing the formation of a more homogenous mixture. Thus, Choice *A* is the correct answer.

74. D: Choice *A* is incorrect because the wrong medication being given to the patient was not due to an error in the pharmacy but rather the prescriber writing an order for the wrong medication. Choice *B* is incorrect and resulted in two errors; the incorrect patient received and administered a medication that was not intended for them, and the patient that should have received the medication did not receive the medication they were supposed to be taking. Choice *C* is incorrect because the pharmacy and the patient were both unaware there was an allergy to the prescribed medication. Therefore, Choice *D* is correct because the medication was entered incorrectly and yet no harm was done because the pharmacist discovered the error during the prescription verification process, before it could be dispensed to the patient.

75. A: Active pharmaceutical ingredients that are sensitive to light must be protected during all aspects of development, production, storage, and dispensing. Precautions must be taken during the manufacturing processes to prevent exposure to light for both the active ingredient as well as any inactive ingredients that may also be sensitive to light. Medications that are sensitive to light can begin to degrade following exposure, which can break down the active ingredient, causing impurities that result in a potentially harmful and nontherapeutic product. For these reasons, Choices *B*, *C*, and *D* are incorrect. Choice *A* is correct because placing a light sensitive medication in an amber colored prescription bottle will protect it from light.

76. C: High-alert/risk medications have the potential to cause significant harm if prescribed in error or administered incorrectly. Choice A is incorrect because lidocaine is not a look-alike medication. Choice B is incorrect because is not a sound-alike medication. Choice D is incorrect because lidocaine is not available in a form that can be crushed.

77. B: Hazardous waste is waste produced in a pharmacy that could produce harmful effects on a person's health and safety. Choice A is incorrect because biological waste is not a recognized category of waste produced in a pharmacy. Choice C is incorrect because infectious waste includes blood, blood products, bodily fluids, infectious sharps, and laboratory waste. Choice D is incorrect because solid waste includes all solid, liquid, and gaseous waste.

78. D: Choice A is incorrect because DEA regulations require schedule II medications to be locked in a safe, vault, or cabinet that can be secured with a lock. Choice B is incorrect because DEA regulations state that if schedule III-V medications are not kept in a locked cabinet they can be inconspicuously stored along with noncontrolled inventory. Choice C is incorrect because access to the pharmacy, noncontrolled medications, and controlled substances should be granted only to authorized pharmacy staff. In addition to restricting access to controlled drugs, it is important to minimize the number of controlled drugs on hand at a given time; therefore, Choice D is correct.

79. C: A verbal order is a prescription order received by telephone and is a valid way of submitting a new prescription to the pharmacy. Choice A is incorrect because e-prescriptions may be transmitted electronically through secure software, but they are not emailed. Choice B is incorrect because patients may request refills on existing prescriptions but may not request new prescriptions themselves. Choice D is incorrect because U.S. mail is not a valid form of submission for prescriptions.

80. D: Gabapentin. The effects of answer choices A, Rifampin, and B, ritonavir, have been extensively studied and well documented. Both A and B have been shown to decrease the efficacy of oral contraceptives (OCs). Choice C, St. John's Wort, has also been linked to decreased hormonal OC effectiveness. Answer choice D, Gabapentin has not been shown to interact with hormonal oral contraceptives.

81. B: Pharmacies should avoid using tailing zeroes, which can cause dosage errors. Choice A is incorrect because pharmacies should remove high concentration electrolytes from dispensing areas. Choice C is incorrect because pharmacies should use leading zeroes to help prevent dosage errors. Choice D is incorrect because it includes options I and III.

82. B: Buspirone: 150mg orally daily. The question seeks to determine which medication/dosage combination is incorrect. The usual dosing range for buspirone is 20 – 30 mg daily in divided doses; therefore, it is inaccurate. Answer choices A, C, and D are appropriately paired medication and dosage combinations.

83. A: Ambien (zolpidem) tablets are slow-release and should not be crushed. Choice B is incorrect because aspirin should not be crushed because it is a slow-release, enteric-coated medication. Choice C is incorrect because isotretinoin (Claravis) should not be crushed because it is a mucous membrane irritant. Choice D is incorrect because Nexium (esomeprazole) should not be crushed because it is a slow-release medication.

84. D: Prehypertension. Answer choice A, normotensive, describes normal adult blood pressure – a systolic blood pressure less than 120 mmHg and a diastolic blood pressure less than 80 mmHg. Answer

217

choice B, Stage II Hypertension, occurs when systolic blood pressure is equal to or above 160 mmHg, and diastolic blood pressure is 100 mmHg or higher. Choice C, Stage I Hypertension refers to systolic blood pressures between 140 mmHg and 159 mmHg and diastolic blood pressures between 90 mmHg and 99 mmHg. Choice D, prehypertension, reflects systolic blood pressures between 120 mmHg and 139 mmHg and diastolic blood pressures between 80 mmHg and 89 mmHg.

85. B: Adding the indication, or use, of the medication to a prescription can help to reduce errors. Choice A is incorrect because both the brand name and generic name should be included to help reduce errors. Choice C is incorrect because LASA medications should be stored in separate locations to reduce the chance of one being confused with another. Choice D is incorrect because tall man lettering, which highlights the differences in similar drug names is commonly used to reduce errors.

86. A: Federal law regulating controlled substances are developed under the guidance of the Controlled Substance Act (CSA). Choice B is incorrect because the Drug Enforcement Administration (DEA) is a government agency that set up to implement the laws developed under the guidance of the CSA. Choice C is incorrect because the U.S. Food and Drug Administration (FDA) is the federal organization that oversees the production and safety of food and drugs. Choice D is incorrect because the Resource Conservation and Recovery Act (RCRA) provides the guidelines for the disposal of prescription medications and other pharmaceutical wastes.

87. D: Abilify – aripiprazole. The generic name for answer choice A, Norvir, is ritonavir. Answer choice B, Aldactone, is the brand name for spironolactone. The generic name for choice C, Elavil, is amitriptyline.

88. D: Prescription origin codes are as follows: 0 = Unknown (e.g., a transferred prescription), 1 = Written prescription, 2 = Telephone prescription, 3 = E-prescription, 4 = Fax prescription. Choices A, B, and C incorrectly match the codes with their descriptors.

89. A: Trailing zeroes (zeroes following a decimal point) can cause the 2.0 mg dose to be misinterpreted as 20 mg, resulting in an overdose. Choice B is incorrect because writing 2 mg as 2.0 mg is likely to result in an overdose, not an underdose. Choices C and D are incorrect because 2.0 mg is a different dose than 20 mg, a ten-fold greater concentration.

90. A: Hypertension. Vasodilators are used to treat hypertension. Common side effects include answer choice B – headache, answer choice C – reflex tachycardia, and answer choice D – dizziness.

PTCB Practice Tests #4-#7

To keep the size of this book manageable, save paper, and provide a digital test-taking experience, the 4th-7th practice tests can be found online. Scan the QR code or go to this link to access it:

testprepbooks.com/bonus/ptcb

The first time you access the tests, you will need to register as a "new user" and verify your email address.

If you have any issues, please email support@testprepbooks.com.

Index

Dear PTCB Test Taker,

Thank you for purchasing this study guide for your PTCB exam. We hope that we exceeded your expectations.

Our goal in creating this study guide was to cover all of the topics that you will see on the test. We also strove to make our practice questions as similar as possible to what you will encounter on test day. With that being said, if you found something that you feel was not up to your standards, please send us an email and let us know.

We would also like to let you know about other books in our catalog that may interest you.

NAPLEX

This can be found on Amazon: amazon.com/dp/1637750455

We have study guides in a wide variety of fields. If you're interested in one, try searching for it on Amazon or send us an email.

Thanks Again and Happy Testing!
Product Development Team
info@studyguideteam.com

FREE Test Taking Tips Video/DVD Offer

To better serve you, we created videos covering test taking tips that we want to give you for FREE. **These videos cover world-class tips that will help you succeed on your test.**

We just ask that you send us feedback about this product. Please let us know what you thought about it—whether good, bad, or indifferent.

To get your **FREE videos**, you can use the QR code below or email freevideos@studyguideteam.com with "Free Videos" in the subject line and the following information in the body of the email:

      a. The title of your product

      b. Your product rating on a scale of 1-5, with 5 being the highest

      c. Your feedback about the product

If you have any questions or concerns, please don't hesitate to contact us at info@studyguideteam.com.

Thank you!